T0277938

Sweet
HANDS

3RD EDITION

Sweet
HANDS

ISLAND COOKING FROM
TRINIDAD & TOBAGO

RAMIN GANESHRAM

photography by
JEAN-PAUL VELLOTTI

HIPPOCRENE BOOKS, INC.
New York

For further information, contact:
HIPPOCRENE BOOKS, INC.
171 Madison Avenue
New York, NY 10016
www.hippocrenebooks.com

Book design by Brittany Hince and K & P Publishing

"*The Sweetest Memories*" (page 240) essay first appeared in *Islands Magazine*, September 2008
The "*Fresh Catch*" essay (page 104) first appeaared in *Islands Magazine*, May 2007.

Additional photo credits:
p. xii Pommerac: "Jamaican Apple" © istockphoto.com/JokoHarismoyo
p. 4 Trinidad & Tobago Map: "Trinidad and Tobago Political Map—Illustration" © istockphoto.com/
PeterHermesFurian
p. 50 Accras: "Cod Fritters" © istockphoto.com/carpaumar
p. 73 Colette's Cilantro Chili Wings: "Barbecue Chicken Wings with a Beer" © istockphoto.com/LauriPatterson
p. 78 Soused Lambie: "Conch Salad on a plate" © istockphoto.com/Anna Bryukhanova
p. 134 "An ear of corn field" by Maks Norodenko/shutterstock.com
p. 149 Fried Sweet Plantains: "Fried Plantains" © istockphoto.com/princessdlaf
p. 151 "Two bananas isolated on white background" by Maks Norodenko/shutterstock.com
p. 166 Chicken Pelau "Trinidad & Tobago Chicken Pelau and Fresh Salad" by pansticks/shutterstock.com
p. 193 M'Busbes "Food Photography on a Tablecloth" by Christopher Coates/shutterstock.com
p. 207 Coconut Cream Pie: "Coconut Custard Pie" © istockphoto.com/THEPALMER
p. 226/227 Guava Cheese "Brazilian dessert goiabada with fresh goiaba on wooden table" by Iuliia Timofeeva/
shutterstock.com
p. 248 Coconut Ice Cream "Coconut Ice Cream in the Coconut Shell" by Zoryanchick/shutterstock.com
p. 284 Sorrel: "Cold Brew Hibiscus Tea with ice and Mint Leaves" © istockphoto.com/alpaksoy

Previous Editions:
Original hardcover edition ISBN-10: 0-7818-1125-2
Second edition in paperback ISBN-13: 978-0-7818-1250-4

Library of Congress Cataloging-in-Publication Data

Ganeshram, Ramin.
Sweet hands : island cooking from Trinidad & Tobago / Ramin Ganeshram ;
with photography by Jean-Paul Vellotti ; and a foreward by Molly O'Neill.
 p. cm.
 Includes index.
 ISBN 978-0-7818-1250-4 (alk. paper) (ppk. 2nd Edition)
 ISBN 978-0-7818-1369-3 ppk (3rd Edition)
 1. Cookery, Trinidadian. 2. Cookery--Trinidad and Tobago. I. Vellotti,
Jean-Paul. II. Title.
 TX716.T7G36 2010
 641.5972983--dc22

                                                    2010020761

Printed in United States of America.

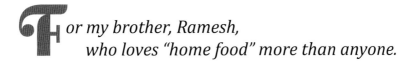*For my brother, Ramesh,*
who loves "home food" more than anyone.

And our parents
Krisnaram and Parvin Ganeshram
— someday we'll be together.

Contents

Sidebars

Acknowledgments

Since the printing of the first edition of this book, I have been fortunate to return to Trinidad many times, meeting folks from every corner of the nation eager to share their love of home food. It has been even more gratifying to meet Trinidadian ex-pats throughout America and even in Europe who have been kind enough to share their experiences and experiments re-creating the dishes of their childhoods using this book.

I would be remiss not to acknowledge the faithful friendship and insights of my good friends Gerard Ramsawak and his wife Oda Van Der Heijden, managers of Pax Guest House at Mount St. Benedict in Tunapuna. They and their daughter Dominique have become my family in Trinidad, and staying with them at Pax is a joyful "homecoming" each and every time.

Here in the United States, the ongoing support and friendship of my brother, Ramesh Ganeshram, is a gift for which I am forever grateful. Thank you to my husband, photographer Jean-Paul Vellotti, whose 20/20 vision always helps put everything in sharpest focus and, never last, to my daughter Sophia, who represents a new generation of pride in our heritage and culture.

Sweet Hands

Foreword

To understand your taste is to appreciate not only what, among other things, distinguishes you from others, but to appreciate the history of flavors that proceeded you, the places your ancestors lived, the households they built, the meals they made.

Families from all corners of the earth are, after all, rift with stories of unexplained habits and food preferences. The six-pronged candlestick to which the Catholic farm wife in Nebraska religiously adds a candle each night in the six days before Christmas turns out to have traveled from a Jewish ghetto in Warsaw to the Midwestern plains. The "family secret" of cutting a pot roast in half and cooking it in two vessels becomes, upon investigation, less about the quality of the dish and more about the fact that a great-great-grandmother did not have a pot large enough to contain the meat.

Habits of the kitchen and the table are not only shaped by ethnic heritage, religious tradition, and financial necessity, they are also sculpted by place. The presence, say, of tomatoes in a Louisiana gumbo says that somewhere along the line the Cajun dish spent time among the Creoles of New Orleans. A wild profusion of meat and herbs in Vietnamese pho is a good indication that the meager beef broth of Hanoi has seen more than a little of Saigon.

The great-granddaughter of an east Indian indentured laborer and Hindu priest, Ramin Ganeshram may not have set out to tease apart the various strands of her own culinary DNA. The Manhattan-born journalist and chef meant to gather and record the recipes of Trinidad & Tobago, her father's homeland. It was a sorely needed task. Her father and Iranian mother lived, she writes, "a life of substitution" after emigrating to New York, and like many ethnically complicated cultures, the dishes of these two Caribbean islands are traditionally passed from mother to daughter and little is written down. But when she returned to the islands where she'd spent the summers of her youth, gathering recipes quickly became an exercise in gathering lost parts of herself and understanding where she came from, who she is, and what she likes to eat.

The result is the first cookbook that teaches the home cooking of these islands in clear, concise recipes. It is also a journey through a dramatic, mountainous spot that has been sculpted by water and wind, as well as by a succession of "overlords." After being spotted by Christopher Columbus, Dutch rule gave way to French rule and that in turn bowed to British rule. And then there were the peoples who were imported from Africa, China, and east India specifically to be indentured to an overlord's cocoa and sugarcane plantations.

At a gentle, all but lyrical pace, Ganeshram has used family stories, snippets of history, lush descriptions, and ambles through village markets, past roadside vendors, to spots like the "Breakfast Shed" and other well off-the-beaten-tourist-path places to lead the reader to the quiet discovery of this beautiful spot where "east" has been meeting "west" day after day for centuries. As I read how to brighten a winter squash soup with coconut and to make a fine shrimp patty and to rethink my relationship with rice, tropical fruits, and plantains, my hands itched to cook—it was difficult to keep my seat.

I like to think that my agitation was a sign of metamorphosis. In Trinidad & Tobago, good cooks may not share a religion, an ethnicity, or the same social status, but they all have magical hands, hands capable of keeping this bright, complicated melting pot of a cuisine simmering, shifting, and vibrantly alive—sweet hands.

—Molly O'Neill

Pomerac, a heart-shaped fruit with a sweet tart flavor

Introduction

When I began researching the first edition of this cookbook, I came to realize that an inordinate number of people didn't know where Trinidad & Tobago (pronounced Toe-BAY-go) was. Now, thanks to a happy confluence of events—a rennaissance of arts, music, literature, and dance, an eagerness among young Americans to travel outside of their comfort zones, as well as a visit from Anthony Bourdain for his popular show *Parts Unknown*—Trinidad & Tobago is now "on the map." It certainly helps that the nation's already well-known epic Carnival (Mardi Gras) celebrations have become equal to those of Rio de Janeiro in the eyes of the world—and a standard to which other Caribbean nations try to keep up.

For me, however, my father's home country of Trinidad & Tobago holds an enchantment of a different kind. When I was a child visiting during summer vacations, I always looked forward to the unusual, exciting, and delicious variety of food.

Among the things I most looked forward to was the enormous array of fruits and vegetables that were simply not to be had back home in New York City. In the weeks leading up to our visits, my brother Ramesh and I would talk endlessly about the fruits we'd pick in our family's yard. For us, it was equivalent to our (never-realized!) dream of going to the corner store with permission to choose any and all candy we wanted.

There was soursop, a tree fruit with a leathery green skin (that reminded me of local iguanas) and a creamy flesh; guava; chinet (a cluster fruit resembling small limes); fresh coconut water and jelly; varieties of cherries and plums different from those we had at home; and pomme cythère (*ambarella*), a dendritic seeded citrus fruit also called golden apple or June apple. Then, of course, there was my personal favorite—pomerac. A small heart-shaped fruit with a thin maroon skin, white flesh, and a single seed, it is sweet and tart and has a consistency between a ripe pear and an apple. Native to the South Pacific, it is also called an *otaheite* apple. It remains my favorite fruit of all time, and even today whenever I visit Trinidad, it's one of the first things I seek out (though my husband says it just tastes like the good old North American strawberry).

Just as the produce available in Trinidad is abundant and varied, so too are the cooking styles, thanks to the country's unique colonial history.

Columbus first spotted Trinidad on his second voyage to the Americas. In fact, it was he who gave the little island its name, meaning "trinity," after the three mountain ranges that crisscross the land. Today we know that those mountains are actually a continuation of the Andes from Venezuela and that at one time in its geological history Trinidad was, in fact, part of the South American mainland.

Once Columbus hit the scene, rampant colonialism ensued. Spain held on to Trinidad for a short time, as evidenced by the name of the capital city, Port of Spain. Shortly after, the Dutch, French, and ultimately the English held sway over Trinidad, with British Colonial rule remaining the longest—until 1962, when the country gained its independence.

My great-grandfather, John Ganeshram (center), came to Trinidad as an indentured laborer.

European colonials were interested in Trinidad for the same reasons they were interested in any other part of the New World—resources. In this case, they sought coconuts and sugarcane. The coconut was used primarily for its oil, and the cane for processed sugar, molasses, and rum.

Someone had to plant and harvest these crops and, in the early days, the rough task fell to enslaved people from West Africa. However, by the 1830s, slavery had been abolished in England and it was necessary to find a new labor source for the backbreaking task of cutting sugarcane and harvesting other crops. Because Britain had also colonized India, the subcontinent was a logical place to obtain laborers as, like Trinidad, India was a tropically hot country. From 1851 to 1917, more than 144,000 East Indians were brought to Trinidad as indentured laborers, typically working a five-year contract in return for a crown land grant, although the system was done away with after the first decade of indentureship in favor of a monetary reward. A small number of Chinese indentured laborers were brought to Trinidad as well.

At least three of my great-grandparents were among the East Indians who came to Trinidad as indentured workers. My grandfather Ganesh Ram was a Hindu priest, but like many of his countrymen, he forged a relationship with Christian missionaries in Trinidad and actually became one of forty-four Presbyterian catechists who were posted around the country teaching Christian doctrine. Eventually he changed his name from simply Ganesh Ram to John Ganeshram.

Yet, for my grandfather as for many African, Indian, and Chinese Trinidadians, conversion to Presbyterianism, Anglicanism, or Catholicism didn't translate into a wholesale abandonment of their birth religions. Instead, a peculiar hybridization of their native religions occurred, including a mixture of West African tribal religion and magic arts called *obeah*, and a type of Hinduism that allowed practitioners to view that religion's many gods on par with Christian saints rather than as polytheistic worship. However, perhaps because of their faith's basic similarity to Christianity, Indian Muslims remained for the most part unconverted.

The end result is a society that is a complex melting pot of people and tradition. One happy consequence is a cuisine that is an organic fusion, without contrivance nor sprung from the mind of a celebrity chef. In Trinidad, items like curry and various Indian breads are a staple in every home—whether there exists an East Indian ancestor or not. *Callalloo*, a soup of West African origin, is the national dish, and the West African tradition of browning meats in caramelized sugar is the first step to most stews. Chinese fried rice is part of any self-respecting cook's repertoire and Christmas feasts have a decidedly Spanish flavor.

Ultimately, this is a book that aims to be both informative and entertaining, painting a rich canvas of the cultural heritage that is a huge part of the evolution of Trinidadian foods. You will find *lagniappe* (what we Trinis, like New Orleaneans, call "that little something extra") in the form of tips and tricks throughout, as well as some other useful information.

I hope you will find *Sweet Hands* not only a culinary resource, but a means of insight into the vibrant and welcoming culture of Trinidad & Tobago.

As for the unusual title: In Trinidad, the best compliment a cook can hope for is to be told he or she has "sweet hands." It means the person is so talented in the kitchen that anything he or she makes—from a sandwich to a seven-course meal—is like manna from the gods.

—**Ramin Ganeshram**
*New York, November 2004,
October 2009, June 2018*

A Few Tips on Using This Cookbook

The glossary of terms at the back of this book should help you understand the ingredients and terms needed to prepare the dishes in this cookbook. For the most part, these ingredients are readily available—now more than ever with online shopping. However, where ingredients are still not easy to come by I have offered suggestions for substitutions. Additionally, while I describe traditional cooking methods, I also give updated directions that make use of modern kitchen utensils and appliances. You'll also find that this third edition features some new recipes and a new section—"Breakfasts."

When a recipe calls for **hot pepper sauce** you can either use a bottled variety (try the Trinidadian Matouk's or Chief brands)72 or make your own using the recipe on page 257.

Whenever **curry powder** is called for, it is Trinidad curry powder or at least Caribbean curry powder, not the East Indian kind. Island specific curry powders are more readily available in regular supermarkets these days and online. Or you can make your own using the recipe on page 253.

Green Seasoning is a fresh herb blend used in a large number of Trinidadian dishes. You can make a batch using the recipe on page 254 and keep it in your refrigerator for about 1 week.

Salt is always coarse or kosher salt.

When **brown sugar** is called for it is measured loosely—not packed.

For my **chili peppers** I use Scotch bonnet peppers as they are the Caribbean's chili pepper of choice. Please be aware that they are a very hot variety, similar in heat to the more common habanero pepper but fruitier, but any hot red chili pepper will do, depending on how much heat you prefer and availability.

Republic of Trinidad & Tobago

Population:
1,300,000 as of 2013

Languages:
English (official), Caribbean Hindustani (a dialect of Hindi), French, Spanish, Chinese

Major Cities:
Port of Spain (capital), San Fernando (south), Tunapuna (north), Chaguanas (central)

Major Religions:
Christianity, Hinduism, Islam

Currency:
Trinidad & Tobago dollar (usually hovers at an exchange rate of between 6 to 6.25 dollars to 1 US dollar.)

Entry/Exit Requirements:
A valid passport is required of U.S. citizens for entry to Trinidad & Tobago (A U.S. passport card alone is not accepted for entry to Trinidad & Tobago or for direct air travel from Trinidad & Tobago back to the U.S.) U.S. citizens do not need a visa for tourism or business-related visits of 90 days or less.

When leaving Trinidad & Tobago visitors are required (as of this writing) to pay a $200 TT, roughly a $30 US departure tax.

Notes to Travelers:
The U.S. Center for Disease Control continues to issue a recommendation of yellow fever vaccine for travelers to Trinidad & Tobago.

———

Source For BOX: CIA World Fact Book; U.S. Department of State

Traveling to T&T

In the years since it was first published, numerous readers, websites, bloggers, and guides have told me that they have used *Sweet Hands* as a cultural as well as culinary guidebook to Trinidad & Tobago. Because of that I thought it would be helpful to readers to have a crib sheet on getting to and around the twin islands.

By no means does this section intend to compete with or cover all the material of a comprehensive guidebook. Instead, it comprises practical information based on research and personal experience. My hope is that this basic travel section will serve as an introduction and quick resource to help plan your own culinary adventure in Trinidad & Tobago.

When to Go

The most popular tourist times to visit Trinidad & Tobago are for the country's famous Carnival (Mardi Gras) which takes place annually the Tuesday before Ash Wednesday and airfares reflect this, so book early. Christmas and summertime travel are popular among expats returning home and so airfares tend to be on the high side then as well. Travelers who can visit T&T during other times of the year will find that they may be lucky enough to find round-trip tickets at much lower prices.

Trinidad & Tobago is, happily, out of the hurricane belt and rarely do large storms hit the islands. Occasionally there are earthquakes, and local lore often correlates the seismic events to periods of uncharacteristic heat. Temperatures in Trinidad & Tobago do not fluctuate widely and tend to be around 85 degrees Fahrenheit, inching closer to 90 degrees during the summer. There is little seasonal change with the notable exception of the rainy season, which is June to December. The dry season from January to May is an ideal time to visit, but brushfires during this time of year are not uncommon.

Trinidad & Tobago is in the Atlantic Standard Time Zone (GMT–4) and is, therefore, in the same time zone as the East Coast of the United States during Eastern Daylight Time, and one hour behind the East Coast the rest of the year during Eastern Standard Time. It is three hours behind the West Coast of the United States during Pacific Daylight Time and four hours behind during Pacific Standard Time.

Getting There & Getting Around

Many major airlines from both America and Europe fly to Trinidad's Piarco International Airport and Tobago's Crown Point International Airport. Among them are American Airlines, British Airways, Liat, Caribbean Airlines, Delta, and Lufthansa. Discounted airfares are available from consolidators such as TravelSpan, though flight days and times are limited if you go that route.

Visitors to Tobago can either fly directly there or fly into Trinidad and either take a commuter plane to Tobago that takes under an hour or a high-speed ferry service that takes two and a half hours. Rates for the ferry vary but are generally between

$10-$15 (US). Vehicles are allowed on ferries and the cost is roughly $75 (US) for a round trip fare. For up-to-date schedules and fares, contact the Port Authority of Trinidad & Tobago at www.patnt.com.

It's best to arrange for transport to your hotel from the airport with your hotel as crimes against tourists by independent taxi drivers—from simply overcharging to actual robbery—have been on the increase. If you do take a taxi from the airport, the National Tourism Authority has established standard rates to hotels and other major stops. You can obtain a rate sheet from the board's tourism site: www.discovertnt.com

Although you can rent a car in Trinidad & Tobago, American visitors should be forewarned that it is right-side driving and follows British traffic patterns. This can be confusing, particularly given the extreme traffic around the capital and winding, narrow roads through rural areas, particularly in higher elevations. If possible, visitors would do better to hire a driver, many of whom can be hired for the day for the same price as it costs to rent a car. Often, your hotel concierge or a reputable taxi service with proper offices can help with this.

Public or municipal buses run by the Public Transport Service Corporation are marked clearly with the corporation's name and run service from the terminal in South Quay in Port of Spain to towns and villages all over both Trinidad and Tobago. Schedules can be found at www.ptsc.co.tt/.

Throughout the island minivans called Maxi Taxis serve as additional quasi-public transportation and service various routes throughout the island, noted by the color of stripe painted on them. I would strongly advise visitors against taking Maxi Taxis as the stops are not well marked and robberies

on Maxi Taxis have become all too common. Maxi Taxis follow set routes, but have no timetable, and after 9 pm this form of transport is unreliable. For the adventurous traveler who wishes to take a Maxi Taxi, Trinidad Development Corporation, the country's official tourism board, has information on the routes.

If you choose to take a car-taxi anywhere in Trinidad, taxi stands are delineated in some of the major cities but taxi cabs are recognizable by their license plates that begin with "H". Cabs in Trinidad take fares along a route until the cab is full, though you can buy the whole cab or the back seat if you want more privacy.

Where to Stay

Major chain hotels have been steadily popping up all over Trinidad and, particularly, Tobago where beach resorts are the norm. On Trinidad, visitors can choose from the Hilton, Marriot Courtyard, Holiday Inn, and Hyatt Regency right in Port of Spain where prices begin at upwards of $150 US per night.

Those looking for a bargain and a true taste of Trinidad can stay at any number of boutique hotels, including the very lovely Coblentz Inn (44 Coblentz Avenue, Cascade, Trinidad; 868-621-0541) and The Chaconia Hotel (106 Saddle Road, Maraval, Trinidad; 868-628-3210). There are a number of small guesthouses throughout the island but safety and security is always an issue in T&T, and readers should note that the large hotels and notable guesthouses are well attended by security guards.

When I visit Trinidad my hands-down preference for accommodations is The Pax Guest House in the hills above Tunapuna, a city about 25 minutes from Port of Spain, and halfway between the capital and Chaguanas, an increasingly bustling metropolis in Central Trinidad that is well known for its shopping, a number of Hindu religious sites, and as the ancestral home of the writer V.S. Naipaul. If you want to have a sense of the Trinidad of days gone by, Pax is the place for you. Nestled in the hillside on the grounds of a Benedictine Monastery, the hotel is peaceful and commodious. While there are no amenities like a pool, the front and rear verandahs are peaceful spots for a rest and a drink. At the front, you'll enjoy remarkable views of the island, nearly all the way to San Fernando, the largest city in the south. At the rear, bird lovers will be delighted at the array of the country's astounding number of bird species that alight there. Proprietor Gerard Ramaswak, an avid birder and eco-guide himself, is pleased to share his knowledge of local bird species and the flora and fauna of the country at large. Ask and he will happily arrange tours for you to see giant leatherback turtles in their laying season, rare red howler monkeys in their native habitat, the scarlet ibis known only in T&T and Venezuela, and many more natural wonders of the islands. (Pax Guest House; 868-662-4084)

And check out the very good accommodation finder at The Official Trinidad & Tobago Tourism Site, www.discovertnt.com

Safety in T&T

Sadly, personal safety has increasingly become an issue in Trinidad & Tobago, both for locals and tourists. Robberies are not uncommon and violent crime is on the rise. The U.S. State Department advises travelers not to wear expensive jewelry or carry electronic equipment with them—there have even been cases of working journalists attacked for their gear. The U.S. State Department has issued warnings to travelers to avoid large crowds and demonstrations in T&T and to specifically seek accommodations with 24-hour security.

Health & Medical Facilities

Port of Spain General Hospital: 160 Charlotte Street, Port of Spain, (868) 623-2951

Eric Williams Medical Sciences Complex: Uriah Butler Highway, Champ Fleurs, (868) 645-4673 (Referrals, Accident & Emergency only), open 24 hours

San Fernando General Hospital: Independence Avenue, San Fernando, Trinidad, (868) 652-3581, open 24 hours

Arima Health Facility: Queen Mary Avenue, Arima, Trinidad, (868) 667-4714, open 24 hours

Chaguanas Health Facility: Main Road, Chaguanas (opposite RBTT Bank), Trinidad, (868) 665-8958, open 24 hours

Sangre Grande Regional Hospital: Ojoe Road, Sangre Grande, Trinidad, (868) 668-2221, open 24 hours

Scarborough General Hospital: Connector Road, Signal Hill, Scarborough, Tobago, (868) 660-4744, open 24 hour

Public Holidays

As elsewhere in the world, public holidays in T&T are marked by school, bank, and government office closures. In many cases, commercial businesses are closed as well. Note that no dates are given for Hindu, Muslim, and some Christian religious days, which are calculated yearly by astronomical events and moon phases. Actual dates are narrowed down more precisely as the specific event draws near.

January 1 New Year's Day

March 30 Spiritual Baptist Shouters Liberation Day

Early Spring Good Friday

Early Spring Easter Monday

May 30 Indian Arrival Day

Late Spring Corpus Christi

End of Ramadan Eid ul Fitr

June 19 Labor Day

August 1 Emancipation Day

August 31 Independence Day

September 24 Republic Day

Autumn Divali

December 25 Christmas Day

December 26 Boxing Day

Some Points of Interest

Fort George—There are two Fort Georges in the nation of Trinidad & Tobago. The older is in Scarborough, Tobago, built in the 1770s. The other, in the hills above Port of Spain overlooking the district of St. James, affords a spectacular view of the west of the nation, the Channel Islands, and the Gulf of Paria.

Hanuman Temple—With nearly half the population of Trinidad being of East Indian descent, there are a number of sites of cultural interest to visitors. Hanuman Temple with its giant statue of the monkey god (*right*), was crafted by artisans brought directly from India and is the largest temple to the god located outside of India.

Indo-Caribbean Museum, Waterloo—Those interested in the rich culture that East Indians brought to Trinidad as indentured laborers will enjoy the Indo-Caribbean Museum in Waterloo, near the Temple In the Sea, founded in 2006.

La Brea Pitch Lake—This natural pitch or tar lake is one of the world's largest resources of tar, the main component of asphalt. Homes and other buildings are constantly being twisted and warped by fingers of pitch that reach out underground from the main lake. Considered one of the natural wonders of the

Giant sculpture of Lord Hanuman (Hindu god), village of Carapichaima, Trinidad

Indo-Caribbean Day Trip

Consider an afternoon outing to Central Trinidad where you can explore the Indo-Caribbean culture of the island among several sites quite close together, including the Hanuman Temple, Indo Caribbean Museum, and Temple In the Sea. Afterwards, hit Chaguanas's main road for a variety of authentic, locally made Indian handicrafts including red clay lamps, clothing, shoes, jewelry, and more.

world, it is said that the lake was first discovered in 1595 by Sir Walter Raleigh, who promptly used it to waterseal his vessels and exported some back to England, where it was first used for road paving on the Westminster Bridge for the opening of the new Parliament.

Temple In the Sea—A monument to the piety of sugarcane laborer Soodas Sadhu, the temple in the sea was originally a stone and mud structure built in the mudflats off the shoreline of the village of Waterloo in central Trinidad. Finished in 1947, the temple was torn down just five years later because it had been built on land owned by the Caroni Sugar Company. Undaunted, Sadhu hauled rocks into the sea itself because, he claimed, only god owned the ocean. Built of cement on a stone base, the temple was never completed though he spent the remaining twenty-five years of his life on the task. In 1994, twenty years after Sadhu's death, the government of Trinidad & Tobago finished the temple as a permanent structure that has become a beloved site for all Trinidadians.

Columbus' Anchor—Trinidad is one of the few New World sites where Columbus actually set foot. The anchor, found in a garden at Point Arenas and bearing the date 1497, has been largely verified to be from one of his sailing vessels and can now be seen on display at the National Museum.

Beaches

While Tobago is most noted for its stunning beaches that surround the whole island, including the famous Pigeon Point, Trinidad has its share of lovely beaches as well. Maracas Bay just outside of Port of Spain on the North Coast is a well-loved spot, especially on Ash Wednesday for a relaxing

Maracas Bay Beach is a popular spot for "lime" or hangout.

day following Carnival Tuesday revelry. Scotland Bay, which is only reachable by boat has serene waters and is almost always nearly empty—perfect for a tranquil swim and relaxing picnic. I particularly love the beaches on the little Channel Islands in the Bocas off the North Coast. Some include Gasparee Grand and Nelson's Island, the former indenture immigration station. On Chacachacare, the former leper colony, the black sands of La Tinta are not to be missed. Several tour companies go "down the islands" as it is called, including Dive TnT (www.divetnt.com) and Caribbean Discovery Tours (www.caribbeandiscoverytours.com/).

Music

Music may be the one thing Trinidadians love more than food. The islands' musical heritage is rich and varied, a complex amalgam of East Indian, African, and natively created music styles.

Calypso—This unique story-telling form of music is thought to have been born from the tradition of African enslaved people who told stories and kept their culture alive through song. Calypso, especially in competition, is most often associated with the celebration of Carnival, brought to the area by French Catholic settlers, but Calypso is a year-round pursuit that has addressed all matters of Trinidadian life through the ages. I have found that you can learn much about the history and tribulations of the twin-island nation by simply listening to Calypso recordings through the ages (the earliest dates to 1912) with their political and socio-cultural messages cloaked in humor and contagious melody.

Steel pan drummer

Some historians date the earliest form of the drum to the mid-nineteenth century when bamboo-based drums that were beat on the ground were created. By the 1930s the discarded oil drums into which depressions were hammered were the first true steel pan. Today, entire pan orchestras play everything from concert classical music to American jazz and pan competitions are another hallmark of Carnival celebrations.

Soca—A recent introduction to the native T&T music repertoire, Soca emerged in the last decade of the twentieth century and is club or dancehall music that marries calypso with heavy drum beats.

Tassa—Not strictly a musical style, but an instrument, the tassa is an Indo-Caribbean drum made from a clay base and goat skin covering that is heated and stretched tightly over the base. The tassa is used at religious events and parades and the drumbeats are both mesmerizing and quite complex.

Chutney—Credited to Indo-Caribbean musicians, chutney mixes Soca (percussion-based dancehall calypso) with Indian musical overlays, including singing in Hindi or Caribbean Hindi.

Parang—This Spanish music form is a testament to the eclectic culture that is easily Trinidad's most valuable gift to the world. Parang comes from the Spanish word *parrenda* meaning "merrymaking." The music, which features guitar, maracas, violin, and various Afro-Caribbean instruments, is sung in Spanish and is a well-loved tradition during Christmastime.

Steel pan—Another completely indigenous musical form, the steel pan or steel drum was created when the African drumming tradition met the burgeoning oil and pitch industry in Trinidad.

Eco-Tourism

Trinidad & Tobago has a remarkable array of native flora and fauna, hiking trails, and natural wonders that will delight anyone, from the hardcore eco-tourist to the erstwhile nature lover. Sites like the Tobago Rain Forest reserve—the oldest reserve of its kind in the Western Hemisphere—demonstrate that communion with the natural world has long been a part of the nation's heritage.

According to the naturalists at the Asa Wright Nature Center in Arima, Trinidad has 97 native mammals, 400 species of birds, 55 types of reptiles, 25 types of amphibians, and 617 species of butterflies, as well as over 2,200 species of flowering plants. In the twenty-first century

Inland waterfalls and their pools offer cool respite from the heat of the jungle.

a number of efforts to preserve T&T's natural wonders, including the endangered leatherback sea turtle, pawi, and red howler monkey, have started to see good success. Here is a list of some major eco-tourist sites on the two islands.

Point a Pierre Wildfowl Trust—Call for guided tour times, (868) 658-4200 ext. 2512, www.papwildfowltrust.org

Asa Wright Nature Centre Arima—(868) 667-5162, www.asawright.org

Caroni Swamp—This mangrove swamp located on the west coast of Trinidad is the largest on the island and home to the scarlet ibis, found only in Trinidad and Venezuela. A wide array of mangrove flora and fauna are here as well. A number of tour operators offer guided tours of the swamp. Ask at your lodgings for recommendations.

Grafton Nature Sanctuary (Tobago)—On the site of an old cocoa estate destroyed by a hurricane in 1963, located near Black Rock Village on the North Side of the island.

Tobago Rain Forest Reserve—The oldest nature reserve in the Western Hemisphere, the Tobago Rain Forest Reserve was created in 1764 and spans the island's forested Central mountain range.

Turtle Watching—Giant leatherback turtles are an endangered prehistoric species that return to the beaches where they were spawned to lay

T&T has a remarkable array of flora and fauna

Shopping

Trinidad & Tobago now has its share of malls, from the most average to the highest end, like West Moorings in Port of Spain. Supermarkets also dot the island, but happily village farmer's markets selling everything from food to DVDs still abound.

Frederick Street in Port of Spain is noted for its textiles, while Chaguanas's Main Road is considered a bargain shopping hub for all manner of goods, not the least of which are authentic East Indian products and handicrafts. At Maracas Bay a number of vendors sell handmade jewelry, bags, and shoes, and while many of them walk among the sunbathers hawking their goods, they often do have lovely items at reasonable prices.

eggs. Hunted to near extinction for their meat, the leatherbacks are today in serious jeopardy of being wiped from the earth. Trinidad & Tobago are fortunate enough to be one of a handful of leatherback breeding grounds in the world. Visitors can observe them laying eggs in the spring. Nature Seekers, a community based non-profit in Matura, Trinidad, works with experts like Dr. Scott Eckert of UNC Chapel Hill, one of the foremost leatherback researchers in the world, to tag and protect giant leatherbacks as well as to aid the hatchlings into the water. The organization has made great strides in saving this remarkable creature. Nature Seekers' work is a testament to the fact that community education and the dedication of the local people is the hope of an environmentally sound future. The group offers tours and nature education: Tel/Fax: (868) 668-7337, www.natureseekers.org.

Festivals

Feasting and food are an integral part of most Trinidad & Tobago holidays. Here are some (but by no means all) of the major festivals not to be missed for their pageantry, culture, and nibbles.

Arrival Day (May 30)—Celebrates the arrival of the Fatel Rozack, the first indenture ship bringing East Indians to labor in the cane fields of Trinidad in 1834.

Carnival—Often called "The Greatest Show on Earth," Carnival celebrations last from Shrove Thursday (the Thursday before Ash Wednesday) to Fat Tuesday (Dimanche Gras). The days are filled with parades, music contests, and high-energy revelry.

A band of Carnival revelers proudly show off the nation's colors

Corpus Christi Day—A major Catholic holiday in Trinidad & Tobago that marks the anniversary of the institution of the Holy Eucharist, this event is marked by processionals in communities on both islands. The largest procession is held at the Catholic church in Independence Square, Port of Spain. Late spring date varies.

Diwali—The Hindu festival honoring the triumph of light over darkness, Diwali is a national holiday in Trinidad marked by elaborate light displays and Hindu vegetarian feasting. While Diwali generally takes place in October or November, the exact day varies annually by astronomical indicators.

Eid Al Fitr—Marking the end of the Ramadan or Muslim fast, Eid Al Fitr features elaborate feasts at mosques and cultural centers throughout Trinidad. The exact day varies annually by astronomical indicators and locality.

Emancipation Day (August 1) —Commemorating the official end of slavery in the Caribbean in 1838, Emancipation Day is a national holiday marked by a parade through Port of Spain featuring traditional African dress and music. At night the Flambeau parade lights up the procession route.

Hosay—Commemoration of the deaths of the Muslim martyrs Hassan and Hossein, Hosay is marked by the construction of elaborate paper mache tadjah, model mausoleums/tombs, that are then marched to the sea in a processional led by tassa drummers and floated away (*right*).

Parang Festival (Sept.-Dec.)—Parang, the music of Spanish settlers in Trinidad, is an integral part of Trinidad's Christmas season. Beginning on September 25th *parranderos* or parang bands are invited to sing in public settings island-wide through to Christmas.

Phagwha (Holi)—Usually held in the Spring, Phagwha is a Hindu celebration of the triumph of good over evil marked by the exuberant throwing of colored water and powder during singing, dancing, and other festivities.

Spirtual Baptist (Shouter) Liberation Day (March 30)— This unusual holiday marks the 1951 repeal of a 1917 law instituted by the colonial government to ban the Baptist religion in Trinidad & Tobago. During the time of the ban, Baptists were persecuted, beaten, and jailed by the Colonial government. Today, jubilant celebrations countrywide mark the holiday.

Tobago Goat Race—Held during Easter weekend, specially trained racing goats run to the wind, their jockeys alongside, in this well-attended and joyful event.

Tobago Heritage Festival—This two-week event is observed by a number of small harvest festivals in towns dotting the island celebrating the African tradition that is the hallmark of Tobago culture. The highlight is the re-enactment of a traditional Tobago wedding, "Ole Time Tobago Wedding," which takes place over two days with the Bachelor's Night, Bride's Affair (preparing the bride), Ceremony, Cake and Wine Reception, and Grand Reception. Dates vary, check yearly calendar.

Hosay commemoration.

For more information on travel to Trinidad & Tobago, visit Go Trinidad & Tobago at www.discovertnt.com.

BREAKFASTS

FRESH CORN PORRIDGE

Despite the warm climate, hot porridges are very popular for breakfast in Trinidad and much of the Caribbean. In Trinidad as in the rest of the Caribbean, porridges are more often made from starchy vegetables such as cassava, pumpkin, and corn instead of from grains. This porridge may be served warm, or if allowed to cool in a greased bowl or loaf pan, it will form a custard that can be inverted onto a plate and sliced for a cold dessert.

6 ears fresh corn

1 tablespoon butter

3 cups coconut milk

½ cup brown sugar

½ teaspoon ground cinnamon

1 Grate the corn niblets off the cob into a bowl.

2 Melt the butter in a large deep saucepan and add the corn. Cook over medium-low heat, stirring often, until the corn begins to soften. Do not allow it to brown.

3 Add the coconut milk and brown sugar and continue to cook and stir until the sugar dissolves. Stir in the cinnamon.

4 Continue to cook the porridge over medium heat, stirring constantly so the bottom does not burn, for about 5 to 7 minutes or until the mixture is reduced by one-quarter.

5 Serve the porridge hot for breakfast or cool completely then pour into a greased loaf pan and chill in the refrigerator overnight, covered in plastic wrap, until it forms a custard. Slice and serve for dessert with whipped cream.

CORNMEAL PORRIDGE

Cornmeal Porridge differs from Fresh Corn Porridge (opposite page) in that it uses cornmeal instead of fresh corn and evaporated milk instead of coconut milk. Use finely ground cornmeal for this dish or you'll have a porridge that is more grainy, like grits.

⅓ cup finely ground cornmeal

¼ teaspoon ground nutmeg

1-inch cinnamon stick or 1 teaspoon
ground cinnamon

¼ cup light brown sugar

1 cup evaporated milk

⅛ teaspoon coarse salt

1 Bring 2 cups of water to a boil in a medium saucepan and add the cornmeal.

2 Add the nutmeg and cinnamon stick and reduce heat to low. Simmer until the mixture is thickened, about 10 to 12 minutes.

3 Stir in the sugar, milk, and salt and mix well. Simmer for 2 to 3 minutes more. Serve hot.

CASSAVA PORRIDGE

Cassava or yucca is extremely starchy and therefore excellent for a thick porridge. You'll find that this finished porridge is shiny and almost translucent, with a toothsome texture, especially since the porridge is sweetened with condensed milk. If you like tapioca pudding, you will like this porridge as tapioca is made from cassava.

6 ounces fresh or frozen cassava root, peeled and cut into chunks

½ teaspoon coarse salt

1-inch piece cinnamon stick

¼ teaspoon ground nutmeg

½ teaspoon mixed essence

½ cup condensed milk, or more to taste

1 Place the cassava cubes into a food processor or heavy-duty blender with 2 cups of water. Process until smooth and thick without any lumps.

2 Bring 2 more cups of water to a boil along with the salt and cinnamon stick. Stir in the pureed cassava mixture. Lower heat to medium-low and simmer, whisking often, for 10 to 15 minutes or until thick and smooth.

3 Stir in the nutmeg, mixed essence, and condensed milk and continue to simmer for 3 to 4 more minutes, whisking often. Serve hot.

COCONUT BAKE

Slightly sweeter than traditional *bake* (page 183) which is a savory fried donut, coconut *bake* is baked in the oven and more cake-like in appearance and texture. It can be eaten with tea for breakfast or as a snack.

2 cups all-purpose flour

¼ cup unsweetened coconut flakes

2 teaspoons baking powder

¾ teaspoon coarse salt

2 tablespoons cold butter or vegetable shortening, plus butter for serving

¾ cup coconut milk

1 Preheat the oven to 350°F. Grease a baking sheet.

2 Sift together the flour, coconut flakes, baking powder, and salt into a large bowl. Cut in the butter with a fork and crumble the mixture together until pea-sized balls form.

3 Gradually add the coconut milk to form a soft dough. Turn out the dough onto a floured board and knead until smooth and elastic, adding more flour as necessary if the dough is too sticky.

4 Pinch off a 2-inch piece of dough and form into a ball. Flatten the ball into a 4-inch disk with the palm of your hand. Repeat using the rest of dough.

5 Place the disks on the greased baking sheet and bake until golden brown, about 20 minutes. Split the hot bakes in half horizontally, butter them, and serve.

TOMATO CHOKHA

Grilling the tomatoes gives this dish the best flavor, but blistering them under a broiler works well, too. Be sure to choose ripe but firm tomatoes. This dish is often served for breakfast as an accompaniment to eggs scrambled with onions, or with Buljol (page 29) and Fry Bake (page 183).

4 large beefsteak tomatoes

1 tablespoon canola oil

½ medium onion, chopped

2 cloves garlic, finely chopped

¼ teaspoon nigella seeds

1 small tomato, chopped

¼ teaspoon coarse salt, or to taste

Freshly ground black pepper to taste

1 tablespoon coarsely chopped cilantro

1 Preheat a grill or broiler. When it is hot, place the beefsteak tomatoes on the grill or under the broiler. Turn frequently, as the tomatoes become brown and blister. Cook until completely charred and soft, about 10 minutes. Remove and cool.

2 Once the tomatoes are cooled, carefully peel them. Place the peeled tomatoes in a bowl and mash. Set aside.

3 Heat the oil in a frying pan. Add the onion and sauté until translucent. Add the garlic and fry until it turns a dark golden brown, then add the nigella seeds and fry until they just begin to pop.

4 Stir in the mashed tomatoes and chopped tomato and sauté for about 2 minutes. Season with salt and black pepper to taste. Garnish with the cilantro and serve with roti (pages 174-177).

PUMPKIN CHOKHA

This dish is often eaten at breakfast with roti, but it also makes a wonderful vegetable side dish for any menu.

1 tablespoon canola oil

1 small onion, chopped

2 cloves garlic, finely chopped

¼ teaspoon cumin seeds

2 cups chopped (1-inch pieces) calabaza, butternut squash, or cheese pumpkin

1 teaspoon brown sugar

2 teaspoons green seasoning (page 254)

1 Roma tomato, chopped

½ teaspoon coarse salt, or to taste

Freshly ground black pepper to taste

1 Heat the oil in a deep saucepan. Add the onion and fry until translucent, then add the garlic and fry until light golden brown. Add the cumin seeds and fry until they begin to pop and release their aroma, about 30 seconds.

2 Mix in the calabaza, squash, or pumpkin and brown sugar and sauté for 1 to 2 minutes. Cover the pot, lower the heat to medium-low, and cook for about 10 minutes.

3 Remove the lid and mix well. The squash should have released some liquid. If the pot is dry, add about ¼ cup of water. Stir in the green seasoning, tomato, salt, and black pepper. Cover the pot and simmer for about 15 to 20 minutes, or until the pumpkin/squash can be mashed easily.

4 Remove the pot from the heat, mash the pumpkin/squash until smooth, and return it to the heat. Cook for 1 to 2 minutes. Serve as a side dish with rice (page 160) or roti (pages 174-177).

SMOKED HERRING AND DUMPLINGS

If saltfish was brought to Trinidad by the Spanish and Portuguese, it's most likely that smoked herring was brought by the English. This dish, which is similar to Buljol (page 29) served with Fry Bake (page 183), uses herring in place of saltfish and is served with boiled dumplings instead of fried bread.

¾ pound smoked herring fillets

2 teaspoons canola oil

1 small onion, chopped

1 tablespoon finely chopped fresh chives

1 tablespoon finely chopped shado beni or cilantro leaves

2 cloves garlic, finely chopped

1 large roma tomato, chopped

1 small red chili pepper, finely chopped (optional)

DUMPLINGS:

½ cup all-purpose flour

½ cup cornmeal

Pinch of coarse salt

1 Bring about 4 cups of water to a boil in a medium saucepan and add the herring fillets. Boil for 2 to 3 minutes and drain. Allow the fillets to cool and then finely shred. Set aside.

2 Make dumplings: Mix together the flour, cornmeal, and salt. Add 6 tablespoons of water and knead to form a stiff dough, adding more water if necessary. Knead until smooth and set aside to rest for 15 minutes. Pinch off 1-inch pieces of dough and roll between the palms of your hands to form ovals. Pinch both ends of the ovals, then flatten between palms or against a cutting board. The dumplings should resemble small flat footballs. Bring a large pot of salted water to a boil and add the dumplings. Simmer until dumplings float to the surface. Drain and set aside, keeping warm.

3 Heat a medium sauté pan and pour in the canola oil. Add the onion, chives, shado beni, and garlic and sauté for about 2 minutes, stirring often. Add the tomato and red chili pepper, if using, and mix well and cook 2 to 3 minutes more. Add the herring and fry for about 5 minutes.

4 To serve, divide the dumplings between four plates and put the smoked herring mixture on top, dividing evenly.

A TRIO OF EGG DISHES

In Trinidad guests are usually treated to the most elaborate dishes a cook can make. As a result, much of the simple and delicious daily fare that is eaten at home is never experienced by the visitor. My good friend Gerard Ramsawak, manager of Pax Guest House in Tunapuna, is a faithful devotee to the notion that the skill of the cook and the quality of the ingredients are most clearly revealed in those dishes that seem most rudimentary—because there is little room for error. Among his favorites are these three egg dishes that are served not just at breakfast, but as a protein-rich meal any other time of the day as well.

EGG CHOKHA

SERVES: 4

2 teaspoons canola oil

½ small onion, finely chopped

2 cloves garlic, finely chopped

¼ green Scotch bonnet pepper or other hot chili pepper, finely chopped

1 large tomato, chopped

8 large eggs, beaten

4 leaves shado beni or cilantro, chopped

1 Heat the canola oil in a medium saute pan and add the onion. When the onion is translucent, lower heat to medium-low and add the garlic and chili pepper and fry until garlic is golden brown.

2 Add the tomato and cook for 2 to 3 minutes or until the tomato is almost broken down.

3 Stir in the beaten eggs and allow to cook 1 minute or until the edges begin to set. Using a spatula, gently push in the edges of the eggs toward the middle of the pan and swirl the uncooked eggs onto the pan surface so they may cook too. Sprinkle the eggs with the shado beni and cook 1 minute more. Flip the omelet (it's ok if it breaks into pieces when flipping) and cook another minute or two. Serve with Sadha Roti (page 176) or Plain Rice (page 160).

INDIAN EGGS

1 teaspoon canola oil

½ small onion, finely chopped

1 teaspoon butter

2 cloves garlic, finely chopped

¼ green Scotch bonnet pepper
  or other hot chili pepper, finely
  chopped

8 large eggs, beaten

1 Heat the canola oil in a medium saute pan and add the onion. When the onion is translucent, add the butter and stir well until butter melts.

2 Lower heat to medium-low and add the garlic and chili pepper and fry until garlic is golden brown.

3 Add the beaten eggs and allow to cook 1 minute or until the edges begin to set. Using a spatula, gently push in the edges of the eggs toward the middle of the pan and swirl the uncooked eggs onto the pan surface and cook 1 minute more. Flip the omelet (it's ok if the it breaks into pieces when flipping) and continue to cook another minute or two. Serve with Sadha Roti (page 176).

EGG CURRY

2 tablespoons canola oil

1 small onion, chopped

3 cloves garlic, finely chopped

1 tablespoon Trinidad curry powder
  (page 253)

4 medium yukon gold potatoes,
  peeled and cut into 1-inch chunks

8 hard-boiled eggs, peeled and sliced
  in half lengthwise

1 Heat 1 tablespoon of the canola oil in a large, deep fry pan and add the onion. Cook until the onion is translucent, about 2 minutes. Add the garlic and cook for 1 minute more. Stir in the curry powder and fry, stirring constantly, until the curry begins to release its aromas.

2 Add the potatoes and stir well, frying for 1 minute. Add 1 cup of water, mix well, and lower heat and simmer for 15 minutes.

3 While potatoes are cooking, heat another fry pan, preferably non-stick and heat the remaining 1 tablespoon oil. Add the egg halves in a single layer and fry gently until lightly browned on all sides. Remove from the heat.

4 Gently add the egg halves to the potato mixture, being careful not to separate the yolks from the whites. Simmer 10 minutes. Serve with Plain Rice (page 160) or Sadha Roti (page 176).

BULJOL

Despite its strong flavors, Buljol—fried codfish with onions and tomatoes—served with Fry Bake is a traditional breakfast dish. If you find the salt cod too strong, you can substitute any white fish fillet—catfish is a good option. There are two ways to prepare Buljol—as a cold salad or as a fried dish. My father always prepared the latter.

½ pound boneless salt cod or fresh white fish filet

1 tablespoon canola oil

1 large onion, finely chopped

2 cloves garlic, finely chopped

1 fresh pimiento pepper, stemmed, seeded, and finely chopped; or 1 teaspoon paprika

1 Scotch bonnet pepper or other hot chili pepper, stemmed, seeded, and finely chopped

1 large tomato, finely chopped

Freshly ground black pepper

1 Rinse salt cod by soaking in cold water for 5 minutes. Drain and repeat 2 more times. SThen drain well and shred the cod. (If using fresh fish do not soak; broil until just cooked through, cool, and shred.)

2 Heat the oil in a skillet and add the onion. Sauté until soft and then add the garlic, sautéing for 1 minute more. Stir in the shredded fish, pimiento pepper, and hot pepper. If using fresh fish, add 1 teaspoon of coarse salt. Fry for 1 to 2 minutes.

3 Add the tomato, mix well, and cook until soft. Season with black pepper, and serve with Fry Bakes (page 183).

Syrian Trinidadians' Culture & Food

Nearly every afternoon around five, Mrs. Antoinette George and several other ladies meet for mezzes of tabbouleh, hummus, olives, and shankleesh at Adam's Bagels, the Syrian-Lebanese eatery owned by her son-in-law in Port of Spain, Trinidad. The women, who comprise an extended network of grandmothers, aunts, cousins, and in-laws living on the Caribbean island, move from the small plates to Arabic coffee and pastries, stopping to greet others coming and going as they shop for delicacies imported from the Middle East.

These ladies represent the matriarchs of Trinidad's Syrian-Lebanese community, descendants of émigrés from what was once known as Greater Syria, encompassing modern-day Iraq, Syria, Palestine, and Lebanon. Their forebears arrived in Trinidad more than one hundred years ago, and their cuisine has been their bridge to Trinidadian society at large.

"In the days when our parents and grandparents came, there weren't the things we needed for our cuisine," said Mrs. George. "So they adapted." Some of those adaptations included substituting the local Mexican culantro (*recao*) for cilantro and instead of spinach using the locally popular *patchoi* (bok choy) brought by Chinese indentured laborers to the island nearly two hundred years ago. The popular fresh sheep's milk cheese called *shankleesh* was made in Trinidad using cow's milk.

The first Arabic immigrants came to Trinidad in 1898 from Beirut, Lebanon, believing they had boarded ships bound for the United States. They were men who worked as simple door-to-door peddlers hauling suitcases filled with sundries.

Working hard they eventually prospered, earning enough money to bring their wives and families to the island as well.

Almost fifty years later, at the onset of the Second World War, fellow Arabs—Syrians from the Crac Des Chevaliers—arrived, supported by those families who had gone before and had successfully made Trinidad their home. Today, history is repeating itself and new immigrants with ties both within this community and outside of it are arriving at a steady pace.

Among the many varied emigrants to Trinidad, the Syrian Lebanese community has remained the most insular, holding fast to their traditions, doing business with and marrying each other almost exclusively. Their numbers remain small, but today these families, now in their fourth and fifth generations, comprise a power base in Trinidad with holdings in real estate, oil, media, construction, and food service.

Newly popular gyro stands are the bailiwick of the newest Syrian immigrants, and they line the major boulevards in towns from the capital of Port of Spain all the way down to San Fernando, and everywhere in between. They are in malls as well and represent small independent operators as well as franchises rapidly overtaking foods like doubles, a curried chickpea sandwich, and oyster shooters from mangrove oysters, as the go-to after-party food for the clubbing crowd.

"The people line up for gyros every night," said Zuher Dukhen who, along with his brothers arrived in Trinidad within the last few years. At their take-out stand, Sami's Arabian, they make their gyro meat daily, hand forming it using traditional methods. They stay open from five in the evening to three or four in the morning, with customers often waiting hours for the gryos to be finished cooking.

Like the earliest wave of their countrymen, families like the Dukhens remain extremely close-knit. Regardless of religious or neighborhood affiliations, the newcomers have proven themselves eager adoptees of their new home. Nothing exemplifies this more than their love of a full table—a "good lime"—the Trinidadian term for easy companionship featuring food, laughter, and chatter among family and friends.

Adam's Bagels owner Adam Abboud is the hallmark example of a man who has straddled these two worlds nicely. Proud of his Syrian-Lebanese roots, he is also in many ways, "Trini to the bone"—as locals would describe someone whose Trinidadian nature is more than skin deep. "I love my heritage but I love my Trinidadian things too," said Mr. Abboud, whose favorite breakfast is a Trini-Syrian bagel of his own devising: smeared with labneh and topped with Buljol, a cold salt cod salad (page 33).

Mr. Abboud is a master limer, happy to sip coffee and chat for hours. Like any good Trinidadian, his catch-phrase is "relax," but he watches his establishment with an expert eye toward service and works the dining room like the local food celebrity he is. Between shaking hands with male patrons and dispensing kisses and compliments to the ladies, Abboud gestures to his staff to demand extras for his customers—a taste of the newly made shankleesh salad, a nibble of a mamoul date pastry. At Adam's Bagels, the Arabic tradition of lavish hospitality is in full-effect.

Like the bagels, other Arabic pastries are baked onsite like fresh pita bread, sesame bread, baklava, and various cookies using aleb molds from the Middle East. They are prepared by a United Nations of workers who represent what Trinidadians call their "callaloo" culture. The pita are made by a recent Venezuelan immigrant; Haitian pastry chefs make the puff pastry and short dough for the Arabic cookies; and the master baker managing the ovens is a native Trinidadian.

For other traditional goodies, in years past Syrian and Lebanese Trinidadians depended upon visiting relatives or those who made a trip back "home" to bring the rare ingredients they needed. Today in Trinidad, extras like olives, stuffed grape leaves, Arabic coffee, and dates have finally made their appearance on the table thanks to importers like Vabat who serves the growing demand for goods from that part of the world. Olive oil, sumac, mahlab, coffee, and other items now regularly arrive on container ships to Port of Spain's harbor, often initially coming through the United States.

ADAM'S BULJOL & BAGEL

Foods from the Middle Eastern tradition have influenced Trinidadian cuisine. At Adam's Bagels in Port of Spain, Syrian-Lebanese owner Adam Abboud tops his bagels (house made in the New York style) with *labneh* (yogurt cheese) and *buljol*, a cold salad made from salted cod fish that is a common and beloved local breakfast food. Mr. Abboud tops the salad with thin slices of Scotch bonnet pepper—a final touch that is not for the faint of heart.

¾ pound salt cod

1 small onion, finely chopped

1 clove garlic, finely chopped

1 pimiento pepper, stemmed, seeded, and finely chopped

1 medium tomato, chopped

1 tablespoon finely chopped shado beni (Mexican culantro) or 2 tablespoons finely chopped cilantro

1 teaspoon freshly ground black pepper

4 bagels, any style

1 cup labneh

1 small Scotch bonnet pepper, stemmed, seeded, and sliced very thin (optional)

1 Place the salt cod in a large pot with enough cold water to cover and bring to a boil. Reduce heat to medium-low and simmer for 20 minutes. Drain the water and repeat the process two more times to soften the fish and remove most of the salt.

2 Put the drained salt cod in a large bowl and using a fork pull it into shreds. Add the onion, garlic, pimento pepper, and tomato, and mix very well.

3 Add the shado beni and ground pepper and mix well. Set aside in the refrigerator until chilled, about 1 hour.

4 Slice the bagels in half and smear each side with equal portions of labneh. Top each with 2 to 3 tablespoons of buljol salad. Top with thin slices of Scotch bonnet pepper, if desired. Serve open faced.

Shark & Bake vendors at Maracas Bay Beach

SOUPS, STREET FOODS & SMALL BITES

One of my greatest pleasures on trips back to Trinidad is the first taste of doubles the morning after I arrive. Spiced chickpeas with onions and pepper sauce folded between rounds of fried bread, *doubles* are Trinidad's equivalent of a New York bagel purchased at a coffee truck. *Doubles* do double-duty, however, as a wee hours snack for late night clubbers. In fact, the only way to eat them is from the various stands on the side of the road, and everyone has their favorite. I like the ones sold inside Brooklyn Bar in Woodbrook, one of the few remaining old-style rum shops in Trinidad. My husband Jean-Paul swears, as does our good friend Gerard Ramsawak, that Curepe is the only place for any kind of decent *doubles*.

Food stands are a tradition in Trinidad, probably dating back to times when day laborers on sugar and cocoa estates had nowhere else to procure a hot midday meal. Today, vendors dot the country, hawking fried oysters, roti, kacheena, shark & bake, beef patties, shaved ices, spiced roasted peanuts, as well as gyros, sold by recent waves of Syrian immigrants to the island. Every one of them has their followers. The more elegant stands may have a table or two, while others cook the food ahead of time and sell it out of galvanized metal or plywood shacks. In my experience, the best street-food vendors operate out of trucks similar to the hot dog trucks that we find at beachfronts in the U.S. The food is cooked or reheated on site, so the meal is hot and tasty.

Perhaps the most famous iteration of the Trinidad food stand was the Breakfast Shed, an old warehouse building on Port of Spain's waterfront. It began in 1926 under the auspices of Audrey Jeffers, a philanthropist who started the venture as a way to provide lunches to poorer schoolchildren. In Port of Spain, the tradition, lore, and local patronage of this eatery is not unlike that of New York's Nathan's Famous or New Orleans' Café du Monde. The Breakfast Shed offered traditional home-style breakfast and lunch to schoolchildren, dockworkers, and political types working in the city center. Cruise-ship travelers eventually joined the mix and the place became a "must-see" pit stop for tourists hoping to savor a taste of the real Trinidad. For a time, newfound tourism fame resulted in a facelift for the old Breakfast Shed, and it was housed in a bright yellow concrete building plastered with packaged food ads, far different from the old galvanized shed I remembered as a child. In 2007-2008, the waterfront area where Breakfast Shed stood was redeveloped with an ultramodern promenade, complete with an elaborate fountain and the luxury Hyatt Regency Hotel a few hundred yards away. A clean, bright new building called the Femmes De Chalet now houses the old Breakfast Shed vendors and the food is as good as ever, but it sure feels odd to go back "home" and not get a meal in the colorful cacophony that was the old establishment.

Visitors who want to sample a large array of street food in one locale should head to the Queen's Park Savannah in Port of Spain. Vendors have set up shop around the perimeter to serve the constant flow of walkers, joggers, and event-goers in the large park, although the government is trying to monitor and crack down on street-food vending. A new and popular street-food event at the Savannah is nighttime food truck gatherings. Port of Spain residents have been known to hit the stands and set up picnic blankets or chairs and small tables on the grass and eat under the stars.

Soups are also among the food traditionally eaten out, and stands selling cow heel soup or *sancoche* (a classic Caribbean stew) abound.

In the home, appetizers don't really exist as a separate course in the traditional sense, but small self-contained foods that are eaten as snacks at breakfast or teatime make wonderful starters for the American table.

AVOCADO SOUP

Avocado, or *zaboca* as it is called in Trinidad, is widely available and it's not uncommon to see large avocado trees overladen with ripe fruit in front yards. One afternoon, while I was taking tea on the balcony at Pax Guest House, a football-size avocado burst free from a branch and landed on the ground with a huge thud. The avocado was so large and ripe that small birds walked into the burst shell, ate their fill, and left—for two days straight!

5 ripe Haas avocados, peeled and chopped (about 4 cups)

1 teaspoon green seasoning (page 254)

2 teaspoons coarse salt

¼ teaspoon ground white pepper

1 cup heavy cream

4 cups chicken broth

⅓ cup sherry

Avocado slices for garnish

1 Place the avocados, green seasoning, salt, white pepper, and cream in a blender or food processor and puree until smooth.

2 Heat the chicken broth in a large saucepan and bring just to a boil. Stir the avocado mixture into the broth. Simmer for 1 to 2 minutes and then add the sherry and simmer for 1 minute more. Adjust the seasonings to taste. Serve the soup warm or cold.

CALLALLOO

This thick soup is considered the national dish of Trinidad. It makes use of dasheen/taro leaves, which lend a particular almost tangy flavor. A mixture of fresh spinach and Swiss chard is a good substitute if you cannot get dasheen. Callalloo can be made with or without crabmeat or pork, according to taste.

1 pound dasheen/taro leaves, or ½ pound each spinach and Swiss chard, stemmed and chopped

6 cups chicken stock

1 onion, finely chopped

1 clove garlic, chopped

3 scallions, green and white parts, chopped

2 tablespoons finely chopped fresh chives

¼ teaspoon fresh thyme leaves

4 ounces lean salt pork or Canadian bacon, cut into ½-inch cubes

½ pound fresh, canned, or frozen crabmeat

½ cup coconut milk

½ pound young okra or 1 (10-ounce) package frozen okra, sliced

Salt and pepper to taste

¼ teaspoon hot pepper sauce, or to taste

1 Place the greens in a soup pot with the chicken stock, onion, garlic, scallions, chives, thyme, and salt pork. Cover and simmer over low heat until the pork is fork tender, about 30 minutes.

2 Using a slotted spoon, remove most of the solids from the pot and place them in a food processor or blender. Puree to a rough paste. Return mixture to the pot, mixing well.

3 Add the crabmeat, coconut milk, and okra, and stir until thoroughly combined. Simmer over medium heat for another 10 minutes. Season to taste with salt, black pepper, and hot pepper sauce.

SQUASH SOUP

Coconut milk, hot pepper, and herbs give this popular soup a little tropical kick. If you have a supply of Green Seasoning (page 254) on hand, you can use that in place of the collected herbs in this recipe—use about 2 tablespoons.

Calabaza, also called West Indian pumpkin, is now more readily available in your standard supermarket, but if you can't find it you can substitute butternut squash. Cinderella or "cheese" pumpkins are actually the best substitute because of their high sugar content. They are generally available in autumn and can be stored in a cool dry place right through the winter. Alternatively, if using them for purees or soup, I peel and cut the pumpkin into large chunks and freeze in individual zip-top bags of about one pound each.

2 tablespoons canola oil

2 cups chopped calabaza, pumpkin, butternut squash, or acorn squash

1 small onion, finely chopped

3 cloves garlic, crushed

4 cups chicken or vegetable stock

1 bay leaf

1 sprig fresh thyme

½ teaspoon dried oregano

1 tablespoon chopped fresh parsley

1 tablespoon chopped fresh cilantro

½ teaspoon coarse salt

½ teaspoon dark brown sugar

1 cup coconut milk

¼ teaspoon hot pepper sauce

Sour cream (optional)

Chopped chives (optional)

1 Heat the oil in a 4-quart saucepan and add the calabaza, tossing to coat. Cook for 2 to 3 minutes, then add the onion and garlic. Cover and sweat the vegetables for about 3 minutes.

2 Add the stock, bay leaf, thyme, oregano, parsley, cilantro, and salt. Cover and simmer for 10 minutes; then remove the lid and simmer over low heat for 10 minutes more, or until the calabaza is fork tender.

3 Remove the bay leaf and discard. Remove the vegetables and herbs from the soup with a slotted spoon and place in a blender or food processor and puree until smooth. Return the puree to the pot and add the sugar and coconut milk and mix well.

4 Simmer the soup uncovered for 5 minutes, or until reduced by one-quarter. Add the pepper sauce and simmer for 2 minutes more. Serve hot, garnished with a dollop of sour cream and some chives.

SANCOCHE
(DUMPLING SOUP)

This is the Trinidadian version of a popular meal that was often prepared on Sundays throughout the Caribbean because it could be left to simmer over the fire while laborers spent the day at church or worked in the fields. One of my childhood favorites, this thick soup features dumplings shaped like pointy-ended ovals. My father always seemed to have a pot of Sancoche, which my brother and I called "Dumpling Soup," on the back burner of the stove or in the refrigerator or freezer.

SOUP

3 tablespoons canola oil

1 pound boneless beef or chicken, cut into 1-inch cubes

2 large onions, chopped

2 cloves garlic, finely chopped

8 cups beef or chicken stock

1 teaspoon chopped fresh thyme

1 bay leaf

1 cup brown lentils

1 pound white boiling potatoes, peeled and cut into chunks

½ pound calabaza or butternut squash, peeled, seeded, and cut into chunks

1 whole Scotch bonnet pepper or other hot chili pepper

Salt and freshly ground black pepper

DUMPLINGS

¾ cup all-purpose flour

½ cup cornmeal

⅛ teaspoon coarse salt

⅛ teaspoon sugar

1 tablespoon cold butter

1 Heat the oil in a Dutch oven or 4-quart saucepan. When the oil is hot, add the meat and sauté until lightly browned. Add the onions and sauté for 5 minutes, stirring from time to time. Add the garlic and cook for 1 minute more, then add the stock, thyme, bay leaf, and lentils. Lower the heat and simmer for about 1 hour.

2 Meanwhile make the dumplings: Mix together the flour, cornmeal, salt, and sugar. Cut in the butter, making sure it is well incorporated into the flour. Gradually add ¼ cup of water or more as needed until you get a firm dough that is not sticky. Pinch off 1-inch pieces of dough and roll between the palms of your hands to form ovals. Pinch both ends, then flatten the ovals between palms or against a cutting board. The dumplings should resemble small flat footballs. Set aside.

3 Add the potatoes, calabaza, and whole Scotch pepper to the soup, and simmer for an additional 20 minutes, adding more stock if necessary. Add salt and black pepper to taste. Add the dumplings and check for seasonings, adding more salt or pepper if needed. Simmer for 15 minutes more. Remove the Scotch pepper, and serve soup hot. (Note: If you'd like to freeze some Sancoche, do so before you add the dumplings; then add them to the soup once you've reheated it.)

COW HEEL SOUP

Cow Heel Soup is one of the street foods found at stands and shops all over Trinidad. The soup originated in colonial times when enslaved people received the offal of slaughtered animals as part of their provisions. Cow heel is more than the name implies—it includes the area from the hoof to the knee. The gelatin in the actual hoof makes this thick soup a more-than-hearty meal.

1 cow heel, or 2 pounds beef soup bones, cleaned and cut into 2-inch pieces

2 teaspoons coarse salt

1 onion, chopped

1 stalk celery, chopped

½ small cassava, peeled and cut into ½-inch chunks

1 small yam, peeled and cut into ½-inch chunks

1 small taro, peeled and cut into ½-inch chunks

Pinch of grated nutmeg

1 small Scotch bonnet pepper or other hot chili pepper

1 pound calabaza or butternut squash, peeled, seeded, and cut into ½-inch chunks

1 teaspoon chopped parsley

2 teaspoons freshly squeezed lime juice

1 Place the cow heel or soup bones and 6 cups water in a soup pot and add the salt. Bring to a boil, skimming the surface as impurities rise to the top. When the water is simmering clear, reduce the heat and add the onion and celery. Cover and simmer for 1 hour.

2 Add the cassava, yams, taro, nutmeg, and hot pepper to the pot. Cover and simmer until the vegetables are tender, about 15 minutes, adding the calabaza in the last 10 minutes of cooking.

3 Remove from heat and remove the chili pepper. Add the parsley and lime juice and serve hot.

Tip
Ask your butcher to cut the cow heel or soup bones to the appropriate size.

OXTAIL SOUP

The traditional way to prepare this soup is to place all the ingredients together in one pot and simmer. My French culinary training has convinced me of the importance of first browning meats and vegetables to develop flavor, and this recipe has been adapted to reflect that process.

1 cup dried black-eyed peas, soaked overnight in 3 cups water, or 1 cup canned

1 tablespoon canola oil

2 small onions, chopped

2 pounds lean oxtails

2 or 3 medium carrots, peeled and chopped

2 or 3 cloves garlic, finely chopped

3 tablespoons finely chopped chives

2 sprigs fresh thyme

1 whole Scotch bonnet pepper or other hot chili pepper

1 teaspoon coarse salt, or to taste

1 tablespoon sherry

1 If using dried black-eyed peas, drain and set aside. If using canned peas, drain in a colander, rinse with cold water, and set aside.

2 In a Dutch oven or heavy-bottomed soup pot, heat the oil. Add the onions and cook for 1 minute. Add the oxtails and brown on all sides. Stir in the carrots and cook until they are light brown. Stir in the garlic and cook for 1 minute.

3 Pour 4 cups of cold water over the oxtail mixture. Make sure there is enough water to completely cover the ingredients. Mix well, scraping the bottom to loosen any caramelized bits. Add the chives, thyme, and hot pepper. Bring to a simmer, cover, and cook for 1 hour, skimming the surface as needed.

4 Add the black-eyed peas. Simmer for 30 minutes more, or until the oxtails and peas are tender. Add the salt and mix well. Simmer for 10 minutes more. Remove the thyme sprigs and chili pepper. Stir in the sherry just before serving.

Tip: Dried Beans

Dried beans have better flavor and are far more economical than canned, but they are not as convenient. I use the following method to get the benefits of dried with the convenience of canned: Soak dried beans at a ratio of 3 cups of water to 1 cup of beans overnight. Drain and bring three times the amount of water as beans to boil in a large pot. Add beans and simmer for 15 minutes. Drain and cool beans. Freeze in one-pound portions in individual ziptop freezer bags.

FISH BROTH

Although this soup is called a broth, it's a far cry from the thin, clear liquid usually bearing that name. Actually a fish soup, it makes a good meal in itself paired with some crusty bread and a glass of white wine. I have seen this prepared in Jamaica, where a whole fish is used and pumpkin puree is added to the broth—it is called "Steamed Fish."

2 pounds firm-fleshed fish fillets, such as tilapia or catfish

2 cloves garlic, finely chopped

1 teaspoon coarse salt

1 teaspoon finely chopped habañero pepper

1 tablespoon freshly squeezed lime juice

2 tablespoons green seasoning (page 254)

1 medium Yukon Gold potato, peeled and cut into 1-inch chunks

1 large carrot, peeled and cut into 1-inch chunks

1 large unripe banana, peeled and cut into 1-inch chunks

1 medium onion, coarsely chopped

1 medium tomato, coarsely chopped, or ½ cup canned stewed tomatoes

1 tablespoon unsalted butter

Hot pepper sauce (optional)

1 Cut the fish into ½-inch-wide slices and toss with the garlic, salt, habañero pepper, lime juice, and green seasoning. Set aside in the refrigerator for 1 hour.

2 Place the potato and carrot in a saucepan with 4 cups of water and bring to a boil. Simmer for 15 minutes.

3 Add the fish mixture, banana, onion, tomato, and butter, and simmer for 20 minutes more, until the fish is flaky. Taste and adjust the flavor with salt, hot pepper sauce, and more lime juice, as desired.

TRINI-SYRIAN HUMMUS

The Middle Eastern chickpea dip called hummus is now as popular as peanut butter in the United States, a development that took place over the last ten years. In Trinidad, hummus has been eaten for nearly one hundred years, arriving with Syrian-Lebanese refugees in the late 1800s. As with many immigrant foods, Syrian hummus was adapted to local ingredients and flavors so that today it features seasoning peppers—or aji dulce—and shado beni (Mexican culantro). I like to use dried chickpeas that are reconstituted and cooked for this recipe because I believe they process to a nice smooth texture without being watery. However, you can use canned chickpeas if you desire.

1 cup dried chickpeas, soaked overnight in 3 cups of water

2 cloves garlic

1 small seasoning pepper (aji dulce*), stemmed and seeded

6 leaves shado beni or cilantro

2 tablespoons freshly squeezed lime juice

1 tablespoon tahini

¼ cup olive oil or more as needed

1 teaspoon coarse salt or to taste

---

*If you cannot find aji dulce, ¼ cup finely chopped red bell pepper is a good substitute.

1 If using dried chickpeas, bring 3 cups of water to a boil in a medium saucepan. Drain the chickpeas and add them to the pot. Reduce heat to a simmer and cook the chickpeas until tender, about 30 minutes. Drain. (If using canned, drain and rinse in colander.)

2 Place the cooked chickpeas, garlic, seasoning pepper, and shado beni in the bowl of a food processor and process into a coarse paste. Mix the lime juice and tahini together and add to the chickpea mixture.

3 With processor on, drizzle in olive oil, adding enough to achieve a thick paste. Add water a teaspoon at a time until the hummus reaches a smooth, easily spreadable consistency. Scrape the hummus into a bowl and stir in the salt. Serve with pita bread or crudite.

ACCRAS

These delicious fritters make use of salt cod (*baccalà*), a popular ingredient brought to the West Indies by the Portuguese and Spanish. The only downside is that the smell of cooked fish permeates the house for some time, so I suggest making accras on a fine day when you can have the windows open!

½ pound boneless salt cod

1 teaspoon active dry yeast (see Tip)

¾ cup warm water (100–110°F), divided

½ teaspoon sugar

1 cup sifted all-purpose flour

1 teaspoon baking powder

¼ teaspoon freshly ground black pepper

1 scallion, finely chopped

¼ teaspoon hot pepper sauce

1 teaspoon green seasoning (page 254)

2 tablespoons finely chopped fresh cilantro

1 egg, lightly beaten

1 cup canola oil for frying

1 Place the salt cod and 2 cups of cold water in a medium pot over medium heat. Bring to a boil and then reduce heat and simmer until the liquid is reduced by half, about 10 minutes. Drain and repeat this process two more times. After draining the salt cod the last time, place in a large bowl and finely shred with a fork. Set aside.

2 In a small bowl, combine the yeast, ¼ cup warm water, and sugar. Stir well and set aside until foamy, about 1 to 2 minutes.

3 Sift together the flour, baking powder, and black pepper. Add the yeast mixture, remaining ½ cup warm water, scallion, pepper sauce, green seasoning, cilantro, and egg. Beat very well until you have a smooth, thick batter. Set aside to proof for 1 hour.

4 Once the dough has proofed, stir in the flaked salt cod.

5 Heat the oil in a deep saucepan (test by dropping ¼ teaspoon of dough into the oil; when it bobs to the surface and fries vigorously, the oil is ready). Drop tablespoons of batter into the oil in batches, being sure not to overcrowd the pot. Fry until golden brown, about 1 minute, then remove with a slotted spoon. Drain on paper towels. Serve hot.

Tip

If you don't want to use yeast, baking powder will work as well but the accras won't be as airy. Substitute 1 tablespoon of baking powder for the yeast and allow the dough to sit for 20 minutes rather than 1 hour.

DOUBLES

This popular breakfast food of spiced chickpeas served between two pieces of fried dough is also a late-night favorite after a good "lime," the Trini term for "hanging out." On Friday and Saturday nights, smart doubles vendors take to their open-air stands to serve hungry revelers seeking a midnight snack.

DOUGH

⅓ cup warm water (100–110°F)

¼ teaspoon sugar

1 teaspoon active dry yeast

2 cups all-purpose flour

½ teaspoon coarse salt

1 teaspoon ground turmeric

½ teaspoon ground cumin

½ teaspoon ground black pepper

FILLING

2 cups dried chickpeas, soaked overnight in 6 cups water, or 1 (16-ounce) can chickpeas

1 tablespoon canola oil

1 onion, thinly sliced

3 cloves garlic, finely chopped

4½ teaspoons Trinidad curry powder (page 253)

Pinch of ground cumin

Coarse salt and freshly ground black pepper to taste

MAKE DOUGH:

1 Place the warm water, sugar, and yeast in a small bowl. Set aside until the mixture bubbles, about 1 to 2 minutes.

2 In a large bowl combine the flour, salt, turmeric, cumin, and black pepper. Stir in the yeast mixture and add additional lukewarm water as needed, about ½ cup, until the mixture comes together into slightly firm dough. Knead until smooth and elastic and cover with a damp cloth. Set aside in a warm place to rise until doubled in size, about 1 hour.

MAKE FILLING:

3 If using dried chickpeas, drain, place in a pot with 6 cups of fresh water. Simmer for about 1 hour, or until tender. Drain and set aside. If using canned chickpeas, drain in a colander and rinse well with cold water. Set aside.

4 Heat the oil in a heavy skillet and add the onion. Cook until translucent. Add the garlic and stir well, frying for 1 minute. Add the curry powder and mix well. Cook for 30 seconds and then add ¼ cup of water.

5 Stir in the drained chickpeas, cover and simmer for 5 minutes. Remove the lid and add 1 more cup of water, the cumin, and salt and pepper, and lower the heat. Simmer until the chickpeas are very tender, about 45 minutes. Set aside.

Canola oil for frying

Hot Pepper Sauce (page 257), for
  serving

Kuchela (page 266), for serving

Finely shredded cucumber, for garnish

ASSEMBLE & FRY:

6 Punch down the dough and allow it to sit for 10
  minutes. Pinch off walnut-size pieces of dough
  and flatten each into a circle about 4½ inches in
  diameter (dampen your hands with water if the
  dough is sticky).

7 Heat about 1 cup of canola oil (at least 3 inches
  deep) in a frying pan or medium saucepan. Test
  the temperature of the oil by sprinkling a bit of
  flour into it; if the flour bubbles and sizzles the
  oil is ready. Add the dough circles in batches and
  fry turning once, until lightly browned on both
  sides, about 40 seconds. Remove from oil with a
  slotted spoon and drain on paper towels. Keep
  warm.

8 To serve, place 2 tablespoons of chickpeas on a
  piece of fried dough. Top with the pepper sauce,
  Kuchela, and cucumber, if desired. Top with
  another piece of fried dough.

KATCHOURIE

Vegetable fritters are popular Trinidadian snacks and are largely East Indian in origin. Katchourie is often sold at the same street stands that sell Phoulourie (page 53) and Sahina (page 54). This dish requires a little planning ahead since the split peas need to be soaked overnight.

2 cups dried yellow split peas, soaked overnight in 6 cups water

3 cloves garlic, finely chopped

1 small onion, finely chopped

3 fresh pimiento peppers, finely chopped, or 1½ teaspoons paprika

¼ cup chopped chives, or 2 scallions, chopped

⅓ cup all-purpose flour

½ teaspoon ground turmeric

2 teaspoons coarse salt

1 Scotch bonnet pepper or other hot red chili pepper, finely chopped

1 cup canola oil, for frying

1 Drain the split peas and grind in a food processor to a coarse paste.

2 In a bowl, combine the ground split peas with the garlic, onion, pimiento, chives, flour, turmeric, salt, and hot pepper. Add enough water to form a loose dough, about the consistency of uncooked meatloaf.

3 Form the dough into patties 3 inches wide and ½ inch thick.

4 Heat the oil in a saucepan until hot (test by dropping a little flour into the pot; if it sizzles vigorously, the oil is ready). Add the patties in batches (do not overcrowd). Fry on each side until golden brown. Remove and drain on paper towels. Serve hot.

Tip: Pimiento Peppers

Pimiento peppers are available at Latino markets, supermarkets that have a good variety of Latino goods, and online. They are sometimes called by the Spanish name *aji dulce*.

PHOULOURIE

These split-pea fritters are just one of many fried snacks found in Trinidad. No one knows the origin of the name but it's generally agreed that they were created by East Indian indentured laborers. Phoulourie has a close resemblance to the batter used for *pakora*—Indian battered fried vegetables. Like *pakoras* these fried treats are usually served with Tamarind Sauce or Shado Beni Sauce, but Mango Chutney and other fruit chutneys are popular too. (Note: This batter is also used for making Sahina, page 54.)

2 cups dried yellow split peas or 1½ cups besan (chickpea flour)

2 cloves garlic, finely chopped

½ teaspoon ground turmeric

¼ teaspoon ground cumin

4 teaspoons baking powder

2 cups all-purpose flour

1 teaspoon coarse salt

½ teaspoon chili powder

2 cups canola oil for frying

1 Place the dried split peas in a pot with 6 cups of water and bring to a boil. Lower the heat and simmer until soft, about 45 minutes.

2 Drain the split peas and place in a food processor. Grind into a coarse meal, resembling couscous. Add the garlic, turmeric, cumin, baking powder, flour, salt, and chili powder and grind by pulsing until well combined. (Or, if using besan, stir into a bowl with the other ingredients until well combined.)

3 Gradually add about 1 cup of water to the split pea mixture, stirring to form a thick batter.

4 Heat the oil in a deep frying pan. Working in batches, drop the batter into the hot oil by tablespoonful. Fry the phoulourie until golden brown, turning often. Remove from the oil with a slotted spoon and drain on a plate lined with paper towels or a wire rack set over a baking sheet.

5 Serve with Tamarind Sauce (page 265), Shado Beni Sauce (page 263), Mango Chutney (page 267), or other fruit chutneys.

SAHINA

Sahina, batter-dipped greens filled with ground split peas, are often sold along with Doubles (page 51) for breakfast. The traditional recipe makes use of dasheen/taro leaves, which are available in Caribbean markets, but you can substitute collard greens, which are about the same width and consistency if a little more bitter. More tender kale provides a lovely variation as well.

6 large dasheen/taro, collard, or kale leaves

Juice of 1 lime

2 cups dried split peas

2 cloves garlic, finely chopped

1 small onion, finely chopped

1 teaspoon ground turmeric

1 scallion, chopped

2 tablespoons flour

2 teaspoons coarse salt

Freshly ground black pepper to taste

1 cup canola oil

¼ cup Phoulourie batter (page 53)

Kitchen twine

1 Wash the leaves with the lime juice being careful not to tear them and set aside.

2 Cook the split peas in 6 cups of water for about 45 minutes, or until soft. Drain and grind in a food processor to a coarse meal about the consistency of couscous.

3 Pulse in the garlic, onion, turmeric, scallion, flour, salt, and black pepper. Slowly add enough water to make an easily spreadable paste.

4 Spread 4 tablespoons of the paste over each leaf, then sandwich 2 leaves together, paste sides facing. Roll the leaves into a long cylinder and tie firmly at both ends with kitchen twine, taking care not to tear the leaves.

5 Place a steamer basket or colander in a large pot, and add water to the base. (The water should not touch the bottom of the steamer basket.) Cover the pot and bring the water to a boil. Place the sahina in the steamer basket or colander and cover the pot. Steam for 15 minutes. Remove the rolls and cool. Once cool, slice the sahina into 1-inch rounds.

6 Heat the oil in a heavy-bottomed skillet or saucepan. Dip the sahina rounds in the phoulourie batter and drop into the hot oil in batches. Fry until golden brown on all sides. Drain on a plate lined with paper towels or a wire rack set over a baking sheet. Serve hot.

SHRIMP PATTIES

Shrimp Patties are very popular in Trinidad since much of the population doesn't eat beef—the traditional filling for this type of turnover (page 56). You can also make the patties half the size suggested below for an interesting cocktail party appetizer.

3 tablespoons canola oil

½ small onion, finely chopped

2 cloves garlic, finely chopped

½ cup finely chopped green cabbage

1 pound shrimp, shelled and deveined

3 scallions, finely chopped

2 tablespoons green seasoning (page 254)

¼ teaspoon hot pepper sauce

Salt and freshly ground black pepper to taste

½ cup dry breadcrumbs

1 recipe patty dough (page 56)

1 egg beaten with 1 tablespoon water

1 Heat 2 tablespoons of the oil in a heavy-bottomed skillet. Add the onion and cook until translucent. Stir in the garlic and cook for 1 minute, then stir in the cabbage. Cover the pan and allow the cabbage to wilt. Once the cabbage wilts, remove the lid, and stir well. Continue to cook until all the liquid evaporates and the cabbage is tender.

2 Mince the shrimp into a paste or grind in a food processor using the steel blade. Heat the remaining 1 tablespoon oil in another skillet and add the scallions. Fry for 1 to 2 minutes, then add the shrimp. When the shrimp begins to turn pink, add the green seasoning, hot pepper sauce, and some salt and black pepper. Mix well and continue to cook until the shrimp is totally pink. Add the breadcrumbs and mix very well. Remove from the heat and allow to cool.

3 Remove the patty dough from the refrigerator. Dust a clean work surface with flour and flour a rolling pin. Roll out the pastry ⅛-inch thick, using additional flour as necessary to keep the dough from sticking. Use a pastry brush to dust away any excess flour. Cut circles from the dough using a 5-inch round pastry cutter.

4 Place 2 to 3 tablespoons of the shrimp mixture in the center of each round. Brush the edges of pastry with the beaten egg and fold in half over the filling. Use a fork to crimp the edges of each patty closed. Brush top of each patty with more beaten egg, then, using the fork, poke a few air vents in the top of each patty.

5 Place the patties on an ungreased baking sheet and refrigerate for 15 minutes. Preheat the oven to 425ºF. Bake the patties until lightly browned, about 15 to 20 minutes. Serve warm.

MEAT PATTIES

Meat patties, or particularly beef patties, are largely credited to Jamaica, but they are made in Trinidad as well using a particular mix of local spices. Annatto, locally called *ruku*, gives the pastry its deep yellow color, and green seasoning with curry gives these patties a totally Trini taste. They can be made with ground chicken, turkey, or beef.

DOUGH

2 tablespoons canola oil

1 teaspoon annatto seeds

2 cups all-purpose flour

Pinch of coarse salt

¾ cup (1½ sticks) cold butter, diced

Ice water, as needed

FILLING

2 slices white bread, crusts removed, ripped into large pieces

¼ cup whole milk

1 tablespoon canola oil

1 small onion, finely chopped

2 cloves garlic, finely chopped

1 pound ground chicken, turkey, or beef

1 Scotch bonnet pepper or other hot red chili pepper, finely chopped

½ cup finely chopped tomato

2 teaspoons Trinidad curry powder (page 253)

1 tablespoon green seasoning (page 254)

Salt and freshly ground black pepper

ASSEMBLE

1 egg beaten with 1 tablespoon cold water

MAKE DOUGH:

1 Heat the oil in a heavy skillet and add the annatto seeds (you should keep well away from the pot or use a spatter screen, as the seeds may pop). Swirl the oil in the pot and fry the seeds for 1 to 2 minutes, until all their color is released into the oil. Strain out the seeds and pour the oil into a heatproof bowl. Let cool and then refrigerate until cold.

2 Place the flour in a bowl with the salt and cut in the butter pieces with a pastry blender until it reaches the consistency of coarse meal with pea-size pieces. (Alternatively, place the flour in the bowl of a food processor fitted with a plastic blade, and pulse quickly.) If using a food processor, remove the dough from the machine and place in a mixing bowl. Using a spoon, stir the dough while adding drops of cold water, until the mixture just comes together in a ball, being careful not to overwork the dough.

3 Wrap the dough in plastic wrap and flatten to form a disk. Chill in the refrigerator for at least 2 hours, or as long as overnight. (Note: The dough may be frozen and then thawed in the refrigerator for later use.)

MAKE FILLING:

4 In a bowl, soak the bread pieces in the milk. Set aside.

5 Heat the oil in a heavy-bottomed skillet and add the onion. Sauté for 1 to 2 minutes or until translucent. Add the garlic and cook for 1 minute more. Stir in the ground meat and sauté until golden brown, breaking up chunks of the meat with a fork, as needed. Add the chili pepper, mix well, and cook for 1 minute. Add the tomato, mix well and cook for 1 minute more. Stir in the curry powder and continue to cook for 3 to 4 minutes, then add the green seasoning, mixing well. Season to taste with salt and black pepper. Remove the meat mixture from the heat and place in a bowl to cool.

6 Once the meat mixture is cool, squeeze the excess liquid from the milk-soaked bread and add it to the meat mixture. Mix very well.

ASSEMBLE PATTIES & BAKE:

7 Remove the dough from the refrigerator. Dust a work surface and a rolling pin with flour. Roll out the pastry to ⅛ inch thick, sprinkling with additional flour as necessary to keep the dough from sticking. Use a pastry brush to dust away any excess flour. Cut circles from the dough using a 5-inch round pastry cutter. Place 2 to 3 tablespoons of the meat mixture on the center of each round. Brush the edges of the pastry with the beaten egg and fold in half covering the filling. Use a fork to crimp the edges of each patty closed.

8 Brush the top of each patty with the reserved annatto oil. Using a fork, poke a few air vents in the top of each patty. Place the patties on an ungreased baking sheet and refrigerate for 15 minutes so that the butter in the crust becomes firm. (Once baked the butter will melt and release steam to create a flaky crust.)

9 Preheat the oven to 425ºF. Bake the patties until lightly browned, about 15 to 20 minutes. Serve warm.

Tip

The **Meat Patties** and **Shrimp Patties** (page 55) may be frozen, uncooked, in a well-sealed container or zip-top plastic bags, for up to 3 months. To cook, place the frozen patties on a baking sheet and bake in a preheated 425ºF oven for 30 to 40 minutes, or until golden brown.

FRIED WONTONS

Chinese takeout is just as popular in Trinidad as it is in the United States—but of course it has a Trinidadian twist. This popular snack is livened up with the addition of hot peppers. You can make them with your choice of proteins.

½ pound shrimp, chicken breast, or lean pork, coarsely ground in a food processor or meat grinder

1 scallion, trimmed and finely chopped (both white and green parts)

2 cloves garlic, finely chopped

½ fresh hot red chili pepper, finely chopped

1 teaspoon soy sauce

24 wonton skins

1 cup canola oil, for deep-frying

½ cup sweet soy sauce

¼ cup rice wine vinegar

1 Combine the ground shrimp, chicken, or pork with the scallion, garlic, chili pepper, and 1 teaspoon soy sauce and set aside.

2 Have a small bowl of cold water ready. Place a wonton skin flat on a work surface and put 1 teaspoon of the shrimp/meat mixture in the middle of the square skin. Dip a finger in cold water and run it along the edges of the wonton skin (this will help the skin stick together when folded). Fold the skin in half over the meat to form a rectangle. Fold it over one more time so the rectangle is half its width. Fold the rectangle horizontally over the stuffed section of the rectangle so that the short ends meet each other. Pinch the lower flaps of the short ends together, leaving top folds free. Use a little water to pinch the dough closed. The wonton will resemble a little nurse's hat. Repeat until all the skins are filled or all the filling is used up.

3 Heat the oil in a saucepan until hot (test by dropping a little flour into the pot; if it sizzles vigorously, the oil is ready). Add the wontons a few at a time, so they are not crowded in the pan. Fry until golden brown, then drain on paper towels.

4 Whisk the sweet soy sauce and vinegar together in a small bowl. Serve as a dipping sauce for the hot wontons.

ALOO PIES

My father came to New York from his native Trinidad in 1954, a time when even that great city had few creature comforts familiar to West Indian immigrants. There he lived a life of substitutions. Although he slathered knishes with hot pepper sauce to mimic these spicy potato turnovers, it was never quite the same. Aloo Pies are not usually served with any condiments since they are well spiced, but I like the popular convention of serving them with Tamarind Sauce, similar to the way a traditional Indian samosa would be eaten.

DOUGH

2 cups all-purpose flour

Pinch of coarse salt

2 teaspoons baking powder

FILLING

1 pound Yukon Gold or other boiling
  potatoes, boiled and peeled

½ teaspoon coarse salt

Hot pepper sauce, to taste

5 large cloves garlic, crushed

½ cup canola oil for frying

MAKE DOUGH:

1 Mix together the flour, salt, and baking powder. Add just enough water to bring the dough together, about ½ cup, and knead until smooth and elastic, about 5 minutes. Form the dough into 2-inch balls and set aside to rest for 15 minutes.

MAKE THE FILLING:

2 Mash together the potatoes, salt, pepper sauce, and garlic.

ASSEMBLE AND FRY:

3 Flatten a ball of dough into a 4-inch patty. Place 1 to 2 tablespoons of the potato filling in the middle of the circle and pinch the sides together covering the filling and reforming into a ball. Holding the ball in one hand, gently flatten into an oblong shape, roughly 5 inches long, taking care not to squeeze out the potato filling. Repeat with remaining dough ball.

4 Heat the oil in a heavy-bottomed frying pan and working in batches, add the aloo pies, being careful not to crowd the pan. Fry on both sides until golden brown, remove, and drain on paper towels. Serve hot, with Tamarind Sauce (page 265) if desired.

PASTELLES WITH EGGS

Pastelles resemble tamales. They are widely sold by street vendors at Christmastime and also made at home as a must-have part of the holiday meal. My father's version is heavily influenced by his years living in Venezuela and contains eggs, but the traditional Trinidadian version does not. I give you both, beginning with the egg version. In either case, pastelles are traditionally wrapped in a soharee leaf, which is similar to a banana leaf, or in a banana leaf itself, and boiled or steamed. However, heavy-duty plastic wrap or corn husks work well too.

DOUGH

2 tablespoons butter

2 teaspoons coarse salt

2 teaspoons sugar

2 cups masa harina

FILLING

2 tablespoons canola oil

1½ pounds lean pork, chicken, or beef, cut into ¼-inch cubes

½ pound chorizo or andouille sausage, cut into ¼-inch cubes

3 red onions, finely chopped

1 clove garlic, finely chopped

2 teaspoons Worcestershire sauce

1 tablespoon tomato paste

1 cup chicken or beef stock

1 tablespoon finely chopped fresh thyme, or 1 teaspoon dried

1 tablespoon finely chopped fresh basil, or 1 teaspoon dried

MAKE DOUGH:

1 Bring 6 cups water to a boil in a large pot and add the butter, salt, and sugar. When the butter melts, add the masa harina and mix vigorously with a heavy spoon. The mixture should be smooth but not sticky, and should slightly come away from the sides of the pot. Set aside to cool.

MAKE FILLING:

2 Heat the oil in a Dutch oven or deep saucepan. Add the meat and sausage and sauté until lightly browned. Add the onions and cook until translucent. Add the garlic and cook 1 minute more. Stir in the Worcestershire sauce, tomato paste, and ½ cup of the stock. Lower the heat and simmer for 5 minutes. Add the chopped herbs, olives, chili peppers, and remaining ½ cup stock and continue to simmer until the meat is tender and almost all the liquid is absorbed. Add salt to taste.

ASSEMBLE & STEAM

3 Scald the banana leaf squares in boiling salted water until malleable. Remove them from the water and set aside to cool.

1½ teaspoons fresh oregano or
¼ teaspoon dried

10 green olives, sliced

1 Scotch bonnet pepper or 2 fresh red
chili peppers, stemmed, seeded, and
finely chopped

ASSEMBLE & STEAM

Fresh banana leaves* or heavy-duty
plastic wrap, cut into 24 12-inch
squares

Canola oil, as needed

2 large hard-boiled eggs, sliced

Kitchen twine

---

*Banana leaves are available in the freezer
section of many Latino or Caribbean markets.

4 Brush a leaf square with oil and spoon 1 heaping
tablespoon of the masa harina dough onto the
leaf. Pat the dough into a square about ¼ inch thick
using the back of a spoon. Place 2 tablespoons
of the meat mixture in the center of the dough
and place a slice of hard-boiled egg on top. Add
another heaping tablespoon of the dough on
top of the meat mixture and smooth. Fold the
leaf in half to form a long rectangle and smooth
it with your fingers so that the filling is evenly
distributed. Fold each end under to form a
rectangular package and tie with twine. Repeat
with remaining leaf squares.

5 Place a steamer basket or colander in a large
pot halfway filled with hot water (the water
level must be below the bottom of the steamer
basket). Put a single layer of pastelles in the
steamer basket and cover the pot. Simmer for
about 45 minutes if using banana leaves or 20
minutes if using plastic. Remove from the water
and drain, then place in a baking dish covered
with foil in a warm oven while you steam the
rest of the pastelles. Serve hot.

Soups, Street Foods & Small Bites 63

KAREN FELICIAN'S PASTELLES

Karen Felician of Maraval serves these traditional pastelles on Christmas Eve. She uses homemade green seasoning made from the local herbs that have made the Paramin region famous and from which her husband, Carlos, hails.

DOUGH

2 cups masa harina

3 cups hot water

¼ cup canola oil, plus more as needed

FILLING

2 tablespoons canola oil

1 small onion, finely chopped

2 cloves garlic, finely chopped

2 pounds ground beef

2 tablespoons Paramin green seasoning (page 255)

½ Scotch bonnet pepper or other hot red chili pepper, stemmed, seeded, and finely chopped

½ pimiento pepper, stemmed, seeded, and finely chopped, or 1 teaspoon paprika

2 teaspoons coarse salt

½ teaspoon ground black pepper

1 teaspoon Worcestershire sauce

3 tablespoons capers

½ cup raisins

MAKE DOUGH:

1 Combine the masa harina, hot water, and oil. Mix until the dough comes together in a ball.

MAKE FILLING:

2 Heat the oil in a large skillet and add the onion. Cook until translucent, then add the garlic and cook for 1 minute more. Add the ground beef, mix well, and brown using a fork to break up any chunks. Add the green seasoning, chili and pimiento peppers, salt, black pepper, Worcestershire sauce, capers, and raisins. Cook for 2 to 3 minutes more, then remove from the heat and cool.

ASSEMBLE & STEAM:

3 Scald the banana leaves in boiling salted water until malleable. Remove them from the water and set aside to cool.

4 Brush a leaf (or plastic square) with oil and spoon 1 heaping tablespoon of the masa dough onto the middle of the square. Pat the dough into a square about ¼-inch thick using the back of a spoon. Place 2 tablespoons of the meat mixture in the center of the dough. Add another heaping tablespoon of the masa dough

Banana leaves* or heavy-duty plastic wrap, cut into 24 8-inch squares

Kitchen twine

---

*Banana leaves are available in the freezer section of many Latino or Caribbean markets.

on top of the meat mixture and smooth. Fold the square in half to form a long rectangle and smooth it with your fingers so that the filling is evenly distributed. Fold each end under to form a rectangular package and tie with twine. Repeat with remaining leaf /plastic squares.

5 Place a steamer basket or colander in a large pot halfway filled with hot water (the water level must be below the bottom of the steamer basket). Put a single layer of pastelles in the steamer basket and cover the pot. Simmer for about 45 minutes if using banana leaves and 20 minutes if using plastic. Remove from the water and drain, then place in a baking dish covered with foil in a warm oven while you steam the remaining pastelles. Serve hot.

SHARK & BAKE

SERVES: 4

Shark & Bake is a fish sandwich in which fried bake—a savory fritter—is sliced open and a piece of breaded, fried nurse shark is tucked between. Nowadays, shark is often substituted with other fish, which is a point of great contention, followed only by what condiments should be used in the sandwich—tamarind sauce, cilantro sauce, or hot pepper sauce are the acceptable choices—and only surpassed by the debate as to whether it is "Shark & Bake" or "Bake & Shark." I learned it as the former so that's what I stick with. At Maracas Bay Beach, eating Shark & Bake is a tradition not unlike eating Nathan's Famous hot dogs on the boardwalk at Coney Island in Brooklyn. If you don't like or can't get shark, you can use any firm-fleshed white fish, such as tilapia or catfish.

1 pound boneless shark meat or other firm-fleshed white fish, cut into 4 x 1-inch strips

2 tablespoons lime juice

2 cloves garlic, finely chopped

2 tablespoons green seasoning (page 254)

2 cups all-purpose flour

1 teaspoon coarse salt

1 teaspoon freshly ground black pepper

½ teaspoon cayenne pepper powder

½ teaspoon dried oregano

1 cup canola oil

4 large bakes (page 183), sliced in half horizontally

Shado Beni Sauce (page 263) or Hot Pepper Sauce (page 257)

1 Put the fish in a glass or non-reactive bowl and pour the lime juice over it. Let stand for a few minutes. Add the garlic and green seasoning and toss to coat fish. Cover and refrigerate for 1 hour.

2 Combine the flour, salt, black pepper, cayenne pepper, and oregano. Heat the oil in a large skillet until hot. Dredge the shark pieces on all sides in the seasoned flour, then drop into the hot oil. Fry until golden brown on all sides, about 10 minutes. Drain on paper towels or on a rack set over a baking sheet.

3 Place some of the fried fish on each of the sliced *bakes* and sprinkle with Shado Beni Sauce or Hot Pepper Sauce.

MÉLANGE CRAB AND DUMPLINGS

Curried Crab and Dumplings (page 118) is a traditional, if laborious, Trini favorite that features cooked crab backs that must be picked for their meat. Moses Reuben, the chef at Mélange restaurant in Port of Spain, has an elegant take on this dish that pairs succulent chunks of crabmeat with delicate dumplings in a spicy curry sauce that stimulates the appetite for courses to come.

DUMPLINGS

1 cup all-purpose flour

2 pinches coarse salt

CRAB

1 teaspoon canola oil

1 tablespoon finely chopped onion

3 cloves garlic, finely chopped

2 pimiento peppers, finely chopped

2 teaspoons Trinidad curry powder (page 253) mixed with 2 teaspoons water

1 teaspoon ground cumin

⅓ cup lump crabmeat

3 tablespoons coconut milk

Salt to taste

MAKE DUMPLINGS:

1 Mix together the flour and a pinch of salt. Add 6 tablespoons of water and knead for 1 to 2 minutes, until the dough forms a firm ball. Set aside to rest for 10 to 15 minutes. Meanwhile, bring 2 cups of water to boil and add the remaining pinch of salt.

2 Divide the dough into three equal parts and role each section into a rope 1 inch thick and 6 inches long. Cut each rope on the bias into ½-inch pieces. When all the dumplings are cut, put them in the boiling water and cook for 3 to 4 minutes at a rapid boil. Drain and set aside.

MAKE CRAB:

3 Heat the oil in a 9-inch skillet. Add the onion and garlic, and sauté for 1 minute. Add the peppers and sauté for 30 seconds more. Add the curry paste and cumin, and sauté for 1 minute, stirring constantly. Add the crabmeat, toss well to coat, and sauté for 30 seconds. Add the coconut milk and simmer over low heat, stirring constantly, for 15 seconds. Add salt to taste.

4 To serve, divide the dumplings between four small serving dishes and spoon 1 heaping tablespoon of the crabmeat mixture on top of each.

OYSTER COCKTAIL

Oysters are a well-loved street food, although the government made it illegal to sell the mollusks along the roadside. Trinidadian oysters grow on the roots of mangrove trees in the large Caroni swamp that covers hundreds of acres in the middle of the island. Although small, they are meatier than sea oysters. Simple though it may be, this appetizer packs a unique punch. It's the seasoning sauce that really makes this dish. While the sauce's respective ingredients are kept in separate bottles by street vendors and squirted onto paper cones full of oysters, my recipe mixes them together to be dolloped onto oysters on the half shell, as desired.

12 Blue Point oysters, or oysters of your choice, shucked, with top shell removed

½ cup coarsely chopped cilantro

1 tablespoon freshly squeezed lime juice

3 cloves garlic, finely chopped

2 tablespoons ketchup mixed with 1 teaspoon sugar*

½ teaspoon hot pepper sauce

1 Arrange the oysters on a bed of crushed ice.

2 Place the cilantro and lime juice in a blender and puree to a smooth paste. Add the remaining ingredients and puree. Drizzle ¼ to ½ teaspoon of the sauce on each oyster. Serve.

---

*Trinidadian ketchup is much sweeter than American versions, hence the addition of sugar in this recipe. You may omit the extra sugar if you like, or use Hunt's ketchup, which is the sweetest of the American brands.

COLETTE'S CILANTRO CHILI WINGS

SERVES: 6 TO 8

I met Colette Cyrus Burnett when she was a contestant and I was a judge on the Food Network show *Throwdown! With Bobby Flay*. Colette had built a business selling hot wings in a variety of Caribbean flavors at her restaurant Superwings in Brooklyn, New York, so the challenge on the show was a Trinidad hot wings recipe. Colette won the competition handily, and although her wings were scrumptious it was her infectious good vibe that impressed me most. More than that, Colette's drive to succeed reminded me of my father and so many other Caribbean immigrants before and after him. After the show, we became fast friends and remain so to this day.

In addition to being a food business entrepreneur, Colette has been an inspiration to countless young people whom she has mentored. She also remains a staunch voice for Caribbean cuisine. Colette calls this wings recipe—a particular favorite in her restaurant—her homage to all things Trinidadian, particularly the Trini love of hot peppers. This recipe even won in the U.S. National Buffalo Wing Contest Spicy category. Blending tartness with high heat in just the right balance, these wings are a perfect appetizer for a Super Bowl party or summer picnic, especially accompanied by an ice cold Carib beer.

WINGS

3 pounds chicken wings, tips removed

4 tablespoons freshly squeezed lime juice

1 teaspoon coarse salt

2 teaspoons garlic powder

½ teaspoon ground black pepper

1 cup all-purpose flour

¼ cup cornstarch

⅓ cup canola oil

SAUCE

2 bunches fresh shado beni or cilantro

½ cup freshly squeezed lime juice

6 cloves garlic, finely chopped

2 Scotch bonnet, habanero, or jalapeño peppers, stemmed and seeds removed

Pinch of ground black pepper

Salt to taste

1 Put the wings in a large bowl and pour the lime juce over them and add the salt. Rub the salt into the wings and then add enough cold water to cover the wings. Set aside.

2 In a large bowl, whisk together the garlic powder, black pepper, flour, and cornstarch.

3 Heat the canola oil in a large, deep skillet over medium heat. When a pinch of flour dropped into the oil sizzles, the oil is ready. Pat the chicken wings dry. Dredge each wing in the flour mixture and shake off excess. Place the wings gently in the hot oil without overcrowding them. Fry until golden brown on each side and cooked through, about 5 to 7 minutes per side. Remove the wings from the pan and place on a wire rack over a sheet tray or on a plate lined with paper towels.

MAKE SAUCE:

4 While the wings are frying, make the sauce: Blend the shado beni, lime juice, garlic, chili peppers, and black pepper in a blender until smooth. Add salt to taste. Pour the mixture into a medium saucepan and cook over medium heat for 20 minutes, or until reduced by half. Cool completely.

ASSEMBLE:

5 Place the fried wings in a dry skillet over medium heat. Pour enough sauce over the wings to coat completely while stirring to heat them through. Serve garnished with additional chopped shado beni, cilantro, or parsley. (You can store any remaining sauce in the refrigerator for up to 2 weeks.)

CHINESE FRIED CHICKEN WINGS

F ried chicken is not only popular from outlets like KFC but also from Chinese restaurants throughout Trinidad. There, the chicken is cut up into bite-size pieces with the bone as it is with nearly every Trinidadian chicken dish. While I find the bone imparts good flavor, I am not too fond of whacking the pieces with a huge cleaver in order to get the same result, so I've adapted this dish using chicken wings which makes it ideal as a party nibble for a crowd.

3 pounds chicken wings, tips removed, drummettes separated

Corn flour (maseca) for dredging

Canola oil for frying

MARINADE

1 cup soy sauce

½ cup rice wine

1 small Scotch bonnet pepper or 1 medium red chili pepper, finely chopped

⅓ cup brown sugar

⅓ cup hoisin sauce

½ teaspoon five spice powder

3 cloves garlic, crushed

1 scallion, white and green parts, finely chopped

DIPPING SAUCE

1 cup chicken stock

1 tablespoon oyster sauce

1 tablespoon thick soy sauce

½ teaspoon cornstarch

1 Rinse and pat dry the chicken wings and place in a deep non-reactive bowl. Whisk together all the ingredients for the marinade and pour over the chicken wings. Cover with plastic wrap and marinate in the refrigerator at least 3 hours, but preferably overnight.

2 Remove the chicken wings from the refrigerator, and take them out of the marinade (discard the marinade). Pat each wing dry and dredge very lightly in the corn flour.

3 Heat about 2 inches of canola oil in a wide, deep skillet to 375°F, or until a pinch of flour dropped into the oil sizzles. Place some of the chicken wings in the hot oil and fry until lightly browned, about 10 to 12 minutes. Place on a rack over a baking sheet and keep warm. Repeat until all the wings are cooked.

4 Make the dipping sauce: Combine the chicken stock, oyster sauce and soy sauce in a saucepan and bring to a boil. In a small bowl, mix the cornstarch with ⅓ cup cold water and whisk well. Add the cornstarch mixture to the stock mixture, lower heat and simmer until thickened. Remove from heat and serve dipping sauce along side the chicken wings.

Spanish Flavor: A Trinidad Christmas

Venezuelan Spanish cocoa laborers first arrived in Trinidad as early as the late sixteenth century, a time when the island was under Spanish control. Highly influential in the cocoa industry from estate owner to common laborer, the Venezuelans are largely credited with building Trinidad's cocoa industry as its king crop until well into the twentieth century (see King Cocoa in Trinidad & Tobago, page 278).

These immigrants were soon known as *Cocoa Espanols* or "the Cocoa Spanish," which was shortened to *Cocoa Paynol*, a term that came to be largely derogatory in meaning but today is a descriptive term for those few retaining Spanish descent and the Spanish ways.

Those Spanish ways are still evident in the larger Trinidadian culture, particularly around Roman Catholic holidays, especially Christmas. To enjoy a Christmas in Trinidad is to enjoy true Latino flavor in everything from food and drink to music.

One of the most delightful aspects of Trinidad at Christmas time, which lasts until Three Kings Day on January 6, is *parang*, Venzuelan troubador music. During the Yuletide season it is common for parang bands or "*parrenderos*" to sing in public areas, and the radio stations are nearly taken over with Christmas *parangs* of old, much in the way that holiday music is piped through American radio from Thanksgiving to New Year's Day. Just as carolers do in America and Europe, parang bands go "house to house" singing songs of the Nativity. A good time to witness an authentic house-to-house is at the Lopinot Parang Festival held in December. One of the more well-known bands is Los Amigos Cantadores (The Singing Friends) of Arima, headed by Neal Marcano.

← Tip

For a lighter version of "Chinese Fried Chicken Wings," I often omit the corn flour dredging and simply place the marinated wings under the broiler or, in the summer, on a hot barbecue grill. This marinade is excellent for whole chicken as well. Simply double or triple the measurements as needed and marinate the chicken overnight, then roast as normal in the oven.

MEATS, POULTRY & FISH

Because of the strong Asian heritage of much of Trinidad's population, red meat generally makes up a small component of a dish rather than the main part of the meal. Also, Trinidad and Tobago are small islands that cannot sustain large herds of beef cattle or pig farms and many meat products must be imported from Venezuela or other South American countries at great cost. In addition, at least some portion of the population is Hindu and doesn't eat beef or pork and the Muslim population abstains from pork. As a result, few dishes feature a large piece of cooked meat served with side dishes. Notable exceptions are holiday ham and turkey, and some steak cuts can now be found in finer restaurants.

Chicken sells so well in Trinidad that while McDonald's couldn't sustain business on the island because of its beef-heavy menu, Kentucky Fried Chicken does a brisk trade— with some cultural adjustments. Not only is the chicken at this eatery very fresh, in true Trini fashion, but the Colonel's secret recipe is liberally doctored with pepper sauce.

Fish, which is widely available, fresh, and varied, is very popular except for the most devout, strictly vegetarian Hindus. Some common fish on the island include king fish, flying fish, and various kinds of river fish. Shrimp and crab are abundant as well.

Soused Lambie (Conch Salad), page 110

BEEF STEW WITH DUMPLINGS

Caramelized sugar for browning the meat adds a rich body to this dish, while dumplings make it a complete meal—perfect for a cold day!

STEW

1½ pounds stew beef, cut into 1-inch cubes

2 tablespoons green seasoning (page 254)

2 tablespoons canola oil

2 tablespoons sugar

1 large onion, thinly sliced

2 cloves garlic, finely chopped

¾ cup dark beer

2 teaspoons soy sauce

2 teaspoons Worcestershire sauce

1 bay leaf

½ teaspoon coarse salt

½ teaspoon hot pepper sauce

2 cups beef stock or water, or more as needed

DUMPLINGS

½ cup all-purpose flour

½ cup cornmeal

Pinch of coarse salt

MAKE STEW:

1 Mix the beef with the green seasoning and refrigerate for 2 hours.

2 Heat the oil in a heavy-bottomed pot. Add the sugar and cook until dark brown. Add the seasoned beef and stir well to coat. Cook for 5 minutes, stirring constantly. Add the onion and garlic, and cook for 5 minutes more. Stir in the beer, soy sauce, Worcestershire sauce, bay leaf, salt, and hot pepper sauce. Add enough stock or wate to cover the beef. Bring to a boil, and then lower heat. Cover and simmer until the meat is tender, about 30 to 40 minutes, adding the dumplings as instructed in Step 4.

MAKE DUMPLINGS:

3 While the stew is simmering, mix together the flour, cornmeal, and salt. Add 6 tablespoons of water and knead to form a stiff dough, adding more water if necessary. Knead until smooth and set aside to rest for 15 minutes. Pinch off 1-inch pieces of dough and roll between the palms of your hands to form ovals. Pinch both ends, then flatten the ovals between palms or against a cutting board (the dumplings should resemble small flat footballs).

4 Drop the dumplings into the beef stew in the last 15 minutes of cooking. Adjust the seasonings to taste and serve hot.

BEEF CURRY

Beef dishes are not ubiquitous in India or in Trinidad, but currying is a popular preparation for all kinds of meat. This curry differs from Indian versions because it employs milder Trinidad curry powder and hot pepper sauce rather than whole chili peppers.

2 pounds stew beef, cut into 1-inch cubes

1 tablespoon green seasoning (page 254)

1 teaspoon coarse salt

½ teaspoon freshly ground black pepper

1 tablespoon canola oil

1 medium onion, thinly sliced

2 cloves garlic, finely chopped

2 tablespoons Trinidad curry powder (page 253)

½ teaspoon hot pepper sauce

1 In a large bowl, mix the beef, green seasoning, salt, and black pepper, and refrigerate for at least two hours and up to overnight.

2 Heat the oil in a heavy-bottomed saucepan. Add the onions and cook until translucent. Stir in the garlic and cook for 1 minute. Add the curry powder and sauté, stirring constantly, for 30 seconds. Add the beef mixture and mix very well. Add 3 cups of water and cover.

3 Simmer over medium-low heat for 30 to 40 minutes, or until the beef is fork tender. Mix in the hot pepper sauce and adjust the seasonings to taste. Serve with rice (page 160) or roti (pages 174-177).

PEPPERPOT

This dish is traditionally credited to Guyana but has become part of the Trinidadian cooking repertoire as well. Although often referred to as a "soup," it's really a thick stew that is served over plain rice.

½ pound oxtail, cut into 1-inch pieces

½ pound stew beef, cut into 1-inch pieces

1 pound pork shoulder, cut into 1-inch pieces

3 tablespoons green seasoning (page 254)

2 cups white vinegar

2 cups cassareep syrup (available in West Indian markets or online)

6 whole cloves

¼ teaspoon ground allspice

2 whole Scotch bonnet peppers or other hot red chili peppers

1 cinnamon stick, snapped in half

2 teaspoons coarse salt, or to taste

1 Rinse the meats in cold water, pat dry, and place in a large bowl. Add the green seasoning and mix well to coat the meats. Refrigerate for at least 2 hours or as long as overnight.

2 Place the seasoned meats in a heavy-bottomed pot and add the vinegar, cassareep syrup, cloves, allspice, hot peppers, cinnamon stick, salt, and 8 cups of water. Cover and simmer for 1 to 1½ hours, or until the meats are tender. Serve with plain white rice.

BEEF PELAU

SERVES: 6 TO 8

Here is a version of *pelau* made with stewing beef. You can also use lamb. Beef pelau is commonly eaten among Muslim Trinidadians following Eid al Adha, a sacrificial feast day. Note that if you use dried peas you need to allow time for them to soak overnight.

1 cup dry pigeon peas, pinto beans, or black-eyed peas, or 1 (12-ounce) can

2 cups long-grain rice

3 tablespoons canola oil

¾ cup sugar (white or brown)

3 pounds stewing beef, cut into 1-inch chunks

1 small onion, chopped

1 clove garlic, finely chopped

1 cup canned coconut milk

1 bay leaf

2 teaspoons green seasoning (page 254)

½ cup chopped parsley

1 sprig thyme

2 carrots, peeled and chopped

5 scallions, ends trimmed and minced (white and green parts)

2 cups cubed fresh calabaza or butternut squash

1 small whole Scotch bonnet pepper or other red chili pepper

½ cup ketchup

1 tablespoon butter

1 If using dried peas, soak them overnight in 3 cups of water. Drain. Bring 3 fresh cups of water to a boil in a saucepan and add the peas. Simmer for 15 minutes, or until cooked almost completely through. Drain and set aside. (If using canned beans, drain, rinse with cold water, drain again, and set aside.)

2 Wash the rice by placing it in a colander or fine-mesh sieve and running cold water over it until the water runs clear, about 1 minute. Drain well and set aside.

3 Heat the oil over medium heat in a Dutch oven or other heavy, deep pot. Add the sugar and swirl in the pot, stirring constantly, until it caramelizes to a dark brown color. Add the beef pieces and stir well to coat. Add the onion and garlic and cook for 1 to 2 minutes, stirring constantly.

4 Stir in 1 cup of water, the coconut milk, bay leaf, green seasoning, parsley, thyme, carrots, and scallions. Reduce the heat to medium-low, cover, and simmer for 10 minutes.

5 Stir in the cooked or canned peas, rice, squash, chili pepper, ketchup, and butter. Cover and cook for 20 minutes, or until the peas and vegetables are tender. Remove lid and fluff the rice. The rice should be moist but not sticky.

CURRIED GOAT

Because goat is tougher than beef, it has to simmer longer on a low heat in order to become tender. Washing the meat with both lime juice and water will help remove some of the gamey taste.

2 pounds boneless goat meat, cut into 1-inch cubes

2 tablespoons freshly squeezed lime juice

2 tablespoons green seasoning (page 254)

1 teaspoon coarse salt

½ teaspoon freshly ground black pepper

1 tablespoon canola oil

1 medium onion, thinly sliced

2 cloves garlic, finely chopped

2 tablespoons Trinidad curry powder (page 253)

½ teaspoon hot pepper sauce

1 In a large bowl, rinse the goat meat with cold water. Drain and add the lime juice. Set aside for 10 minutes. Rinse again, drain, and place back in the bowl. Add the green seasoning, salt, and black pepper, and toss to coat the meat. Refrigerate overnight.

2 Heat the oil in a heavy-bottomed saucepan. Add the onions and cook until translucent. Add the garlic, mix well, and cook for 1 minute. Add the curry powder and sauté, stirring constantly, for 30 seconds.

3 Add the meat mixture to the saucepan and mix very well. Add 3 cups of water and cover. Simmer over medium-low heat for 1 hour, or until the meat is fork tender. Mix in the hot pepper sauce and adjust the seasonings to taste. Serve with rice (page 160) or roti (page 174-177).

GARLIC PORK

Pickling meat and fish is often considered a Jamaican cooking technique, but it occasionally finds it's way into Trini dishes as well. You need to plan ahead for this dish but the long marinating time for the pork yields a tender, flavorful meat.

2 pounds boneless pork shoulder, cut into ½-inch thick slices

¾ cup white vinegar

1 head garlic, peeled

¼ cup fresh oregano, or 1 tablespoon dried

1 Scotch bonnet pepper or other hot red chili pepper, seeded

2 teaspoons coarse salt

1 Rinse the pork with ¼ cup of the vinegar and place in a glass or other nonreactive dish.

2 Using a food processor, grind the garlic, oregano, chili pepper, and salt into a coarse paste. Add the remaining ½ cup of vinegar and spread the paste over the pork. Cover with plastic wrap and refrigerate for 2 days.

3 Preheat the oven to 350ºF. Remove the pork from the marinade and wrap in aluminum foil. Set in a roasting pan and bake for 30 minutes. Open the foil and bake for 20 minutes more. Cut the pork slices into ½-inch cubes and serve.

DASHEEN PORK

Dasheen Pork is one of those dishes that melds local ingredients and Old World cooking style and it is an iconic Trinidad Chinese dish. *Dasheen* is the local word for taro.

2 pounds boneless pork shoulder

1 bay leaf

1 clove garlic, slightly crushed, plus 2 cloves garlic, finely chopped

5 whole cloves, slightly crushed

4 medium dasheen/taros, peeled and cut into ½-inch slices

2 tablespoons soy sauce

2 tablespoons dark rum

2 tablespoons canola oil

1 teaspoon peeled and grated fresh ginger

1 (1-inch) piece red bean curd, chopped

3 tablespoons finely chopped onion

2 tablespoons green seasoning (page 254)

1 teaspoon five-spice powder

1 Place the pork shoulder in a pot with the bay leaf, crushed garlic, and cloves. Add just enough water to cover and bring to a simmer. Cook, covered, for 30 minutes, or until the pork is tender.

2 While the pork is cooking, bring a pot of salted water to a boil and add the taro. Simmer for 10 minutes, drain, and set aside to cool.

3 When the pork is tender, remove it from the pot, cool, and cut into ½-inch-thick slices. Place in a bowl and add the soy sauce and rum. Mix well to coat all sides of the pork.

4 Heat the oil in a large skillet and add the pork slices (reserving the soy-rum mixture), and brown on both sides. Remove and allow to cool. Place the pork in a bowl and add the finely chopped garlic, ginger, bean curd, onion, green seasoning, and five-spice powder. Toss to coat the meat.

5 Preheat the oven to 350ºF. In a large baking dish, arrange the taro and pork slices in alternating layers, and pour any leftover soy-rum mixture on top. Cover with aluminum foil and bake for 45 minutes, or until the taro is fork tender and slightly translucent.

Bush Meat & Buccaneer Cooking

Trinidad is known for unusual species of plants and animals, many of which find their way into a cooking pot. Hunting wild game or "bush meat," as it is called on the islands, dates back to the Caribs and Arawaks, Amerindian tribes that first lived on Trinidad and Tobago and throughout the Caribbean. It was they who developed a cooking style of smoking or roasting meat in pits with smoldering wood and wet leaves—a method known today as pit barbecuing.

The tradition of eating bush meat is waning in Trinidad but there are still those who prefer the pickings of the wild— especially on Tobago. Bush meat includes, among others, *manicou* (opossum), *agouti* (hare), and iguana. Sadly, even endangered leatherback sea turtles and red howler monkeys—treasures of the animal kingdom that exist only in Trinidad and South America—are fair game. They are being driven to near extinction in Trinidad as a source of meat. Along the same lines, the Trinidad *piping guan*, a bird that exists only in Trinidad and is locally called *pawi*, is a popular bush meat because its friendly nature makes it easy to poach. It,

too, is now considered endangered and is under the protection of the government. The giant sea turtle, another recognized endangered species, has suffered the same fate at the hands of those seeking its flesh as a local delicacy.

Among the descendants of Amerindian natives high in the northern range of Trinidad, in cities like Paramin and Brasso Seco, pre-Colombian cooking methods of bush meat are still practiced. In Brasso Seco, Mr. Felix, who was a village leader and one of the true Creoles (people of mixed Amerindian, Spanish, and French heritage), practices what has come to be called "buccaneer" or *boucanee* cooking—a method of smoking highly seasoned meats over a fire of native woods, like the superhard long-smoldering samaan tree, dampened with wet leaves.

But while buccaneer cooking is especially suited for tougher bush meats, which require a long, slow heat to become tender, it is a delicious way to prepare chicken too (page 91), which I enjoyed at Mr. Felix's generous table.

Mr. Felix smokes chicken using the "buccaneer" method

BUCCANEER SMOKED CHICKEN

This is a wonderful barbecue dish and travels well for picnics too. In the hills above Arima in the Northern Range, a village leader named Mr. Felix smokes his chicken using local hardwoods like tonka or samaan. For best flavor, I suggest using fruit woods, such as apple or cherry, if you can get them. If you don't have a charcoal grill you can use a gas grill set on a low temperature or bake the chicken in the oven at 250ºF for about two hours; however, you will miss out on the smoky flavor.

1 (3- to 4-pound) chicken, cut into
  8 pieces

2 tablespoons freshly squeezed lime
  juice

2 teaspoons coarse salt

Freshly ground black pepper

¼ cup green seasoning (page 254)

1 tablespoon dark brown sugar

6 cups fruit wood briquettes for grilling

1 Rub the chicken with the lime juice and then rinse with water. Pat dry and rub on the salt and black pepper. Mix the green seasoning with the brown sugar and rub on the chicken. Place the chicken in a shallow nonreactive bowl, cover, and refrigerate overnight, or up to 2 days.

2 Soak 3 cups of the wood briquettes in water for 1 hour.

3 In a charcoal grill, create a smoldering fire on only one side of the grill pan, using the 3 cups of dry wood briquettes. Once the embers are glowing, place the chicken on the grill and cook for 2 to 3 minutes per side, or until grill marks form.

4 Move the chicken to the opposite side of the grill, away from the fire. Add the 3 cups of damp briquettes to the fire and let smolder. Close the grill lid and allow to smoke for about 1 hour. If necessary, occasionally spray the fire with fresh water during cooking, using a spray bottle—just enough to maintain smoke without putting out the fire.

5 Remove the chicken and serve with Foo Foo (page 148), Callaloo (page 39), Trini Coleslaw (page 123), Pigeon Peas and Rice (page 165), and/or Fried Sweet Plantains (page 149).

DAD'S CURRIED CHICKEN

East Indians account for nearly half the population of Trinidad and curry is a staple ingredient throughout the country. Religious food proscriptions against beef and pork among Trinidad East Indians of Hindu and Muslim descent make chicken the most widely consumed meat, so it's only natural that curried chicken is practically a national dish. This is my father's version.

1 (4-pound) chicken, cut into 8 pieces, skin removed

1 tablespoon freshly squeezed lime juice

2 tablespoons green seasoning (page 254)

1 teaspoon coarse salt

1 Scotch bonnet pepper or other hot red chili pepper, finely chopped

2 cloves garlic, crushed

¼ cup Trinidad curry powder (page 253)

2 tablespoons canola oil

1 medium onion, chopped

1 cup chicken stock or water

1 Place the chicken pieces in a bowl and toss with lime juice. Drain, rinse the chicken with cold water, and drain again. Remove the chicken from the bowl and pat dry with paper towels.

2 Place the chicken in another bowl and add the green seasoning, salt, chili pepper, and garlic. Toss well to coat and refrigerate for at least 30 minutes but ideally overnight.

3 Combine the curry powder with just enough water to form a thick paste. Heat the oil in a heavy-bottomed pot. Add the curry paste and onion. Cook, stirring constantly, for 1 to 2 minutes over medium-low heat—do not allow the curry to scorch. Add the chicken pieces and stir well to coat. Add the stock or water, cover, and simmer for 30 to 40 minutes, or until the chicken is tender.

4 Remove the lid and simmer for 5 minutes more over medium-high heat, until the sauce reduces by one-third. Serve with roti (pages 174-177) or white rice (page 160).

MÉLANGE CURRIED CHICKEN

Moses Reuben, executive chef and owner of Mélange Restaurant in Port of Spain, adds elegance to everyday Trinidadian foods with French technique and delicate seasoning. His version of curry chicken can be paired with roti for a more traditional feel or plain rice for a more sophisticated presentation.

4 boneless chicken breasts, cut into ½-inch cubes

3 tablespoons chopped onion

2 cloves garlic, chopped

1½ teaspoons chopped shado beni or cilantro leaves

1 teaspoon ground cumin

3 tablespoons Trinidad curry powder (page 253)

2 tablespoons canola oil

1 cup chicken stock

1 medium Yukon Gold potato, peeled and cut into ½-inch chunks

½ teaspoon coarse salt

¼ cup coconut milk

1 Mix the chicken with the onion, garlic, shado beni, cumin, and 2 teaspoons of the curry powder. Set aside to marinate for at least 20 minutes but preferably overnight in the refrigerator.

2 Mix the remaining curry powder with ½ cup of water to make a smooth paste. Heat the oil in a deep saucepan and add the curry paste and cook for about 30 seconds or until it releases its aroma. Add the marinated chicken, mix well, and sauté for 2 to 3 minutes.

3 Add the stock, potato, and salt. Simmer until the sauce thickens, about 15 minutes. Add the coconut milk and simmer for 3 minutes more. Taste to adjust the seasonings. Serve with rice (page 160) or roti (pages 174-177).

Meats, Poultry & Fish   93

STEWED CHICKEN

Trinidadians cut meat or chicken for stew into many small pieces, not more than two inches long, with the bones generally left intact. This adds flavor to the meat but can make for difficult eating, a problem solved by picking up the pieces with one's fingers and sucking off all the meat and juices. I prefer to cut my chicken for stews and curries into just eight pieces, only going so far as to cut the breast (with bone) in half.

1 (3- to 4-pound) chicken, cut into 8 pieces and skinned

3 tablespoons green seasoning (page 254)

2 tablespoons canola oil

2 tablespoons sugar

1 large onion, thinly sliced

2 cloves garlic, finely chopped

½ red bell pepper, seeded and chopped

2 teaspoons soy sauce

2 teaspoons Worcestershire sauce

1 bay leaf

½ teaspoon coarse salt

½ teaspoon hot pepper sauce

3 cups chicken stock or water

1 Mix the chicken pieces with the green seasoning and set aside in the refrigerator for 2 hours.

2 Heat the oil in a heavy-bottomed pot and add the sugar. Caramelize the sugar until dark brown. Add the seasoned chicken and stir well to coat. Cook for 5 minutes, stirring constantly.

3 Add the onion and garlic. Cook for 5 minutes more. Add the red bell pepper and mix well. Add the soy sauce, Worcestershire sauce, bay leaf, salt, hot pepper sauce, and stock or water. Add additional stock or water if necessary to cover the chicken.

4 Bring to a boil, then lower to a simmer. Cover and cook until the meat is tender, about 30 to 40 minutes. Serve with rice.

CHAGUANAS-STYLE FRIED CHICKEN

SERVES: 6 TO 8

Kentucky Fried Chicken and the local chain, Royal Castle, are very popular in Trinidad, but not without a Trini twist. The KFC chicken from my father's home town of Chaguanas is widely agreed to be the best because of the copious amounts of pepper that somehow found its way into the Colonel's recipe. I got the idea for this fried chicken as a result, which might call to mind the "Hot Chicken" popular in Tennessee.

1 (3-4 pound) chicken, cut into 8 pieces with bones

2 tablespoons freshly squeezed lime juice

2 teaspoons coarse salt

¼ teaspoon hot pepper sauce

1 cup evaporated milk

2 cups all-purpose flour

⅓ teaspoon baking powder

⅓ teaspoon freshly ground black pepper

¼ teaspoon ground thyme

2 teaspoons garlic powder

½ teaspoon dried oregano

⅓ teaspoon paprika

Canola oil for frying

1 Rub the lime juice all over the chicken pieces and then rinse with cold water. Drain completely and pat dry. Place the chicken in a bowl and sprinkle with 1 teaspoon of the salt. Using a spoon, mix in the hot pepper sauce and toss well to coat. Add the evaporated milk and mix well. Cover with plastic wrap and refrigerate overnight.

2 Using a whisk, mix the flour, baking powder, remaining 1 teaspoon salt, black pepper, thyme, garlic powder, oregano, and paprika until well combined. Remove chicken from the refrigerator and shake off excess milk mixture from each piece (reserving milk mixture) then dredge them in flour mixture. Set them in a single layer on a large platter.

3 Once again, dip the chicken pieces in the spiced milk and then again in the flour mixture. When all the pieces have been coated twice, place the platter in the refrigerator for 30 minutes.

4 Heat oven to 400°F. Heat about 2 cups of canola oil in a deep frying pan or large Dutch oven. Test oil with a frying thermometer (it should be between 350 and 375 degrees) or by dropping a pinch of flour into the oil—if it bubbles vigorously the oil is ready.

5 Remove chicken from the refrigerator and gently place chicken pieces in the hot oil. Do not overcrowd the pan, allow about ½ inch space between each piece. Fry chicken until golden brown on one side, about 8 to 10 minutes, then turn over and brown the other side. Remove the chicken pieces with tongs and place on a wire rack placed over a sheet tray. Place the sheet tray in the preheated 400°F. oven and bake for 10 minutes. Serve with Fry Bake (page 183) and Trini Coleslaw (page 123).

Tip

Breading the chicken pieces twice is called a double breading procedure and creates a crispier crust, as does chilling the chicken pieces before frying. Finishing the cooking process in the oven allows for a drier, less greasy fried chicken while maintaining a nice golden color.

CURRIED DUCK

Curried duck is a popular dish to serve at a "river lime," an all-day outing when family and close friends hangout, or "lime," by the beds of Trinidad's many rivers or at the ocean beaches. One of the pleasures of a river lime is cooking foods on site, so marinated meats are brought, along with precooked rice, ground provisions, salads, and drinks. The men tend the cooking of the meat over an open fire while downing Caribs or Stags, both locally made beers, and joking. The women lounge and watch the children who splash in the water or play along the shores.

1 (4-pound) duck, cut into 8 pieces with bone, skin removed

2 tablespoons freshly squeezed lime juice

3 tablespoons green seasoning (page 254)

¼ cup Trinidad curry powder (page 253)

2 tablespoons canola oil

1 whole Scotch bonnet pepper or other hot red chili pepper

Salt to taste

1 Toss the duck pieces with the lime juice, and then rinse with water, drain, and pat dry. Sprinkle on the green seasoning and toss to coat. Set aside in the refrigerator for at least 3 hours and up to overnight.

2 Mix the curry powder and ¼ cup of water to make a paste. Heat the oil in a heavy-bottomed pot over medium-low heat. Add the curry paste and chili pepper. Mix well and cook, stirring constantly, for 1 to 2 minutes, or until the curry has a grainy consistency.

3 Add the duck pieces and turn to coat. Reduce the heat to a simmer, cover, and cook until all the liquid has evaporated.

4 Add salt and additional water to just cover the meat. Simmer for 40 minutes, or until the meat is tender. Remove the chili pepper before serving. Serve with rice or roti.

CURRIED FISH

This is a simple yet tasty preparation for any kind of fish. This recipe calls for fillets, but traditionally whole fish would be used, since it is believed the head and bones give the most flavor.

2 tablespoons canola oil

1 medium onion, chopped

2 cloves garlic, finely chopped

½ Scotch bonnet pepper or other hot red chili pepper, stemmed, seeded, and finely chopped

1 small tomato, chopped

2 or 3 fresh curry leaves (optional)

2 tablespoons Trinidad curry powder (page 253)

2 pounds firm-fleshed white fish fillets, such as tilapia or catfish, or kingfish steaks

1 tablespoon coarsely chopped cilantro

1 Heat the oil in a deep skillet. Add the onion and cook until translucent. Add the garlic and sauté for 1 minute more. Add the chili pepper and sauté for 30 seconds. Add the tomato and curry leaves, and stir for 1 minute more. Add the curry powder and continue to cook, stirring often, for 1 minute.

2 Stir in ½ cup of water and simmer for 5 minutes. Add the fish and cook, uncovered, for 15 to 20 minutes, or until the sauce is reduced and the fish is flaky. Garnish with the cilantro. Serve with rice.

SALTFISH & PROVISIONS

G round provisions, or simply "provision," refers to the tubers and starchy vegetables that were given to enslaved people and indentured laborers working on the estates as the main part of their food rations. It remains an incredibly popular staple, much like potatoes in America or Ireland.

1 pound boneless salt cod

½ teaspoon coarse salt

1 medium yam, peeled and cubed

1 medium cassava, peeled and cubed

2 taros, peeled and cubed

2 tablespoons canola oil

1 medium onion, chopped

1 Soak the salt cod in cold water for 5 minutes. Drain, add fresh cold water and soak again for 5 minutes. Drain again, add fresh cold water and then soak for 1 hour. Drain and shred finely.

2 While the cod is soaking, bring 4 cups of water to a boil with the salt. Add the yam, cassava, and taro and simmer for 15 to 20 minutes, or until tender. Drain and set aside.

3 Heat the oil in a deep frying pan. Add the onion and sauté until translucent. Add the shredded salt cod and fry for 10 minutes. Add the cooked yam, cassava, and taro. Stir well and sauté for 1 to 2 minutes until lightly brown. Serve immediately.

FRIED FISH

The best fish for this recipe is flying fish, a sweet fish found largely in the waters between Tobago and Barbados. Flying fish can sometimes be found frozen in West Indian markets, but if you can't find it, substitute any firm-fleshed white fish fillet, such as tilapia or catfish.

FISH

2 pounds flying fish fillets or other firm-fleshed white fish

2 tablespoons green seasoning (page 254)

1 teaspoon garlic powder

½ teaspoon coarse salt

½ teaspoon freshly ground black pepper

BREADING

1½ cups dry breadcrumbs

1 teaspoon dried oregano

1 teaspoon dried parsley

½ teaspoon dried thyme

½ teaspoon paprika

¼ teaspoon coarse salt

1 teaspoon garlic powder

1 teaspoon onion powder

½ cup canola oil, for frying

Sliced tomato for garnish (optional)

Lime wedges, for garnish (optional)

MARINATE FISH:

1 Rinse the fish and pat dry. Mix together the green seasoning, garlic powder, salt, and black pepper, then rub onto the fish. Place the fish in a nonreactive dish, cover and refrigerate for 20 minutes.

MAKE BREADING:

2 Mix all the breading ingredients in a shallow bowl. Remove the fish from the refrigerator and dip in the breading mixture, coating both sides of each fillet evenly. Place the fillets on a clean plate and refrigerate again for 15 minutes.

FRY FISH:

3 Heat the oil in a deep frying pan and add the fish fillets in batches, frying until golden brown on both sides (do not crowd the pan). Remove and drain on a wire rack set over a baking sheet or on paper towels.

4 Place fried fish on a platter and garnish with tomato slices and lime wedges. Serve with Pigeon Peas and Rice (page 165) or a green salad; or use the filets to make fish sandwiches.

CURRIED CASCADURA/SWORDFISH

Cascadura is a thick-scaled fish that lives in slow-moving fresh water. With long tendrils around its mouth, it resembles catfish. The local superstition in Trinidad is that if you eat cascadura you are destined to eventually return to the island. Since cascadura is rare even in the Caribbean, it's not likely you'll find it in American markets. The closest substitute for flavor is swordfish.

2 pounds whole cascadura or swordfish steaks

4 tablespoons freshly squeezed lime juice

2 cloves garlic, finely chopped

3 tablespoons green seasoning (page 254)

1 teaspoon coarse salt

2 tablespoons canola oil

¼ cup Trinidad curry powder (page 253)

1 medium onion, thinly sliced

4 cups coconut milk

¼ teaspoon hot pepper sauce

1 If using cascadura, have the fishmonger scale and gut the fish. Lightly score the surface of the flesh with a paring knife. Wash the surface and cavity of the fish with the lime juice and then rinse with water. Pat dry. If using swordfish, rinse the steaks with the lime juice and then with water. Pat dry.

2 Rub the garlic, green seasoning, and salt onto the fish (and into the cavity, if using cascadura).

3 Heat the oil in a deep frying pan. Add the curry powder and sauté for 20 to 30 seconds, stirring constantly. Add the onion and cook for 1 minute. Add the fish and turn to coat with the curry. Lower the heat and cook for about 5 minutes.

4 Add the coconut milk and bring to a boil. Add the hot pepper sauce and adjust the seasonings to taste. Serve with rice.

Fresh Catch

Some things are worth a risk. For me, Tobago's flying fish is one of them. Eat it, and you put your life in the hands of the filleter. The slightest nick of the fish's poisonous innards while cutting can turn the succulently sweet flesh into a deadly dish. But my yen knows no fear.

My first bite was while visiting Tobago with my Trinidadian father some twenty-five years ago. We stayed with his favorite niece, Pinky, who had relocated there from Trinidad as a young woman. She was an accomplished cook, and the fish that she served us that day was so remarkable that, even at twelve years old, I realized I was eating the first delicacy of my young life. Flying fish are so prized that when they changed migration patterns beginning in the 1960s from the waters around Barbados to those nearer Tobago, bitter tensions arose between the two islands, bordering on an international incident.

Fresh flying fish was not to be had at home in New York City, where my father settled back in the 1950s. Sometimes the West Indian fishmonger in Brooklyn sold it frozen, a watery imitation of itself. It is rarely seen fresh even on sister-island Trinidad, twenty-one miles away from Tobago.

So, on a recent trip to Tobago, the moment my husband and I land at Crown Point International Airport on the southern tip of the island, I ask the driver to take us somewhere for flying fish.

"None 'round here, Miss," he says.

"How 'bout Charlotteville?" I counter.

"Yuh wan' go way out dere?" He looks at me in surprise. "De fast road being fix."

"Yes," I say unflinchingly and get into his twenty-year-old Toyota.

The fishing village of Charlotteville is tucked into a bay on the north coast, about twenty miles from the airport as the crow flies. But since the more direct south road is closed, we have to take the narrow paved road along the island's leeward coast that skirts the dense rainforest preserve at the island's heart. This trip will likely take two and a half hours.

We drive along in silence punctuated by the driver's here-and-there comments. As we pass a group of hunters at the forest edge, their dogs straining hard against the leashes and the day's heat, he says, "Is manicou dey gettin'." Manicou, a type of opossum, is a delicacy here. The driver says he makes it into a stew.

"I have sweet hand, ya know," he says smiling, using the local slang to say he is a good cook.

We drive on, and the flashes of turquoise from the Caribbean bays and inlets below are like sparkles off a diamond. The car slows until a group of barefoot children trying to coax a cow out of the road moves aside.

It is May, and many of the fruit trees are bearing. I search for a glimpse of my favorite: pommerac (also known as the Malay apple), a thin-skinned red fruit with a sweet-tart flesh that grows in the yard of my family's ancestral home in Trinidad. I see none and share this disappointment with the driver, which gets us to talking about our beloved foods. His favorite dishes are made during Christmastime.

Suddenly he starts to sing local carols. I lean toward the window to feel the breeze and, in my mind, the different ways to cook flying fish bounce along with his tune: fried fish, creole fish, curry fish, fish with tamarind sauce.

About halfway there we pull over for a soda at a rum shop squatting on a precipice over the sea. Below, Parlatuvier Bay on the leeward coast arcs into a perfect horseshoe, like an impossibly pretty postcard. Inside, three old men are sitting at a table. There is a bottle of rum in the center and each has a bottle of Stag beer. They will sit for hours teasing and telling stories as they pour fingers of rum and drink them with beer chasers.

"How you goin' baby?" one of them calls out to me.

"Fine, uncle," I answer politely. In Trinidad & Tobago, it's improper for a "decent woman" to lime in a rum shop. But in the company of my husband and the driver, I won't be judged a "fast woman." The old men smile and nod in return.

Back in the car I cannot concentrate on the driver's banter. I barely notice the traditional outdoor mud-oven that we pass. Old ladies man the volcano-shaped structure, using water-filled rum bottles for rolling pins and banana-leaf squares as baking trays for their fat coconut tarts. It is the flying fish I want.

The car dips down a low hill toward Charlotteville and, in the distance, fishermen haul their pirogues onto the shore. I see the glistening of fish flesh when the boats tip side to side as they are dragged. My mouth starts to water.

At Sharon and Phebs restaurant in the village we take a table on the veranda. It is mid-afternoon and we are the only customers.

"Fish fresh?" I ask the waitress, although I know the answer. She juts her chin toward the fishermen.

"Flying fish?" I ask.

She nods, "How ya wantin' it?"

I close my eyes. I can't decide. I want to order ten plates and taste each one. Instead I choose the local style. "Creole," I answer.

We sit back to look out at Man of War Bay, a little-visited spot that reminds me Tobago is sometimes thought to be Robinson Crusoe's original isle. We watch ripples of warm, clear water hypnotically roll over the soft sand, and we wait.

Finally, finally it comes: a huge plate, the fish smothered in tomato, onion, and green pepper. I inhale deeply and my eyes begin to water. It's not from the steam; it is from joy. I take my first bite. It is delicate and delectable and, most of all, sweet. As sweet as the memory of my now-gone father holding out a little morsel of fish for me to nibble from his hand.

KINGFISH CREOLE

Creole-style dishes are usually stewed or braised and feature a tomato-based sauce. The kingfish's hearty flesh makes it ideal for this type of cooking.

2 tablespoons canola oil

4 (6-ounce each) kingfish steaks

1 medium onion, thinly sliced

2 cloves garlic, thinly sliced

1 (16-ounce) can stewed chopped tomatoes

1 tablespoon green seasoning (page 254)

½ teaspoon hot pepper sauce, or to taste

1 tablespoon freshly squeezed lime juice

½ teaspoon coarse salt

Freshly ground black pepper to taste

1 Heat the oil in a large, deep frying pan. Add the fish and brown on one side, about 4 to 5 minutes. Turn and brown on the other side. Remove and drain on paper towels.

2 Place the onion slices in the frying pan and sauté until soft. Add the garlic and cook for 1 minute more. Stir in the remaining ingredients. Cook for 1 to 2 minutes, and then reduce the heat to low.

3 Return the fish to the pan and spoon the sauce over it. Cover tightly and simmer over low heat for 15 to 20 minutes. The fish should flake easily. Serve with rice.

SPICY STUFFED RED SNAPPER

This dish is largely Creole in style since it makes use of tomatoes and olive oil. It is primarily served for special occasions or holidays.

FISH

2 (2-pounds each) whole red snappers, scaled and gutted

2 tablespoons white vinegar

2 pimiento peppers, seeded and stemmed; or 2 tablespoons jarred pimientos; or 1 teaspoon paprika

1 large beefsteak tomato, chopped

½ Scotch bonnet or other hot red chili pepper, stemmed, seeded, and finely chopped

1 teaspoon coarse salt

Freshly ground black pepper to taste

2 tablespoons fresh lime juice

2 tablespoons olive oil

STUFFING

1 cup dry breadcrumbs

1 tablespoon chopped chives

1 tablespoon chopped parsley

1 teaspoon fresh thyme

½ red bell pepper, seeded and finely chopped

1 small onion, finely chopped

4 tablespoons (½ stick) butter, softened

PREPARE FISH:

1 Rub the fish, including the cavity, with the vinegar and rinse with water. Pat dry. Score the fish three times on each side with a sharp knife.

2 In a food processor or spice grinder, grind the pimiento peppers, if using, tomato, hot pepper, salt, and black pepper to a paste. Place the fish in a shallow baking dish and spread the pimiento paste evenly on the outside of the fish and in the cavities. If using paprika, simply sprinkle, along with the salt and pepper, outside and inside the fish. Squeeze the lime juice over the fish, cover with plastic wrap, and place in the refrigerator for 1 hour.

MAKE STUFFING:

3 While the fish is marinating, combine all the stuffing ingredients and set aside. Preheat the oven to 425 degrees F. Remove the fish from the refrigerator and stuff evenly with stuffing mixture.

COOK FISH:

4 Drizzle with the olive oil, cover with foil, and place in the oven. Bake for 10 to 15 minutes, then remove the foil and reduce the oven temperature to 375 degrees F. Bake for 25 minutes longer, or until the fish flakes easily. Serve hot.

TAMARIND FISH

Tamarind is a fruit that is used often in Indian cooking and this dish is East Indian in origin. The simplest way to use this ingredient is to purchase pre-made tamarind syrup, which is available in Middle Eastern and Indian grocery stores.

2 tablespoons canola oil

1 pound fish fillets, such as tilapia or catfish

1 small onion, finely chopped

1 tablespoon chopped fresh ginger

2 cloves garlic, finely chopped

1 tablespoon tamarind syrup

2 teaspoons sugar

1 small Scotch bonnet or other hot red chili pepper, stemmed, seeded, and chopped

1 (1-inch) cinnamon stick, or ¼ teaspoon ground cinnamon

Grated zest of ½ lemon

Coarse salt to taste

Freshly ground black pepper to taste

4 bay leaves

1 Heat 1 tablespoon of the canola oil in a deep skillet and add the fish. Fry until golden brown, about 4 to 5 minutes, then turn and fry the other side. Remove the fish to a plate lined with paper towels.

2 Heat the remaining oil in the same skillet and add the onion and ginger and sauté until the onion is soft, about 2 to 3 minutes. Add the garlic and fry for about 1 minute more.

3 Place the tamarind syrup, sugar, and ¼ cup of water in a small saucepan. Bring to a simmer and cook until the sugar is just dissolved. Remove from heat.

4 Stir the tamarind mixture into the onion mixture and add the chili pepper, cinnamon stick, lemon zest, salt, pepper, and bay leaves. Cover and simmer for 5 minutes.

5 Remove the lid and add the fish, turning to coat well. Simmer for 15 minutes, or until the sauce has thickened and the fish flakes easily. Serve with rice.

SWEET & SOUR FISH

SERVES: 4

This is another popular Trinidadian Chinese dish, and while folks in the United States will recognize the "sweet and sour" from American Chinese takeout menus, the Trinidadian version makes use of the ubiquitous hot pepper and the French method of first poaching the fish in a court bouillon, perhaps a culinary holdover from the very brief period of French colonization.

1 tablespoon chives

3 cloves garlic, lightly crushed

½ teaspoon coarse salt

5 Sichuan peppercorns

10 thin lemon slices

1-inch piece fresh ginger, peeled and thinly sliced

2 pounds pompano or butterfish fillets

SAUCE

1 tablespoon soy sauce

½ cup tomato sauce

3 teaspoons brown sugar

1 teaspoon ginger paste

1 teaspoon coarse or kosher salt

1 small Scotch bonnet or other hot red chili pepper, finely chopped

½ cup shredded Napa cabbage

2 tablespoons cornstarch

POACH FISH

1 Prepare a poaching liquid for the fish by combining 1 cup of water in a wide sauté pan with the chives, garlic, salt, peppercorns, lemon slices, and ginger. Bring to a simmer and add the fish fillets. Poach on a low simmer until cooked, about 15 to 20 minutes.

PREPARE SAUCE:

2 While fish is poaching prepare the sweet and sour sauce: Combine 1 cup of water, soy sauce, tomato sauce, brown sugar, ginger paste, salt, and chili pepper in a medium saucepan and bring to a simmer. Add the cabbage and continue to simmer until the cabbage cooks through, about 5 minutes. Dissolve the cornstarch in ½ cup of water and whisk so that the mixture resembles heavy cream. Add to the sweet and sour sauce, stirring constantly. Continue to simmer until the sauce thickens, about 1 minute.

3 Remove the fish fillets from their poaching liquid and place on a deep rimmed platter. Pour the sweet and sour sauce over them. Serve with rice.

SOUSED LAMBIE (CONCH SALAD)

Conch is a popular fish throughout the Caribbean and this method of preparation could be considered a Trini-style ceviche, although because of the conch's tough texture it must be cooked to soften it. To add extra freshness to the dish, I sometimes include julienned jicama with the watercress.

2 pounds conch meat

1 tablespoon green seasoning (page 254)

1 medium red onion, finely chopped

½ English cucumber, cut into ½-inch pieces

½ Scotch bonnet pepper or other hot red chili pepper, seeded, stemmed, and finely chopped

¾ cup freshly squeezed lime juice

Coarse salt and freshly ground black pepper to taste

1 bunch watercress or arugula, washed well

1 small jicama, peeled and julienned (optional)

1 Using a meat mallet, pound the conch for about 2 minutes in order to tenderize it. (It should be pounded flat, like a chicken cutlet and feel less rubbery to the touch.)

2 Cut the conch into bite-size pieces and place in a deep saucepan with 4 cups of water. Add the green seasoning and simmer over low heat until the conch is tender, about 1½ hours. Drain and cool.

3 Combine the cooled conch with the onion, cucumber, chili pepper, lime juice, salt, and black pepper.

4 Divide the watercress between four to six dishes and top with equal amounts of jicama, if using. Spoon an equal amount of the conch mixture onto each pile.

(photo page 78)

CHOW HAR LOOK

Chinese food is as much a part of Trinidadian culture as East Indian or African dishes, though Trinidadians of Chinese descent are today relatively few in number and are largely mixed with the rest of the population. Like American Chinese food, many Trinidadian Chinese dishes, such as Chow Har Look (shrimp in tomato sauce), don't exist back in China, but are hybrids of local taste and Chinese cooking methods.

1 tablespoon cornstarch

¼ cup canola oil

1 (2-inch) piece ginger, peeled and finely chopped

2 cloves garlic, finely chopped

3 scallions, chopped, or 1 small bunch of chives, chopped

2 pounds shrimp, shelled and deveined

1 cup tomato sauce

2 tablespoons Worcestershire sauce

1 teaspoon coarse salt

1 teaspoon sugar

1 teaspoon dark rum

Freshly ground black pepper to taste

½ teaspoon hot pepper sauce, or to taste

1 In a small bowl, combine the cornstarch and 2 tablespoons of water (the mixture should resemble milk). Set aside.

2 Heat the canola oil in a deep frying pan or, preferably, a wok. Add the ginger, garlic, and scallions and fry for 30 seconds. Add the shrimp, and sauté, stirring constantly, until they just turn pink. Add the tomato sauce, Worcestershire sauce, salt, sugar, rum, and black pepper.

3 Add the cornstarch mixture, stirring constantly. Simmer for about 5 minutes or until the sauce thickens. Add the hot pepper sauce and adjust the seasonings to taste. Serve with rice.

Meats, Poultry & Fish   111

KASHIA CAVE'S SHRIMP CEVICHE

I first met Kashia Cave when a mutual friend told me about the work of her nonprofit, My City Kitchen, located in Hamden, Connecticut. My City Kitchen provides cooking instruction to at-risk youth, providing them real world skills as well as self-esteem and positive connections with others. Born and raised in south Trinidad, Kashia is a tireless activist who believes in the power of good home cooking. Fresh produce is a hallmark of all her dishes, no doubt gleaned from her grandfather who was a cocoa farmer. Like our mutual friend Colette Burnett (page 72), Kashia represents the promise and vibrancy of American immigrant culture. An entrepreneur who makes connections with food all over the world, she has recently become involved in importing small-batch, artisanal olive oil from Italy to both America and Trinidad. More than anything, though, Kashia has a joyful spirit that always makes my heart glad—plus she is a stellar cook! I'm proud to call her "sister." This recipe is Kashia's interpretation of the "soused" or "escabeche" fish dishes that are common to the Caribbean. In her version shrimp are enlivened with fresh tropical fruit and the flavorful bite of poblano chili. This ceviche makes a wonderful appetizer for a warm weather dinner party.

2 tablespoons salt

1 pound medium-small shrimp, peeled and deveined

¾ cup freshly squeezed lime juice

¾ cup freshly squeezed lemon juice

1 cup finely chopped red onion

1 poblano pepper, stemmed, ribs and seeds removed, finely chopped

1 sweet mango, peeled, sliced, and cut into ¼-inch pieces

1½ cups chopped papaya

1 cup chopped cilantro

1 Fill a large bowl with 2 cups of ice and 2 cups of water and set aside. In a large saucepan, bring an additional 6 cups of water to a boil and add the salt. Add the shrimp and cook until they just turn pink, about 1 to 2 minutes. Drain the shrimp and immediately put them in the bowl of ice water.

2 Remove the shrimp from the ice bath. Cut each shrimp in half and place them in a glass bowl. Mix in the lime juice, lemon juice, red onion, and poblano pepper. Cover and refrigerate for 30 minutes.

3 In a separate bowl, mix the mango and papaya together and refrigerate.

2 Persian cucumbers, cut into ½-inch pieces

Salt and pepper to taste

Fresh chives, for garnish

4 Right before serving add the cilantro and cucumbers to the shrimp mixture and season with salt and black pepper to taste.

5 Divide the mango/papaya mixture equally among six martini glasses or small plates. Add an equal amount of the shrimp mixture on top of it and garnish with chives.

SHRIMP CREOLE

SERVES: 4 TO 6

Shrimp Creole is quick to prepare but still features a good depth of flavor. Serve with pita bread for a quick lunch or dinner.

2 pounds shrimp, shelled and deveined

2 tablespoons green seasoning (page 254)

1 tablespoon canola oil

1 small onion, chopped

1 stalk celery, chopped

1 small red bell pepper, seeded and chopped

1 clove garlic, finely chopped

1 (16-ounce) can chopped tomatoes

1 teaspoon coarse salt

1 teaspoon hot pepper sauce

1 bay leaf

1 Combine the shrimp and green seasoning and set aside in the refrigerator for 1 hour.

2 Heat the canola oil in a medium deep frying pan and add the onion, celery, and bell pepper. Sauté until the onion is soft. Add the garlic, stir well and cook for 1 to 2 minutes more.

3 Add the tomatoes, salt, and hot pepper sauce. Mix well and add the bay leaf. Simmer, covered, for 20 minutes.

4 Add the shrimp and cook until they only just turn pink. Remove from the heat and serve with rice.

CURRIED SHRIMP

This is a popular curry in roti shops and is often paired with Curried Aloo and Dalpuri or Paratha Roti to make a delicious meal.

1 pound large shrimp, shelled and deveined

3 scallions, white and green parts, finely chopped

1 small onion, chopped

½ teaspoon ground turmeric

½ teaspoon ground cumin

1 tablespoon Trinidad curry powder (page 253)

¼ Scotch bonnet pepper or other hot red chili pepper, finely chopped

2 tablespoons chopped shado beni or cilantro leaves

1 tablespoon canola oil

2 roma tomatoes, chopped

Coarse salt and ground black pepper to taste

1 Mix shrimp, scallions, onion, turmeric, cumin, curry powder, chili pepper, and shado beni together in a large bowl. Cover with plastic wrap and refrigerate for 2 hours.

2 Heat the oil in a large deep frying pan. Add the tomatoes and cook 1 minute. Add the shrimp mixture.

3 Add 1 cup of water and simmer until shrimp turn pink. Season with salt and pepper and mix well.

4 Remove from heat and serve with Aloo Talkari (page 129), Dalpuri (page 180), Paratha Roti (page 174), or rice (page 160).

CURRIED CRAB
& DUMPLINGS

T his dish is from Shairoon Nicholas of Santa Cruz, located in the valley of Trinidad's Northern Range. Most blue crabs come from the Mayaro area along the southeast coast. Popular throughout the country, this dish is a particular favorite on Tobago, Trinidad's sister island.

DUMPLINGS

2 cups all-purpose flour

Pinch of coarse salt

½ teaspoon dried oregano

1 teaspoon garlic powder

CRAB

4 tablespoons freshly squeezed lime juice

8 blue crabs, backs removed and innards cleaned out

1 medium onion, grated

6 cloves garlic, crushed

1 tablespoon each finely chopped fresh chives, oregano, cilantro, and thyme

1½ teaspoons coarse salt

2 tablespoons canola oil

½ cup Trinidad curry powder (page 253)

½ cup coconut milk

Freshly ground black pepper to taste

MAKE DUMPLING DOUGH:

1 Combine the flour, salt, oregano, and garlic powder in a bowl. Using an electric mixer to blend, slowly add about ¾ cup of water, just until dough comes together into a ball. Knead by hand for 2 minutes to form a firm, hard dough. Set aside to rest for 15 minutes.

PREPARE CRAB:

2 Pour the lime juice over the crabs, toss well, and rinse with cold water. Combine the onion, garlic, and herbs with 1 teaspoon of the salt to form a loose paste. Smear this paste over the crabs and set aside.

3 Heat the canola oil in a heavy-bottomed deep pot. Reduce the heat and add the curry powder and cook the curry, stirring constantly, for 1 minute. Add the crabs and toss well to coat.

4 Add the coconut milk, ¼ cup of water, and black pepper to taste. Stir well and cover the pot. Simmer over low heat for 15 minutes, then remove the lid and simmer until the liquid reduces by one-third.

Travel Tip

Every Easter, Buccoo, a small fishing village in Tobago, celebrates with two beloved festivities—goat races and crab races. The crabs, tied to a string, are "guided" toward the finish line by "jockeys" who run beside them. Winners and losers alike get the same dubious accolade—a trip to the curry pot.

COOK DUMPLINGS:

5 While the crabs are cooking, complete the dumplings by dividing the dough into walnut-size balls. Roll each ball between your palms to form an egg shape. Flatten each between your hands to form thick patties. Bring 4 cups of water to a boil with the remaining ½ teaspoon of salt. Add the dumplings and simmer at a moderate boil for 15 minutes. Drain.

6 To serve, place the drained dumplings on a deep serving platter. Arrange the crabs over them and pour the sauce on top.

VEGETABLES & RICE

Vegetarians find it very easy to eat in Trinidad since the abundance of local vegetables, creatively used, means there is always something on the menu for non-meateaters. The wide variety of vegetable dishes has to do with the large East Indian Hindu population, which originally came to Trinidad as vegetarians even if they did not remain that way.

Even those Trinidadians who must have meat at every meal eat a healthy variety of vegetables in addition to the standard starch that, as in America, generally accompanies every meat dish. These are known as "ground provisions," the catchall term for the starchy tubers, fruits, and squash like cassava, pumpkin, plantains, and breadfruit, that were the staple diet for enslaved people and indentured laborers. Now generally referred to as "provision," they remain a major part of the Trinidadian diet, whether elegantly prepared in a curry sauce or casserole or simply simmered in salted water as a side dish.

Plenty of leafy greens, such as spinach, bok choy, and dasheen, the leaf of the taro plant, are consumed. While carrots, sweet peas, and tomatoes are now widely used, they are largely considered flavorings and don't often comprise the bulk of a vegetable side dish. Legumes and beans, however, are enormously popular with Trinidadians of all descent and are prepared in any number of ways, providing a rich source of fiber and protein for a population that doesn't eat a great deal of animal protein besides chicken.

TRINI COLESLAW

Coleslaw is known to have been prepared by the Dutch and later the English in the American colonies, so it is tempting to think those same settlers brought the dish to the Caribbean on one of the many circular trade routes between North America, Europe, Africa, and the Caribbean. Truthfully, I have not been able to find any evidence supporting this idea and I'm not really sure how coleslaw came to Trinidad. It could very well be a latter twentieth century addition to the Caribbean culinary repertoire, like hamburgers and hot dogs.

Trinidadian coleslaw doesn't employ mayonnaise, perhaps a practical food safety measure given the country's heat. A vinegar based dish, it is a particularly refreshing accompaniment to foods like Fried Fish (page 102) and Chaguanas-Style Fried Chicken (page 96).

1 small red onion, thinly sliced

½ cup white vinegar

3 tablespoons brown sugar

½ teaspoon coarse salt

¼ head green cabbage, shredded

¼ head red cabbage, shredded

2 carrots, shredded

3 tablespoons finely chopped fresh or jarred pimiento peppers

5 shado beni or cilantro leaves, finely chopped

1 Place the onion, vinegar, brown sugar, and salt in a large bowl. Whisk together to dissolve the sugar and salt.

2 Add the cabbages, carrots, and pimiento pepper to the vinegar mixture and toss well. Cover and set aside to macerate for at least one hour and up to overnight in the refrigerator.

3 Toss in the shado beni or cilantro leaves just before serving.

WATERCRESS SALAD

This is a refreshing salad that makes a great side dish with any kind of barbecue or can be served as a starter to a meal. It's important to trim the watercress stems to about 2 inches long for both presentation and texture. Watercress is a common salad green throughout the Caribbean and is similar to arugula in its peppery flavor. When in season Asian pear is a nice substitute for the crunchy, fresh jicama in this recipe.

DRESSING

¼ cup freshly squeezed lime juice

½ shallot, minced

2 teaspoons sugar

¼ teaspoon salt

¼ teaspoon freshly ground black pepper

¾ cup good quality extra virgin olive oil

SALAD

2 bunches watercress, stems trimmed

1 small jicama, peeled and sliced into thin matchsticks

12 to 15 grape tomatoes, sliced in half

2 Persian cucumbers, diced (optional)

1 Haas avocado, peeled, pitted, and diced (optional)

MAKE DRESSING:

1 In a medium bowl, mix together the lime juice, shallot, sugar, salt, and black pepper and allow to sit for 10 minutes. Slowly whisk the olive oil into the dressing (you may also do this in a high speed blender for a smoother emulsion).

MIX SALAD:

2 Gently toss all the salad ingredients together in a large bowl.

3 Pour about half the dressing (or more if desired) over the salad and toss well.

Note: You may store any remaining dressing in a sealed container in the refrigerator for up to 1 week. Bring to room temperature before serving.

ZABOCA CHOKHA
TRINI-STYLE GUACAMOLE

My father was a lover of avocados and often ate them spread over bread or simply sliced or even mashed as an accompaniment to a meal. I've seen other Trinidadians do the same and call the dish "*zaboca chokha*." Since I love guacamole, I developed this dish to reflect the best of both worlds.

1 small white onion, finely chopped

2 cloves garlic, finely chopped

4 shado beni or cilantro leaves, finely chopped

2 tablespoons freshly squeezed lime juice

¼ Scotch bonnet pepper or other hot red chili pepper, finely chopped

1 teaspoon coarse or kosher salt

1 large Florida or Caribbean avocado or 4 Haas avocados

1 Combine onion, garlic, shado beni, lime juice, chili pepper, and salt in a bowl and allow to macerate for 20 minutes.

2 Meanwhile, scrape flesh out of the avocados and mash well with a fork.

3 Combine mashed avocado with the onion mixture and mix well. Serve with roti (pages 174-177).

FRY ALOO

Some years ago my friend Gerard Ramsawak was hosting a visiting ambassador to Trinidad at his hotel, Pax Guest House. Gerard asked the ambassador whether he had sampled East Indian food while in Trinidad and got the usual answers of curries, dalpuri, and other elaborate dishes. True to his nature, Gerard insisted the ambassador join him for a "real" Trinidadian Indian meal, the kind that featured simple "not for company" dishes that are a staple in every Trinidadian home. The diplomat had to concur that though seemingly unsophisticated, the meal was both artful and among the most delicious he had on his visit.

4 Yukon Gold potatoes

1 tablespoon canola oil

1 small onion, finely chopped

3 cloves garlic, finely chopped

½ green Scotch bonnet pepper or other hot chili pepper, finely chopped

Coarse salt and freshly ground black pepper to taste

Tip

The trick to a perfect Fry Aloo is to make sure the potato slices are just wet enough to steam and then brown in the pan.

1 Peel the potatoes and thinly slice them into 3-inch-long by 1-inch wide pieces. Place the potato slices in water to cover and set aside.

2 Heat the canola oil in a large frying pan. Add the onion and garlic and fry, stirring constantly, until the garlic is lightly browned. Add the chili pepper and fry 1 minute more.

3 Add some of the potatoes by reaching into the bowl with your hand and grabbing a handful. Shake once or twice to remove most of the excess water and add to the pan. Repeat until all the potatoes are added.

4 Season the potatoes with salt and freshly ground black pepper and stir well. Cover the frying pan and lower heat to medium-low. Cook for 15 minutes.

5 Remove cover from pan and allow the water to evaporate and then brown the potatoes lightly on all sides. Serve with rice or Fry Bake (page 183).

VARIATION: FRY ALOO WITH SALTFISH

Some people like to add salt cod to Fry Aloo. To do so, boil ½ pound boneless salt cod in water for 20 minutes. Drain and shred salt cod into small pieces. Heat a frying pan with 2 teaspoons canola oil and add the salt cod, frying until lightly browned. Remove from heat and using a slotted spoon, add cooked salt cod to the cooked potatoes before serving.

ALOO TALKARI

This curried dish was a specialty of my aunts and is a particular favorite of my husband. It is up to you whether to peel the potatoes. I generally don't, since the skins add flavor.

3 tablespoons canola oil or ghee

4 medium Yukon Gold potatoes, cut into 1-inch chunks

1 pound green beans, trimmed and cut into 1-inch lengths

1 small onion, chopped

2 cloves garlic, finely chopped

1 heaping tablespoon Trinidad curry powder (page 253)

2 cups chicken broth, vegetable broth, or water

1 teaspoon coarse salt

2 teaspoons coarsely chopped cilantro

1 Heat the canola oil or ghee in a deep, heavy-bottomed pan. Add the potatoes and cook and stir for 1 to 2 minutes, browning on all sides.

2 Stir in the green beans and cook for 4 to 5 minutes, or until the beans begin to brown and blister. Add the onion and cook for 1 to 2 minutes more. Add the garlic and stir well and cook for 30 seconds.

3 Mix in the curry powder and stir to coat the vegetables. Cook for about 30 seconds, or until the curry just begins to release its aromas. Add the broth and salt, partly cover, and simmer for 20 minutes.

4 Remove the lid and simmer for 15 minutes more, or until the liquid is reduced by half. Garnish with the cilantro and serve with roti (pages 174-177).

VARIATION:
Omit the string beans if you like just a potato dish.

Tip: Ghee

Many East Indian-based dishes call for ghee as the preferred oil. Ghee is toasted clarified butter, which can be purchased in Eastern markets but can also be easily made at home: Melt 8 tablespoons (1 stick) of unsalted butter in a small saucepan over medium heat. Once the butter melts, reduce the heat to low and simmer for 15 to 20 minutes, or until the sediment settles to the bottom of the pan and the oil is a golden brown color. Strain through a fine mesh sieve and store in a sealed container. Ghee may be stored either refrigerated or in a dry cupboard for up to 2 weeks.

BAIGANI

SERVES: 4

Baigani makes use of *phoulourie* batter for an end product very similar to classic. Indian *pakoras* (battered-fried vegetables). Although it is not traditionally Trinidadian, I will sometimes substitute slices of large zucchini for the eggplant. If you use Chinese or white eggplants, the baigani (*bhaijias*) will have a more delicate flavor and make for a lovely appetizer.

2 large Italian eggplants, 3 white eggplants, or 5 Chinese eggplants (1½ pounds total)

Coarse salt as needed

1 cup canola oil

1 cup all-purpose flour seasoned with coarse salt and pepper

1 recipe phoulourie batter (page 53)

1 Stem the eggplants and slice ¼-inch thick. Place the eggplant slices on a wire rack set over a baking sheet and sprinkle both sides of the slices liberally with salt. Set aside for 20 minutes.

2 Discard the water that has leeched from the eggplants. Rinse each slice and pat dry.

3 Heat the oil in a deep saucepan and, when hot, begin dipping each eggplant slice in the seasoned flour and then in the batter, coating both sides well.

4 Drop the battered eggplant slices into the hot oil, turning as necessary, and frying until golden brown on both sides. Remove with a slotted spoon and drain on a platter lined with paper towels or on a wire rack set over a baking sheet. Serve hot.

BAIGAN CHOKHA

The term "*chokha*" actually refers to any dish of vegetables roasted over a fire or scorched in hot oil, then mashed into a paste, and usually eaten with roti. Although it has of late become synonymous with something simply "mashed."

2 large Italian eggplants

1 tablespoon canola oil

½ medium onion, chopped

2 cloves garlic, finely chopped

1 small tomato, chopped

¼ teaspoon coarse salt, or to taste

Freshly ground black pepper to taste

1 tablespoon coarsely chopped cilantro

1 Prepare a hot grill or preheat the broiler.

2 With a fork, pierce the eggplants all over and place on the grill or under the broiler. Grill or broil until completely charred and soft, about 20 minutes, turning frequently (the eggplants will brown and blister quickly). Remove and allow to cool.

3 Once cool, cut open the eggplants and scrape out the flesh. The flesh should be soft to the touch and pulpy and should easily come away from the skin. Set aside.

4 Heat the canola oil in a frying pan. Add the onion and sauté until translucent. Add the garlic and fry until the garlic turns a dark golden brown, then add the tomato and fry for 1 to 2 minutes.

5 Stir in the mashed eggplant and cook for about 2 minutes. Season with salt and black pepper to taste. Garnish with the cilantro and serve with roti (pages 174-177).

COCONUT CHOKHA

The first time I had this unusual dish was not in Trinidad but at a Guyanese restaurant in Queens, New York. After checking with my Trini-Guyanese friend Darrel, he confirmed that Coconut Chokha is Trinidadian as well, though rarely prepared. I found it to be a wonderful accompaniment to all kinds of dishes, particularly those with less spice that need a kick. It is something akin to a cooked coconut chutney.

1 cup freshly grated or frozen grated
  unsweetened coconut

2 tablespoons canola oil

1 small onion, finely chopped

1 clove garlic, finely chopped

⅓ teaspoon mustard seeds

¼ Scotch bonnet pepper or other hot
  red chili pepper, finely chopped

1 Heat a medium sauté pan over medium heat and add coconut. Cook, stirring often, until the coconut is toasted and light brown. Remove from heat and set aside.

2 Heat another medium sauté pan over medium heat and add canola oil. Add the onion and sauté until translucent. Add the garlic and fry until lightly browned. Mix in the mustard seeds and cook, stirring, until they begin to pop.

3 Add the chili pepper and fry for 30 seconds, then add the toasted coconut. Mix well and fry, stirring often, for 5 to 7 minutes. Remove from heat and serve with roti (pages 174-177).

Tip
The key to success with this dish is to ensure that the grated coconut is relatively dry, so if you use frozen instead of fresh, after defrosting spread the coconut on a baking sheet lined with paper towels so some of the water from freezing is absorbed.

BHAJI

Bhaji, or spinach, is very popular in Trinidad and the North American varieties commonly found in any American supermarket are favored over tougher local Trinidadian varieties.

1 tablespoon canola oil

1 small onion, chopped

1 clove garlic, finely chopped

1 pound spinach, washed well, stemmed, and coarsely chopped

¼ teaspoon coarse salt, or to taste

Freshly ground black pepper to taste

¼ cup coconut milk

1 In a large, wide frying pan, heat the oil until very hot. Add the onion and fry until translucent. Add the garlic and fry until golden brown, about 30 seconds.

2 Stir in the spinach. Cook, stirring constantly, until the spinach begins to wilt. Add salt and black pepper to taste, then add the coconut milk and 2 tablespoons water. Mix well and lower the heat to medium-low. Simmer until all the coconut milk is absorbed and the spinach is soft. Serve as a side dish with rice or roti (pages 174-177).

Two Cocoa Paynol Corn Recipes

When I was young I was always puzzled by the idea of corn in Caribbean cooking, assuming, as I did, that corn was a uniquely American product—one I associated with summertime cookouts. And while corn is certainly most associated with America, it was originally a Central American and native Caribbean crop, no doubt used in very similar ways as Native American people used it. In the colonial period, ground corn, in the form of meal or hominy, became a key commodity in the triangular trade that brought captives from Africa to be enslaved in the Caribbean, and corn grown in the vast fields of the American colonies went to the Caribbean to feed enslaved people. In Trinidad, the various ways that corn is used is most representative of two traditions: our deep West African roots in the form of those original dishes that enslaved ancestors fashioned from corn rations and the influence of South American cocoa laborers, called *cocoa paynols*, who emigrated to the island in the eighteenth century bringing their own native uses for corn.

CACHAPAS

Cachapa is the Venezuelan version of "tortilla" and is also a popular street food in that country where it is often topped with cheese or sour cream.

6 ears fresh corn

2 teaspoons sugar

Pinch of salt

1 tablespoon milk

1½ teaspoons cornstarch

2 tablespoons corn flour (maseca)

Canola oil as needed

Grated manchego cheese (optional)

Sour cream (optional

1 Grate corn niblets off the cob into a large bowl.

2 Add the sugar, salt, milk, cornstarch, and corn flour and mix well. Add more milk as needed to achieve a thick batter.

3 Heat a griddle or a tawa and brush with oil. Pour about 4 tablespoons of batter onto the griddle and spread to make a pancake. Cook pancake until brown on one side and then flip and cook on the other side until brown. Repeat until all batter is used up.

4 Top the cachapas with grated manchego cheese or sour cream or use for tacos or as a side dish with any stewed meat.

BOLLITOS

Bollito means "cake" in Spanish and this simple corn cake is a good accompaniment to hearty stews or other saucy dishes.

6 ears fresh corn

Pinch of salt

1½ teaspoons cornstarch

2 tablespoons corn flour (maseca)

6 banana leaves cut into 12-inch squares

1 Grate corn off the cob into a large bowl.

2 Place one-third of the corn in a large dishtowel and fold closed. Twist tightly in opposing directions over a sink to squeeze out excess water. Repeat with two more batches. Place squeezed corn in a bowl and add salt, cornstarch, and corn flour. Mix well.

3 Scoop corn onto banana leaves in six equal portions and spread with the back of a spoon leaving about ½-inch space all around the edges. Fold one side of each filled leaf halfway over the filling and the other side halfway over to slightly overlap the first side, then fold the leaf in the other direction in the same manner to form a package. Tie tightly with kitchen twine.

4 Bring a large pot of water to a boil and add the bollitos. Boil for 10 to12 minutes, or until firm to the touch. Remove from the water, untie, and serve the corn cakes with stew.

CORN PIE

Corn pie is one of those recipes that is quintessentially Trinidadian because it speaks to a long history. Corn meal, reminiscent of the milled corn sent to the Caribbean as part of the eighteenth-century triangular trade between Africa, North America/Caribbean, and Europe, is married with European cooking methods. Corn pie was an extremely common dish in early America and is similar to baked, casserole-type dishes in England. In the United States, a very similar corn pie is made in Amish country, but it is baked with a flour crust. Evaporated milk appears in this, as it does in many Trinidadian recipes, since tinned milk was at one time more readily available throughout the Caribbean than fresh. Do not substiute fresh milk, however, because it contains more water than evaporated milk and will change the outcome of the recipe.

4 tablespoons unsalted butter

1 small onion, finely chopped

3 pimiento peppers, stemmed, seeded and finely chopped

1 cup evaporated milk

2 large eggs

1 cup canned creamed corn

½ teaspoon coarse salt

½ teaspoon freshly ground pepper

¼ cup fine cornmeal

2 cups fresh corn kernels

1 Preheat oven to 350°F and grease an 8x8 casserole dish.

2 Melt the butter in a medium saucepan over medium heat. Add the onion and pimiento pepper and fry until onion is soft and translucent, about 7 to 8 minutes. Remove from heat and cool completely.

3 Beat together the evaporated milk and eggs. Beat in the creamed corn, salt, and pepper then add the cold onion mixture and mix well. Slowly beat or whisk in the cornmeal so there are no lumps. Add the fresh corn and mix very well.

4 Pour the batter into the prepared dish and bake for 30 minutes or until a tester comes out clean. Serve as a side dish.

VARIATION: CHEESY CORN PIE
Some folks like to add shredded cheddar cheese to their corn pie which gives it a gooier texture and a tangy bite. If you'd like to do this, increase the amount of evaporated milk to 1¼ cups and add 1 cup of shredded sharp cheddar after you beat together the milk and eggs, before adding the remaining ingredients.

COOCOO

This thick cornmeal and okra cake is a delicious—if heavy —side dish that is ideal for sopping up the juices of stewed meats.

1 cup coconut milk

12 okras, stemmed and sliced into ½-inch pieces, or 1 cup frozen sliced okra

1 teaspoon coarse salt

¼ teaspoon freshly ground black pepper

1 cup cornmeal

1 Lightly grease a 2-quart bowl and set aside.

2 Mix 1 cup of water and the coconut milk in a saucepan. Add the okra and bring to a boil. Lower the heat and simmer until soft, about 5 minutes.

3 Add the salt and black pepper and mix well. Slowly add the cornmeal, mixing constantly. Continue stirring vigorously while cooking over medium-low heat until the mixture holds a stiff peak, about 15 to 20 minutes.

4 Pour into the greased bowl and smooth the top. Allow to set for 1 to 2 minutes, then invert onto a plate. Slice and serve warm.

CURRIED CHATAIGNE

This curry, like most vegetable curries, is popular for Hindu holidays such as Paghwa and Diwali, or prayer meetings, where vegetarian fare must be served. *Chataigne* (pronounced Shah-tyne) is the French word for chestnut and the Trinidadian name for breadnut, a starchy tree fruit that is similar to breadfruit in taste and family, but closer to chestnut in appearance. Also called jackfruit or by the Indian name *katahar*, chataigne is available in most Asian, Indian, and Caribbean markets. Canned jackfruit in sweet syrup is available as well and is a popular dessert in East Asia. I have also seen frozen Thai jackfruit pulp but the fruit is generally shredded and seedless.

1 3-pound chataigne (jackfruit), peeled and cut into chunks

1 tablespoon canola oil

1 medium onion, chopped

4 cloves garlic, finely chopped

½ Scotch bonnet pepper or 1 small red chili pepper, finely chopped

3 tablespoons Trinidad curry powder (page 253)

2 teaspoons coarse salt

2 cups coconut milk

1 Using your hands, break the chataigne into smaller pieces and remove the seeds. Peel the covering of the seeds and discard, setting aside the seeds.

2 Heat the canola oil in a large sauté pan and add the onion. Fry the onion until translucent and then add the garlic and sauté until just starting to lightly brown.

3 Add the chili pepper and fry 30 to 40 seconds more. Add the curry powder and fry, stirring often, until the curry begins to release its aromas, about 30 to 60 seconds.

4 Add the chataigne pieces and seeds and mix well so all the pieces are coated. Add 1½ cups of water and the salt and lower the heat to low. Cover and simmer for 10 minutes.

5 Stir in the coconut milk and raise the heat in order to bring the mixture to a boil, then reduce the heat and simmer for 20 minutes more, or until the chataigne flesh and seeds are fork tender. Serve with roti (pages 174-177) or rice (page 160).

CHATAIGNE STUFFING

This unusual stuffing for your holiday bird is from Karen Felician of Maraval. Turkeys, imported from the United States, have become highly popular fare for Christmas and Easter in Trinidad & Tobago. This recipe makes enough stuffing for a 15-pound turkey.

2 to 3 pounds chataigne (jackfruit)

1½ teaspoons green seasoning (page 254)

1 tablespoon Maggi Spicy Seasoning

1 tablespoon canola oil

1 small onion, finely chopped

3 cloves garlic, finely chopped

2 fresh pimiento peppers, stemmed and finely chopped; or 2 tablespoons finely chopped jarred pimientos; or 1 teaspoon paprika

Turkey giblets, finely chopped (*optional*)

1 tablespoon butter

2 teaspoons Hunt's ketchup, or 2 teaspoons other brand ketchup mixed with ½ teaspoon sugar

1 teaspoon soy sauce

½ cup raisins

1 Place the chataignes in a large pot with water to cover and bring to a boil. Simmer until soft, about 30 minutes. Remove from the pan and peel.

2 Cut the chataignes in half and dig out the seeds. Peel the seeds and set aside. Cut the chataigne flesh into chunks and place in the bowl of a food processor with the peeled seeds, green seasoning, and Maggi seasoning. Pulse to a coarse meal about the consistency of wet sand.

3 Heat the oil in a heavy-bottomed pot and add the onion and sauté until translucent. Add the garlic and pimientos and fry for 30 seconds more and then add the giblets, if using.

4 Add the butter to the onion mixture and heat until the butter melts. Stir in the chataigne mixture. Add the ketchup, soy sauce, raisins, and ¼ cup of water. Mix well and cook, stirring often, until all the liquid is absorbed, about 15 minutes. Cool completely.

5 Use this mixture to stuff a turkey following the same directions for bread stuffing. This stuffing can also be baked separately in a lightly greased casserole dish, covered with aluminum foil at 350°F for 30 minutes.

At the Market

Supermarkets, malls, and box stores are nothing new to Trinidad and they dot the landscape as they do in America—nestled in massive shopping plazas, with sprawling parking lots packed with cars. Walk into one of these new, super-modern structures and you'll get everything you need under one roof, from vegetables and meats to spices and baked goods, and even liquor.

Yet, despite their presence, the local "village" markets happily remain a mainstay of Trinidadian existence. While almost every little town has its own market area, even if it is just a simple collection of wooden stalls in a public square, certain cities are known for the massive size of their markets and the large assortment of goods available there. Among these are the markets in Port of Spain, San Fernando, and the town where my father was raised, Chaguanas.

I remember the market as a hodgepodge open-air collection of individual stands selling everything from vegetables to textiles. Today, the Chaguanas market is a concrete structure with high, galvanized metal roofing and an orderly arrangement of stalls and vendors assigned by type of wares. It is an embarrassment of riches, particularly when it comes to fresh vegetables and succulent fruit. The aroma of powdered and whole spices warms the air, while tables are laden with silvery rows of fish so fresh that they have no smell. As in the old days, there are plenty of stands selling clothes, perfumes, and other dry goods, but now CD and toiletry vendors are also part of the mix.

My grandmother sold hand-sewn dresses, shirts, and other clothing in the Chaguanas market, creating a trade from a young lady's hobby after the death of my grandfather in 1925. He left her with a house that was little more than a shack, two building lots, ten acres of arable land in the country, a long bar tab, and six hungry children to feed. The Depression came to Trinidad, and indeed the rest of the world, far earlier than the United States and 1925 was an inopportune time for a family to try and make its way without a father. Also, like those of its worldly neighbors, Trinidad's women were not well-placed to earn enough money to support a family, although their mothers and grandmothers had been used as indentured laborers, cutting cane and picking cocoa right alongside the men. This was largely because the newly-free Indians hoped to marry their daughters to men who would support them instead of forcing them to live a life of self-supporting physical labor. Additionally, Indian tradition rarely encouraged women to gain an education or skills that would afford them non-laboring jobs and most were largely uneducated—my own grandmother could not read and write.

There in the Chaguanas market, my grandmother, Sarah Elikah, came to be known for her fine sewn goods as well as her ingenuity. She would collect empty sugar and rice sacks, cast aside after their contents had

been sold, and bring them home to dampen and beat with stones. This would soften the coarse cloth enough for her to sew it into work clothes for the sugarcane laborers—clothes they could afford while keeping their few nice things aside. She enlisted my then-young aunts into this task, too.

By the time my father brought us to Chaguanas to visit his family, my grandmother was long dead, but my Aunt Toy (so called because she was said to be as pretty as a toy doll when she was a young woman) still sold goods in the market. I remember visiting her there and being fascinated by the spice stand just outside the market gate, manned by three strapping young brothers who cheerfully hawked their wares to passersby.

On a trip to Trinidad in 2004, I stopped in the then-new market, making my way to a spice vendor that seemed to have the best wares. Chatting with the proprietress, I learned that it was the very stand manned by the three brothers, now three old men. Her polite responses to my many questions turned into avid interest when she learned my now-deceased father had grown up mere blocks away. And at the end of our transaction there was a little something extra (or *lagniappe* as they say in Trinidad)—a warm embrace and the heartfelt exclamation, "Welcome home, nuh!"

BREADFRUIT OIL-DOWN

Breadfruit is a starchy tree fruit that was a mainstay for slaves and indentured laborers because it was filling but cheap for plantation owners to provide. It was often flavored with an equally cheap cut of pork, such as pig's feet. "Oil-down" refers to the cooking method by which vegetables are stewed in coconut milk until all of the milk is absorbed and just a bit of coconut oil is left in the bottom of the pan. I find that smoked ham, bacon, or turkey bacon provides good flavor in this dish, but my vegetarian cousin Jerry Kalloo, who lives on Tobago, omits meat altogether and it tastes just as good.

1 tablespoon canola oil

1 large onion, finely chopped

1 fresh pimiento pepper, stemmed, seeded, and chopped; or 1 tablespoon chopped jarred pimientos; or ½ teaspoon paprika

1 clove garlic, finely chopped

¼ pound smoked bacon or turkey bacon, chopped (optional)

3 scallions, finely chopped

½ Scotch bonnet pepper or other hot red chili pepper, stemmed, seeded, and finely chopped

1 teaspoon fresh thyme, or ½ teaspoon dried

4 cups coconut milk

1 large breadfruit, peeled, seeded, and chopped into large chunks*

Coarse salt and freshly ground black pepper to taste

1 Heat the canola oil in a deep saucepan and add the onion and pimiento pepper (if using paprika, add with the coconut milk). Sauté until soft. Add the garlic and bacon and sauté for 1 minute more.

2 Add the scallions, chili pepper, and thyme, and sauté for 1 minute, stirring constantly. Stir in the coconut milk (and paprika if using) and bring to a boil.

3 Mix in the breadfruit and salt and black pepper to taste. Lower the heat and cover. Simmer for 30 to 40 minutes, or until the breadfruit has absorbed all the coconut milk. Serve hot as a side dish.

---

* Breadfruit is available canned. One 16-ounce can is roughly equivalent to one fresh breadfruit. Drain well before using.

SAUTÉED CARAILI

SERVES: 4

C araili, a type of bitter melon, is a standard vegetable in the East Indian diet. It is light green and resembles a knobby-skinned cucumber. If you like collard greens, escarole, or other bitter vegetables, you'll find caraili appealing as well. It is readily available in Asian and Middle Eastern markets and sometimes makes an appearance in the tropical produce section of larger grocery stores. Although you can substitute zucchini in this dish, the characteristic bitter flavor will be missing.

1 tablespoon canola oil

1 small onion, chopped

1 clove garlic, finely chopped

¼ teaspoon nigella seeds

3 caraili, stem ends removed, sliced into ¼-inch rounds

¼ teaspoon coarse salt, or to taste

Freshly ground black pepper

1 Heat the oil in a large, wide frying pan. Add the onion and sauté until translucent. Add the garlic, frying until golden brown, about 30 seconds.

2 Add the nigella seeds and fry until they begin to pop, about 15 seconds. Add the caraili and stir well, frying for 1 to 2 minutes, or until they begin to brown.

3 Stir in the salt and black pepper, reduce the heat to medium-low, and cook until the caraili is soft, about 15 minutes. Serve with rice or roti (pages 174-177).

Vegetables & Rice   143

CHRISTOPHENE AU GRATIN

Although it resembles a large green pear, christophene (also called chayote) is a vine squash. Its thin skin and soft, pear-like flesh are exceedingly mild, making it perfect for combining with stronger-tasting ingredients, like cheddar cheese.

4 christophenes/chayote

¾ teaspoon coarse salt

4 tablespoons (½ stick) butter

1 medium onion, finely chopped

Freshly ground black pepper to taste

2 tablespoons dry breadcrumbs

1 cup (4 ounces) grated cheddar cheese

1 Preheat the oven to 350°F. Place the christophenes in a large saucepan with enough water to cover and ½ teaspoon of the salt. Bring to a boil, then lower the heat and simmer for about 25 minutes, or until the christophenes are tender. Drain and cool.

2 Once the christophenes are cool, slice them in half lengthwise and using a spoon remove and discard any seeds from the center and then scrape out the pulp, reserving the shells. Chop the pulp into bite-size pieces and mash about one-quarter of the pieces with a potato masher until pulpy. Set aside.

3 Heat the butter in a deep frying pan. Add the onion and cook until translucent. Add the mashed and chopped christophene and mix well. Season with the remaining ½ teaspoon of salt and black pepper. Cook, stirring often, for about 2 minutes. Stir in the breadcrumbs and cook for 1 minute. Mix in ½ cup of the grated cheese and remove from heat.

4 Place the christophene shells on a baking sheet and spoon the christophene mixture evenly into each shell. Top with the remaining ½ cup of grated cheese. Bake for 15 minutes, or until the cheese is melted, bubbly, and lightly brown. Serve hot as a vegetable side dish.

CURRIED POMME CYTHÈRE

P omme cythère or "*pomsee-tay*" is also called "golden apple," but is really ambarella, a tree fruit in the citrus family. In Jamaica it is called June Apple. Once upon a time it was near impossible to find this fruit in the United States, but happily, as professional chefs' interest in unusual citrus has grown, fruits like ugli fruit, pomelo, and pomme cythère are pretty widely available. Pomme cythère now makes regular appearances at Caribbean markets everywhere and makes a really wonderful curry.

1 tablespoon canola oil

1 small onion, chopped

2 cloves garlic, finely chopped

1 tablespoon chopped shado beni or cilantro leaves

2 teaspoons ground turmeric

1 tablespoon Trinidad curry powder (page 253)

4 large pomme cythère, peeled and cut into large chunks

1 tablespoon light brown sugar

Coarse salt to taste

Freshly ground pepper to taste

1 Heat the oil in a heavy pot. Add the onion and sauté until soft, then add the garlic and sauté for about 40 seconds. Add the shado beni and cook, stirring often, for 30 seconds. Add the turmeric and curry powder and fry for 30 seconds.

2 Add the pomme cythère and sugar, and stir well to coat. Add enough water to barely cover the pomme cythère, and mix well. Cover and simmer over medium-low heat until the fruit is fork tender, about 30 minutes

3 Remove the lid and continue to simmer until the liquid is reduced to a thick gravy. Season with salt and black pepper to taste, and serve hot with rice or roti.

Tip
In Trinidad, cooks use a cleaver to chop the fruit into small chunks, slicing right through the spiny, dendritic pit. Although you may do the same, this recipe provides for peeling the fruit and cutting off large chunks, which is easier. If you are ever in Trinidad, try the curried pomsee-tay at Shianns' on Cipriani Road in Port of Spain—it is the best I've ever tasted.

MANGO CURRY

This is another lovely fruit curry with a sweet-tart note that perfectly complements the aromatic flavors of the curry powder.

1 tablespoon canola oil

1 small onion, chopped

2 cloves garlic, finely chopped

1 tablespoon chopped shado beni or cilantro leaves

2 teaspoons ground turmeric

1 tablespoon Trinidad curry powder (page 253)

2 teaspoons amchur masala

2 large mangoes, peeled and cut into large chunks

1 tablespoon light brown sugar

Coarse salt to taste

Freshly ground pepper to taste

1 Heat the oil in a heavy pot. Add the onion and sauté until soft, then add the garlic and sauté for about 40 seconds. Add the shado beni and cook, stirring, for 30 seconds.

2 Add the turmeric, curry powder, and amchur masala, and cook for 30 seconds.

3 Add the mangoes and sugar, and stir well to coat. Add enough water to barely cover the mangoes, and mix well. Cover and simmer over medium-low heat until the fruit is fork tender, about 15 minutes.

4 Remove the lid and continue to simmer until the liquid is reduced to a thick gravy. Season with salt and black pepper to taste, and serve with rice or roti (pages 174-177).

FRIED OKRO

O kra, commonly called "okro" in Trinidad, is one of the vegetables carried to the New World by African indentured laborers, although it was widely eaten in India as well. Fried Okro is a popular side dish for Creole-style stewed meats and fish.

1 pound fresh okra, stemmed and cut into ½-inch pieces, or 1 (16-ounce) package frozen okra

1 tablespoon canola oil

1 small onion, chopped

1 clove garlic, finely chopped

¼ teaspoon mustard seeds

¼ teaspoon ground turmeric

¼ teaspoon coarse salt, or to taste

Freshly ground black pepper

¼ cup water, vegetable stock, or chicken stock

1 If using frozen okra, defrost and spread out onto a tray lined with paper towels until the okra dries slightly, about 10 minutes.

2 Heat the oil in a large, wide frying pan. Add the onion and fry until translucent. Add the garlic and fry until golden brown, about 30 seconds.

3 Add the mustard seeds and fry until they begin to pop, about 15 seconds. Stir in the okra, frying for 1 to 2 minutes, or until the okra begins to lightly brown.

4 Add the turmeric, salt, black pepper, and water or stock. Mix well, lower the heat to medium-low, and simmer until all the liquid is absorbed. The okra should be tender but not soupy. Serve with rice or roti.

FOO FOO

This somewhat bland "provision" is traditionally served with Callalloo or sometimes as part of a plate of ground provisions. Its sticky smoothness offers a pleasant consistency.

1 green plantain

Coarse salt and freshly ground black pepper to taste

1 Peel the plantain by trimming the stem end and scoring the skin three times around the plantain from end to end with a sharp knife, then pull away the skin between score marks.

2 Cut the plantain into 1-inch cubes and place in a saucepan with enough water to cover. Simmer until tender, about 30 minutes, and then drain.

3 Place the plantain in a mortar or deep bowl, and mash with a pestle or potato masher. Drizzle water onto the plantain as the mixture becomes sticky and sticks to your pestle. Use enough water to create a smooth and shiny paste. Continue to pound until smooth, and season with salt and black pepper.

4 Form the mixture into 1½-inch balls. You may warm the foo foo in a covered baking dish in a 350°F oven before serving if you like. Serve with Callaloo (page 39).

Tip: Plantains

I have often been disappointed with what seemed to be a ripe plantain that cooked up mealy or bland—a result of ripening off the tree. Sometimes you can find flash-frozen naturally ripened plantain pieces in the freezer section of Caribbean markets. These are what are used by Mexican restaurants to ensure dishes that use *platanos maduros* (ripe plantains) are consistently good. If you can get them, they are ripe, sugary, and worth a try.

FRIED SWEET PLANTAINS

Fried plantains in varying stages of ripeness are one of the usual starchy vegetables offered at most Creole-style meals. I favor the softest plantains because they are the sweetest and have the most flavor. Choose plantains that are almost totally black, as these are the ripest. They should be soft to the touch.

2 large, very ripe plantains

¼ cup canola oil

1 Peel the plantains and cut crosswise into 3-sections. Slice each section lengthwise into three pieces.

2 Heat the oil in a deep frying pan until hot. Add the plantains and fry until golden brown on one side, about 1 to 2 minutes. (Do not overcrowd the pan or allow the plantains to scorch.)

3 Remove the plantains from the pan and drain on a plate lined with paper towels. Serve hot as a side dish or dust the plantains with confectioners' sugar for a simple dessert.

GREEN "FIG" PIE

This is not so much a pie as it is a casserole, and the figs are, in fact, unripe regular bananas since in Trinidad "fig" is the common term for a banana. Although the use of banana might indicate this is a dessert, it is far from it. Instead, Green Fig Pie is yet another clever use of a relatively bland provision for a side dish.

2 pounds green bananas

1 teaspoon freshly squeezed lime juice

2 teaspoons coarse salt

¾ cup milk

1 tablespoon butter

1 small onion, finely chopped

1 clove garlic, finely chopped

1 teaspoon green seasoning (page 254)

¼ teaspoon freshly ground black pepper

¼ cup plain dry breadcrumbs

1 Preheat the oven to 350°F. Grease an ovenproof 8-inch square baking dish.

2 Peel the bananas. If they are difficult to peel, trim the stem ends and score the skin from end to end with a sharp knife. Score three times around the banana, then peel away the skin between the score marks.

3 Cut the bananas into 1-inch pieces and place in a bowl with 1 cup of water and the lime juice. Toss well, drain, and then place banana pieces in a saucepan with 2 cups of water and 1 teaspoon of the salt. Simmer until the bananas are tender, about 25 minutes.

4 Drain and place the bananas in a deep bowl while still hot. Add the milk, butter, onion, garlic, green seasoning, and the remaining 1 teaspoon of salt and the black pepper, and mash well.

5 Pour the banana mixture into the prepared dish. Sprinkle the breadcrumbs evenly on top, and bake until the crumbs are golden brown and the filling is heated through, about 20 minutes.

GREEN "FIG" SOUSE

Souse, or pickled green bananas, makes an interesting cold salad or side dish, in part because of the firm yet smooth texture and in part because of the hint of sweetness that even the unripe fruit retains. The green bananas in this dish are cooked in their skins.

2 pounds green bananas

2 tablespoons freshly squeezed lime juice

2 cloves garlic, finely chopped

½ small red onion, thinly sliced

1 teaspoon coarse salt

1 Scotch bonnet pepper or other hot red chili pepper, stemmed, seeded, and finely chopped

Freshly ground black pepper to taste

½ bunch watercress, chopped

1 Cook the whole green bananas in water to cover in a large, deep saucepan for about 15 minutes, or until they can be easily pierced with a knife. Remove from the heat, drain, peel, and cut into ½-inch-thick slices.

2 Place the sliced bananas in a bowl and stir in the lime juice, garlic, onions, salt, chili pepper, and black pepper. Mix well. Add the watercress and toss thoroughly. Chill for at least 2 hours before serving. Serve cold as a salad or side dish.

In Trinidad, "fig" is the common term for a banana

GREEN "FIG" CURRY

Curry powder is as standard to the Trinidadian kitchen as salt and pepper is to the American cook, as you can see in this recipe for curried unripe bananas.

¼ pound boneless salt cod

2 pounds green bananas

1 tablespoon canola oil

1 small onion, finely chopped

2 tablespoons Trinidad curry powder (page 253)

3 cloves garlic, finely chopped

1 cup coconut milk

1 teaspoon coarse salt

¼ teaspoon hot pepper sauce, or to taste

1 Soak the salt cod in cold water for 1 hour. Drain and shred into small pieces. Set aside.

2 Peel the bananas. If they are difficult to peel, trim the ends and score the skin from end to end with a sharp knife. Score three times around the banana, then peel away the skin between the score marks. Cut into ¼-inch slices.

3 Heat the oil and add the onion and cook until translucent. Add the curry powder and sauté for 30 seconds, stirring constantly. Add the garlic and salt cod and toss well to coat. Fry for about 1 minute, then add ¼ cup of water. Adjust the heat to low and simmer for about 5 minutes.

4 Add the banana slices and stir well to coat. Simmer for an additional 5 minutes.

5 Mix the coconut milk with 1 cup of water and add to the banana mixture with the salt and hot sauce. Simmer until the bananas are tender and the sauce is thickened. Serve with rice (page 160) or roti (pages 174-177).

CHANNA ALOO

Legumes were a traditional source of protein for vegetarian Hindus and they remain a staple in the diet of both East Indian and other-heritage Trinidadians. Unlike East Indian versions of channa-based dishes which are popularly seasoned with garam masala, like so many foods in Trinidad, these chickpeas are curried.

1 cup dried chickpeas, or 1 (15-ounce) can chickpeas

2 tablespoons canola oil

½ small onion, chopped (optional)

6 cloves garlic

1 tablespoon chopped shado beni or cilantro leaves

¼ Scotch bonnet pepper or other hot red chili pepper

2 tablespoons Trinidad curry powder (page 253)

1 pound Yukon Gold potatoes, peeled and cut into ½-inch chunks

1 If using dried chickpeas, soak them in 3 cups of water overnight.

2 Drain the chickpeas and rinse. In a deep saucepan, cook the chickpeas with 3 cups of fresh water, simmering until tender, about 15 minutes. If using canned chickpeas, drain and rinse with cold water. Set aside.

3 Heat the oil in a heavy-bottomed pot and add the onion, garlic, shado beni, and chili pepper. Cook for 1 minute, stirring often.

4 Add the curry powder and cook, stirring constantly, for 30 to 45 seconds (do not allow the curry to scorch).

5 Stir in the chickpeas and potatoes. Cook, covered, for 1 to 2 minutes. Add just enough water to cover the potatoes and simmer, uncovered, for 25 minutes. Serve hot with roti (pages 174-177).

TRINIDADIAN DAL

I t seemed that a pot of dal was always simmering on a back burner of my father's stove. For him, it was the equivalent of fast food because paired with the also-ever-present pot of white rice, it was a quick, hearty, and nourishing meal. Thus dal and rice is one of my first taste-memories. I recall standing by my father's side with my mouth wide open like a baby bird waiting to taste what was on his plate. He often ate with his hands in the traditional Indian way. Using his fingers as a scoop he pushed the food inside my mouth. I remember enjoying the creaminess of the dal with a hint of garlic which he had pureed using an egg beater. These days I use a stick-blender or food processor to the same effect.

1 tablespoon oil

1 small onion, chopped

1 teaspoon peeled and finely chopped fresh ginger

1 clove garlic, finely chopped

½ teaspoon cumin seeds

1 cup dried yellow split peas

1 teaspoon coarse salt, or to taste

1 small whole Scotch bonnet pepper or other hot red chili pepper

1 Heat the oil in a skillet over medium-high heat. Add the onion and sauté until soft. Add the ginger and garlic and fry, stirring, for about 30 seconds more. Add the cumin seeds and fry for 30 seconds.

2 Add the split peas, 2 cups of water, and the salt. Bring the mixture to a boil and then lower the heat to a simmer. Add the whole hot pepper. Simmer until the split peas are very soft, about 25 minutes, skimming foam from the top as necessary.

3 Remove the hot pepper and puree the split peas using a hand (stick) blender or standing blender, in batches if necessary, until smooth. Serve hot over rice.

STEWED PIGEON PEAS

These peas are lovely over rice or as a vegetarian stew. For a heartier meal, add salt pork or sausage to the pot when simmering and serve with a crusty loaf of bread. If using the dried pigeon peas be sure to allot time to soak overnight.

2 cups dried pigeon peas or red kidney beans or 1 (16-ounce) can

2 tablespoons canola oil

½ small onion, chopped

1 teaspoon finely chopped garlic

1 tablespoon green seasoning (page 254)

1 cup 1-inch cubes calabaza or butternut squash

½ cup chopped tomatoes (fresh or canned)

1 teaspoon coarse salt

Freshly ground black pepper to taste

Sour cream for garnish (optional)

1 If using dried beans, soak them overnight in 6 cups of cold water. Drain and set aside. If using canned, rinse the beans under cold running water, drain, and set aside.

2 Heat the oil in a large saucepan. Add the onion and sauté until translucent. Add the garlic and fry for 30 seconds more.

3 Add the peas or beans and green seasoning and cook over medium heat for 15 minutes, stirring from time to time. Add the squash, tomatoes, salt, black pepper, and 4 cups of water.

4 Bring to a boil, then lower the heat and simmer until the peas and squash are soft, about 30 minutes (most of the liquid should be absorbed). Adjust the salt and pepper to taste. Serve hot with rice.

TRINI CHOW MEIN

This is another one of those favorite dishes that demonstrate the Chinese influence on the island. You will note, except for the bean sprouts, the absence of any "traditional" Chinese ingredients like you would find in authentic stir-fries. Although in the United States, crispy noodles are the hallmark of chow mein and non-Trinidadians will recognize this dish as "lo mein," the Trinidadian terminology is closer to the original Chinese meaning: "a dish using soft noodles."

12 ounces lo mein noodles

1 tablespoon canola oil

1 small onion, thinly sliced

1 cup shredded red cabbage

1 carrot, julienned

1 red bell pepper, stemmed, seeded, julienned

1 medium christophene, seeded and thinly sliced

1 cup bean sprouts (optional)

½ small Scotch bonnet pepper or other hot red chili pepper, finely chopped, or ⅓ teaspoon hot pepper sauce

1 large chicken breast, or ½ pound boneless beef, pork, or shrimp, cut into small cubes

1 tablespoon thick soy sauce

⅓ cup vegetable or chicken stock or water

1 Bring a large pot of water to a boil and add the noodles. Lower heat to a simmer and boil noodles until tender, about 5 minutes. Drain, rinse, and set aside.

2 Heat the canola oil in a large deep frying pan or wok and add the onion, cabbage, carrot, and red bell pepper. Fry, stirring often, until the onion turns translucent.

3 Add the christophene, bean sprouts, if using, and chili pepper and toss well. Add your meat of choice and fry until well browned on all sides.

4 Mix in the soy sauce and stock or water and simmer for 5 to 7 minutes to ensure the meat is cooked through.

5 Add the lo mein noodles to the pan and toss well so all ingredients are incorporated and any liquid is absorbed.

Tip: Thick Soy Sauce
Thick soy sauce is available in Chinese and Asian markets and online. It looks very similar to molasses. A little goes a long way so use sparingly and up the amount as you go to suit your personal taste.

PLAIN RICE

R ice connoisseurship is a serious pursuit in my family because of my Persian mother. Many say that Iranians are superior rice cooks, thanks to the high quality basmati rice they use, as well as a steaming method that employs oil or butter. I have adapted the Persian kateh method to cooking rice for Trinidadian dishes because I cannot abide sticky rice. In fact, it is a method I use for all kinds of international one-pot rice dishes including Peas & Rice, Jambalaya, Paella, and Biriyani. Here's how I prepare plain rice to go with many of the dishes in this book.

1½ cups basmati or other long-grain white rice

1 bay leaf

2 teaspoon canola oil or ghee

1½ teaspoons coarse salt

Tip
Persians adore the crust at the bottom of the rice called "*tahdigh*" but it is not a Trinidadian dish and the cooking time in this recipe has been altered to prevent the crust from forming. Should you like crusty rice (which in my opinion is wonderful with any stew-like meal) add 10 more minutes to the cooking time. You should be able to invert the rice pot onto a platter and the rice will emerge as a "cake" with the golden crust on top and the fluffy rice underneath.

1 Place rice in a deep bowl and add enough cold water to cover by 1 or 2 inches. Swirl rice around with your hand until the water becomes cloudy and then gently pour off the water being careful not to pour out the rice. Repeat this process 2 to 3 times or until the water stays clear. Drain rice.

2 Place rice in a 2- quart saucepan (preferably nonstick) and add enough water to cover the rice by ½ inch from its surface. Add the bay leaf, canola oil or ghee, and salt. Mix well and place over medium heat.

3 When the rice begins to simmer, mix well one more time. Now watch carefully. When almost all the water is absorbed and "crab holes" begin to form in the rice, lower heat to low and place a doubled up paper towel or clean dish towel over the top of the pot. Place the pot lid firmly over this, pressing down to make a tight seal. Cook rice on low heat, allowing it to steam, for 15 to 20 minutes more. Remove lid and fluff the rice to serve.

FRIED RICE

Fried rice may seem like a strange thing to have in a Caribbean cookbook, but because Chinese indentured laborers were among the first migrants to Trinidad in the mid-nineteenth century, their influence on the local cuisine is widespread and well-entrenched. As a result, in Trinidad certain Chinese dishes are standard in the repertoire of any home cook, and this is one of them. Unlike true Chinese fried rice, this recipe calls for long-grain rather than short-grain sticky rice.

2 tablespoons canola oil

1 small onion, chopped

½ carrot, peeled and chopped

1 small red bell pepper, stemmed, seeded, and sliced

1 small green bell pepper, stemmed, seeded, and sliced

2 cloves garlic, finely chopped

2 cups cooked long-grain rice

1 tablespoon soy sauce

Freshly ground black pepper

2 eggs, lightly beaten

1 scallion, green and white parts, chopped, for garnish

1 Heat the oil in a large, deep frying pan or wok. Add the onion, carrot, and red and green peppers and sauté until the onion is translucent. Add the garlic and fry, stirring, for 1 minute more.

2 Stir in the rice, soy sauce, and black pepper. While stirring, add the eggs, mixing constantly, so the eggs are dispersed throughout as scrambled pieces. Serve hot, garnished with scallions.

VARIATION: SHRIMP FRIED RICE
Add half a pound of shelled, deveined shrimp to this dish in the last five minutes of cooking.

CREOLE RICE

Creole rice is very similar to fried rice in its method of preparation. Like most Creole dishes, it has a tomato base, in this case provided by tomato paste. The peanut butter no doubt harkens to the West African tradition of using peanuts or peanut products in stews and other heavy dishes.

¼ pound bacon, chopped

1 small onion, chopped

1 green bell pepper, stemmed, seeded, and cut in strips

1 small red bell pepper, stemmed, seeded, and cut into strips

½ pound stew beef cubes

¼ cup tomato paste

1 tablespoon peanut butter

2½ cups beef stock

¼ Scotch bonnet pepper or other hot red chili pepper, finely chopped, or more to taste

1 cup parboiled rice (such as Uncle Ben's)

Fresh chopped parsley, for garnish

1 Heat a skillet and add the bacon and fry for 5 minutes. Add the onion and green and red bell peppers and sauté for 1 to 2 minutes, or until the onion is soft. Add the beef and toss well to coat. Lightly brown the beef on all sides. Add the tomato paste, mix well and fry, stirring often, for 5 minutes.

2 Stir in the peanut butter and mix well. Add the stock and mix well. Reduce the heat and simmer for 15 minutes.

3 Mix in the hot pepper and rice. Cover and simmer until the rice is thoroughly cooked and all the liquid is absorbed (the rice should not be sticky). Serve hot on a platter garnished with parsley.

OKRO RICE

You may omit the pork from this dish for a vegetarian version, but if you do, adjust the salt to taste. If you eat meat but not pork, you can substitute salt beef or cured turkey bacon, and it will be just as flavorful. "Okro" is the Trinidadian word for okra.

24 fresh okra, stemmed and sliced into ½-inch slices, or 1 (16 oz) package frozen precut okra

½ pound boneless salt cod, salt pork, or cured ham (optional)

1 tablespoon canola oil

½ large onion chopped

2 cloves garlic, finely chopped

2 cups long-grain rice

2½ cups beef, chicken, or vegetable broth, or water

1 small Scotch bonnet pepper or other hot red chili pepper, stemmed, seeded, and finely chopped, or to taste

Coarse salt to taste

1. If using frozen okra, place it in a colander to defrost and drain for 10 minutes. Spread on a baking sheet lined with paper towels and pat dry. If you are using salt cod, place it in a bowl with cold water to cover for 1 hour. Drain the water and shred the fish into ½-inch pieces. Set aside. If using salt pork or ham, cut into ½-inch pieces.

2. Heat the oil in a deep saucepan. Add the onion and sauté until translucent. Add the garlic and sauté for 1 minute more.

3. Add the salt cod, salt pork, or ham and toss well to coat. Fry for 1 to 2 minutes. Add the okra and fry for 2 minutes, stirring occasionally. Remove from heat.

4. Place the rice in a deep bowl and add enough cold water to cover by 1 or 2 inches above. Swirl rice around with your hand until the water becomes cloudy and then gently pour off the water being careful not to pour out the rice with it. Repeat the process 2 or 3 times or until the water stays clear. Drain.

5. Add the washed rice to the okra mixture and put pan on heat and toss well to coat. Add the broth, hot pepper, and salt and bring to a simmer. Cover and lower heat and simmer for 30 minutes, or until the rice is tender but not sticky (all the water should be absorbed). Fluff with a fork and serve.

PIGEON PEAS & RICE

Often simply called "peas and rice" this dish can be a meal unto itself with the addition of salt pork or ham. Even omitting the meat, peas, and rice form a complete protein—a vegetarian's delight. If you are using dried peas be sure to allot time for soaking them overnight.

1½ cups dried pigeon peas or pinto beans or 1 (15-ounce) can

2 cups long-grain rice

1 tablespoon canola oil

½ pound salt pork or cured ham, cut into ½-inch cubes (optional)

1 small onion, chopped

1 small green bell pepper, stemmed, seeded, and chopped

1 small red bell pepper, stemmed, seeded, and chopped

2 cloves garlic, finely chopped

1 teaspoon chopped parsley

1 sprig thyme

½ Scotch bonnet pepper or other hot red chili pepper, stemmed, seeded, and finely chopped

1 teaspoon coarse salt or to taste

Tip
You may want to increase the amount of salt if you omit the salt pork.

1 If using dried peas or beans, soak them overnight in 5½ cups of cold water. Drain and set aside. If using canned peas or beans, rinse well under cold running water and set aside.

2 Wash the rice by placing it in a deep bowl and adding enough cold water to cover. Swirl the rice with your hand until the water is cloudy and then pour off the water, taking care not to pour out the rice. Repeat 3 to 4 times or until the water stays clear. Set aside.

3 Heat the oil in a deep saucepan. Add the salt pork or ham, if using, and fry for 1 minute. Add the onion and fry for 1 minute more, then add the green and red bell peppers and sauté until the onions are soft. Stir in the garlic and cook for 30 seconds.

4 Add the peas or beans, parsley, and thyme and stir well to combine. Gently stir in the washed rice so as not to break the rice grains. Add enough water to rise above the surface of the rice mixture by ½ inch (about 2½ cups).

5 Stir in the salt and reduce the heat to low. Simmer, covered, for 30 minutes, or until the rice is cooked but not sticky (all the water should be absorbed). Fluff with a fork and remove the thyme sprig. Spoon the rice onto a serving platter. Garnish with fresh thyme sprigs if desired.

CHICKEN PELAU

Pelau is one of those dishes that really exemplifies Trinidadian cuisine because it is an admixture of various cooking styles. *Pelau* (rice layered with meats and vegetables) is a variation of East Indian *pilau*, which originated in Persia where it is called *polow*. The Anglicized version of the dish is called *pilaf*. The process of browning meat in sugar for *pelau* is an African tradition and ketchup is a New World addition, although I suspect it has its basis in tomato chutneys available in British India and likely brought to Trinidad by the English.

1 cup dried pigeon peas, pinto beans, or black-eyed peas, or 1 (12-ounce) can

3 tablespoons canola oil

¾ cup sugar (white or brown)

1 (3-pound) chicken, cut into 8 pieces, skin removed

1 small onion, chopped

1 clove garlic, finely chopped

1 cup coconut milk

1 bay leaf

2 teaspoons green seasoning (page 254)

½ cup chopped parsley

1 sprig thyme

2 carrots, peeled and chopped

5 scallions, chopped (white and green parts)

2 cups long-grain rice

2 cups cubed fresh calabaza or butternut squash

1 small whole Scotch bonnet pepper or other hot red chili pepper

½ cup ketchup

1 tablespoon butter

1 If using dried peas or beans, soak them overnight in 3 cups of water. Drain peas/beans. Bring 3 cups of fresh water to a boil in a saucepan and add the peas or beans. Simmer for 15 minutes, or until almost cooked. Drain and set aside. If using canned peas or beans, drain, rinse with cold water, drain again, and set aside.

2 Heat the oil in a Dutch oven or other heavy deep pot over medium-high heat. Add the sugar and swirl in the pot; allow it to caramelize to a caramel brown color.

3 Add the chicken and stir well to coat. Lower the heat to medium and add the onion and garlic. Cook for 1 to 2 minutes, stirring constantly. Add 2 cups of water, the coconut milk, bay leaf, green seasoning, parsley, thyme, carrots, and scallions. Cover and simmer over medium-low heat for 10 minutes.

4 Meanwhile wash the rice by placing it in a deep bowl and adding enough cold water to cover. Swirl the rice with your hand until the water is cloudy and then pour off the water, taking care not to pour out the rice. Repeat 3 to 4 times or until the water stays clear. Drain well.

5 Stir the washed rice into the chicken mixture along with the prepared peas or beans, squash, chili pepper, ketchup, and butter. Cover and cook for 20 minutes, or until the peas and vegetables are tender.

6 Remove the lid and fluff the rice. The rice should be moist but not sticky. Remove bay leaf, thyme sprig, and chili pepper. Serve with Trini Coleslaw (page 123).

CRAB PELAU

L ike most Trinidadian crab dishes, this recipe traditionally calls for whole cleaned crabs. My version makes use of lump crabmeat, which is widely available in cans in the seafood section of the supermarket, and makes this recipe much less time-consuming.

1½ cups long-grain rice

2 tablespoons canola oil

1 medium onion, chopped

2 carrots, peeled and chopped

2 Roma tomatoes, chopped

1 tablespoon Trinidad curry powder (page 253)

1 cup lump crabmeat

1 cup coconut milk

1 teaspoon finely chopped chives

1 sprig thyme

1 bay leaf

1 teaspoon coarse salt

1 small whole Scotch bonnet pepper or other hot red chili pepper

1 Wash the rice by placing it in a deep bowl and adding enough cold water to cover. Swirl the rice with your hand until the water is cloudy and then pour off the water, taking care not to pour out the rice. Repeat 3 to 4 times or until the water stays clear. Drain and set aside.

2 Heat the oil in a saucepan, add the onion and carrots and cook over medium-low heat until the onions are soft. Stir in the tomatoes and cook 1 minute. Mix in the curry powder and continue cooking, stirring constantly, for 1 to 2 minutes.

3 Add the crabmeat, mix well to coat, then add the coconut milk and 1 cup of water. Add the chives, thyme, bay leaf, salt, and chili pepper and simmer for 1 to 2 minutes.

4 Add the rice and stir well. Bring to a boil, then lower the heat, cover loosely and simmer for about 20 minutes or until all the liquid is absorbed and the rice is soft but not sticky. Fluff with a fork. Remove bay leaf, thyme sprig, and chili pepper and serve.

MACARONI PIE

Macaroni pie is essentially baked mac n' cheese and is incredibly popular in Trinidad and much of the English Caribbean where it is a standard offering at buffet lunches and dinners. The allure is the cheddar cheese—originally brought to the island by the English and still a local favorite.

1 teaspoon coarse salt

1 (16-ounce) package elbow macaroni

2 tablespoons butter

1 tablespoon all-purpose flour

1 (12-ounce) can evaporated milk, chilled

Freshly ground white pepper to taste

1 cup (4 ounces) grated cheddar cheese, plus additional for topping

1 Preheat the oven to 375°F. Butter an 8-inch square baking dish and set aside.

2 Bring a large pot of water to a boil and add the salt. Add the macaroni and stir to loosen any macaroni that gets stuck to the bottom of the pot. Simmer until the macaroni is al dente, about 15 minutes. Drain and rinse with cold running water.

3 Melt the butter in a frying pan over low heat. Add the flour and cook, stirring constantly, for about 1 to 2 minutes (do not allow the flour to brown). Add the milk all at once, whisking the whole time. Add white pepper and simmer until the sauce thickens. Add the cheese and stir until it melts.

4 Pour the macaroni into the prepared dish and pour the sauce over it. Mix well. Sprinkle with additional cheese and bake for 40 minutes, or until the top is light brown and bubbly. Serve as a side dish with stewed meats.

BREADS

In 1924 when my father Krisnaram was born in Trinidad, the "bush" still extended over most of the land, except where punctuated by vast sugarcane fields managed by English or Scottish estate owners. There was no running water and only a few cars. Electricity was barely heard of, even in the British enclaves.

Although my grandfather, Reuben, had died by the time my father was a year old, leaving my grandmother to struggle with feeding herself and six children, she was considered a well-off woman—a "proprietress"—as Reuben had left her land, including a double lot with a one-room shack. The little house stood on stilts, a common construction in the Caribbean that added living space "under the house" where it was cooler, and also raised the building above torrential rains, vermin, and dust.

A lot of cooking took place under the house, especially when weather did not permit cooking in the yard. The cookstove consisted of a small wood fire, over which iron pots called "coal pots" were placed. From the time they were six years old, my three aunts could be found squatting near that fire in the evenings, making the family meal while their mother was at the village market selling work clothes she sewed to the estate laborers.

Breadmaking was part of the girls' daily culinary chores, largely because flour was cheaper than rice, the other main staple in their Indian culture. Although our everyday bread is a flatbread called "roti," its cooking method is actually closer to a traditional *chapati*, and its ingredients are closer to *naan*. In India, roti and chapati are both unleavened breads and the true roti is finished on an open flame, but in Trinidad the leavened roti is cooked on a round iron griddle called a *tawa* and liberally slathered with ghee (clarified butter).

Kneading any bread by hand requires patience and a firm hand, and making roti is no different. It was a skill my young aunts mastered in childhood but one my father struggled with—and never mastered—his whole life. "My hand isn't set for it," he'd say almost every time he watched the roti lay dull and flat after he'd slapped it down on the cast-iron griddle. Other *tawa* breads escaped him, too: Dalpuri, layered with fine lentil meal that cascades out of its folds, and Buss Up Shut, a bread made from exceptionally soft roti that is gently torn apart.

Even though he lost his battles with the griddle, my father was skillful with "bake," a simple fritter of flour, salt, and baking powder, and he was an absolute master with an oven. In Trinidad, Sunday has always been baking day. For generations, families baked a week's worth of sweet rolls, coconut breads, white breads, and butter cakes after returning home from church. But during his childhood, my father's family was too poor to have a kitchen, much less an oven. And it wasn't until 1945, when my father built a new house with a real kitchen to replace their shack, that Western-style bread baking had a place in his life.

By the time he arrived in America in 1954, my father came with memories of the baked goods his mother and sisters produced in that new kitchen with techniques learned from relatives or neighbors who had been better off for a longer time. In New York in those days, there were few Trinidadians. Most of the island's émigrés headed for England, as Trinidad was still a British colony. Despite the fact that there was an abundance of wonderful baked goods and pastries, my father longed for coconut bread and black cake.

After a few years, he thought he'd have a go at making them himself, and his first attempts were nothing short of disgusting. The breads came out sodden and soggy with no hope of rising—the water he had used to proof the yeast was too hot. Then there were cakes with a consistency of paste that could barely be separated from their tins—he hadn't creamed the butter fluffy enough or had beaten in the sugar too long. These stories were recounted with a little laugh years after he

had become a proficient baker—a laugh that inevitably faded into a sad smile as he remembered the desperate loneliness he had felt in those days, and how those sorry cakes were at least some tie to home.

Once the era of my own childhood had arrived, my father had taught himself well. He had been baking for close to twenty years by the time I was about five. There was no timing or occasion to his baking days; they took place once every four or five months. We only knew the time had come when Saturday morning found pots of yeast starter fermenting around the kitchen and butter softening on the counter. The baking was a two-day affair—two days of total joy for my brother and me. Every bit of it was interesting, from watching my father hand-grate fresh coconut for cakes and knead big batches of dough to rise on the first day, to the punching down of the doughs through the night, and creaming—again by hand—pounds of butter with sugar on the second day. On the evening of the second day came the actual baking. The oven ran for most of the night as row after row of tins went in and came out. There was the smell of raisins caramelizing and bursting their skins inside the sweet breads and of melting butter in the white rolls.

My favorite was the white bread, which I ate much too hot and much too fast—the loaf was still doughlike from the heat and I could feel the gooey mass burning all the way down. My father's choice was the hard rolls, which he made just like the ones he had bought walking home from primary school back in Trinidad. "This big" he'd motion when telling the story, making a grapefruit-size sphere in the air with both hands. The roll had come with a hunk of cheddar cheese, its dimensions indicated by his extended first and second fingers, and all for a penny, which was then the British equivalent of two cents.

PARATHA ROTI

Like my father, I've found that my hand isn't "set for" making roti. I've tried many recipes over the years and have better success with some than others. The best recipe I've found comes from my dear friend Darrel Sukhdeo whom I met shortly after completing the first edition of this book in 2004. Darrel is an entrepreneur and wonderful cook who has prepared food for many an Indian wedding in Trinidad, where sometimes hundreds of guests are served roti that is cooked on a four-foot-wide *tawa*. The secret to this recipe is not to over work the dough. If your dough is sticky enough to be barely able to be handled, then you're doing it right.

2 cups all-purpose flour, plus additional as needed

2 tablespoons baking powder, preferably Lion Brand

¼ teaspoon coarse salt

Warm water as needed

3 tablespoons cold ghee

2 tablespoons canola oil

1 Whisk together flour, baking powder, and salt in a bowl. Gradually add a little warm water, using your fingers to mix the flour and water together—do not knead, just gently combine the flour and water. Continue adding water a little at a time until you achieve a soft sticky dough that just comes together into a ball. Cover and set aside to rest for 15 minutes.

2 Combine the ghee and oil to make a paste. Set aside.

3 Flour a work surface and turn out the roti dough. Cut the dough into 4 large pieces and gently form each into a ball. Flour your hands so you are able to handle the dough and knead just enough to allow the dough to hold together (do not over knead).

4 Roll out a ball of dough into a circle ¼ inch thick. Sprinkle the surface lightly with flour. Make a cut halfway down the middle of the circle. Brush the circle with some of the prepared paste. Roll the dough away from you into a cone shape starting at one side of the slit. Roll the cone into a ball by pushing the narrow end of the cone in towards the wider end and pinching the edges closed.

Tip

You can easily increase the amount of roti you make using this equation: 1 tablespoon of baking powder and ⅛ teaspoon of coarse salt for every 1 cup of flour.

Roll out the dough in to a circle and cut halfway down the middle.

Brush the dough with the butter paste.

Roll the dough into a cone shape.

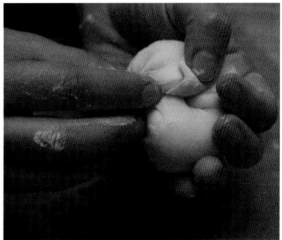
Pinch the dough closed into a ball.

VARIATION: BUSS UP SHUT

This bread's unusual name, meaning "burst up shirt," comes from the way its soft cottony folds are shredded after cooking. Simply make Paratha Roti and when removing the bread from the tawa or griddle, use a wooden spoon and lightly beat the hot cooked bread on a flat surface until it shreds. Alternatively, gently tear into 3-inch-wide strips. Serve hot with the curry of your choice.

Repeat with the remaining circles of dough. Let the balls rest for 15 to 20 minutes on a floured surface.

5 Roll the rested dough balls into ⅛-inch-thick circles and place on a hot tawa or cast-iron griddle. Brush with oil, immediately turn over, and brush with oil again. Continue to flip the discs until puffy. Remove from heat and place on a clean dishtowel. Fold the dishtowel to cover the rotis so they stay warm. Serve warm.

CHANDRA'S SADHA ROTI

This is the simplest of the various griddle breads called roti that are served in Trinidad. Most cooks still knead roti dough by hand, but an electric mixer with a paddle attachment makes the job easier. Miss Chandra Ballyram, a home cook from southern Trinidad, suggests microwaving the roti after cooking, to ensure puffing.

Chandra and Mattie show off a family portrait

2 cups all-purpose flour

2 tablespoons baking powder

Pinch of coarse salt

1 tablespoon canola oil

1 Combine the flour, baking powder, and salt. Slowly add about ½ to ¾ cups of warm water, until the dough comes together into a soft ball. Knead slowly, adding the oil in a slow, steady stream. Continue kneading until dough is smooth, about 2 minutes, then allow to rest for 15 minutes.

2 Divide the dough into four equal balls and allow to rest for 5 minutes more. Heat a 12-inch tawa or a heavy-bottomed skillet over medium heat. Roll one of the balls into a 9-inch circle and place it on the tawa or skillet. Flip after 20 seconds and continue flipping the roti over until fluffy and lightly browned all over. Repeat with the remaining dough.

3 If your roti did not puff up, place it on a plate in the microwave for 40 seconds on HIGH. When all the rotis are cooked, wrap them together in a clean towel. Serve hot with curries or stews.

DOSTI ROTI

This roti is often called a Trini version of puff pastry because of it layers. You can serve it with anything for which you use Sadha or paratha roti. I imagine the name comes from the Hindi word for two: "*doh.*"

2 cups plus 8 teaspoons all-purpose flour

2 tablespoons baking powder

Pinch of coarse salt

¼ cup canola oil

8 teaspoons softened butter

1 Combine the 2 cups flour, baking powder, and salt. Slowly add about ½ to ¾ cup of warm water, until the dough comes together into a soft ball. Knead slowly, adding the oil in a slow, steady stream. Continue kneading until dough is smooth, about 2 minutes. Allow the dough to rest for 15 minutes.

2 Divide the dough into 8 equal balls and allow to rest for 5 minutes more. Roll each of the balls into a 4-inch circle and spread each evenly with one teaspoon of the softened butter. Sprinkle each buttered circle with 1 teaspoon of flour.

3 Take one of the circles and place it butter side down on another circle with butter side up—both buttered sides should face each other. Press firmly and push down on edges to pinch them closed. Repeat with remaining dough circles so you have four layered circles.

4 Roll out each layered dough circle to a circle ⅛ inch thick. Heat the tawa or griddle on medium and brush lightly with canola oil. Place a dosti roti on the tawa or griddle. Flip the roti after 40 seconds and continue flipping the roti over until fluffy and lightly browned all over. Repeat with the remaining dough circles. Serve warm.

PEPPER ROTI

This roti is more like a spicy vegetable pizza and makes a good light lunch or snack.

VEGETABLE PASTE

1 medium Italian eggplant

1 potato

1 tomato

1 carrot, peeled and grated

2 tablespoons chopped shado beni or cilantro leaves

1 Scotch bonnet pepper or other hot red chili pepper, stemmed, seeded, and chopped

SADHA ROTI

2 cups all-purpose flour

2 tablespoons baking powder

Pinch of coarse salt

1 tablespoon canola oil

PREPARE VEGETABLE PASTE:

1 Preheat a grill or broiler. Once hot place the whole eggplant, potato, and tomato on the grill or on a pan under the broiler and roast until the vegetables are charred on the outside. Remove from heat, cool, peel, and process to a paste in a food processor with the carrot, shado beni, and chili pepper. Set aside.

PREPARE ROTI DOUGH:

2 Combine the flour, baking powder, and salt. Slowly add about ½ to ¾ cups of warm water, until the dough comes together into a soft ball. Knead slowly, adding the oil in a slow, steady stream. Continue kneading until dough is smooth, about 2 minutes, then allow to rest for 15 minutes.

MAKE SADHA ROTIS:

3 Divide the dough into four equal balls and allow to rest for 5 minutes more. Heat a 12-inch tawa or a heavy-bottomed skillet over medium heat. Roll one of the balls into a 9-inch circle and place it on the tawa or skillet. Flip after 20 seconds and continue flipping the roti over until fluffy and lightly browned all over. Remove from pan and keep warm. Repeat with the remaining dough. (If your roti did not puff up, place it on a plate in the microwave for 40 seconds on HIGH.)

4 When the four roti are cooked, spread two roti with the vegetable paste. Place a plain roti on top of each. Serve hot.

CHEESE STRAWS

Cheese straws are made from short pastry sprinkled with cheddar cheese and twisted into something akin to a bread stick. While the Guyanese are most noted for their skill with baking in general and items like cheese straws in particular, they are made in Trinidad as well.

2¼ cups all-purpose flour

½ teaspoon coarse salt

½ teaspoon cayenne pepper powder

¾ teaspoon dry ground mustard

½ cup (1 stick) butter, cut into pieces

2 cups grated extra-sharp Cheddar cheese

1 tablespoon finely chopped pimiento pepper

2 egg yolks, beaten

¼ cup cold water

1 Preheat oven to 400 degrees.

2 In a large bowl, sift together the flour, salt, cayenne pepper powder, and ground mustard. Add the butter pieces and using a pastry cutter or fork, rub the butter into the flour until the mixture forms small "peas." (Alternatively, you may place the flour mixture in the bowl of a food processor, add the butter pieces, and pulse until you achieve the desired consistency.)

3 Place flour mixture in a bowl and add the grated cheese and pimiento pepper and mix well. Add beaten egg yolks and cold water and mix well to form a stiff dough.

4 Flour a clean surface and roll the dough out until it is ¼ inch thick. Cut the dough into strips 4 inches long and ½ inch wide. Twist the sticks to form a spiral. (Alternatively, you may roll the dough ½ inch thick and cut into strips 4 inches long and ½ inch wide. Take a fork and holding the round side down on a dough strip, drag the fork down the length of the dough strip, pressing gently to create indentations in the dough.)

5 Place the formed dough strips on a baking sheet lined with parchment paper and bake for 15 minutes or until golden brown. Remove, cool, and serve as a snack.

DALPURI

This fluffy bread is filled with a fine powder made from cooked lentils. Unlike East Indian puris, which contain onion, garlic, or even potatoes, Dalpuri is incredibly light. It has become the standard roti to eat with curry.

FILLING

¾ cup dried yellow split peas

1 teaspoon ground turmeric

4 cloves garlic, crushed

¼ Scotch bonnet pepper or other hot red chili pepper, stemmed, seeded, and finely chopped

1 tablespoon chopped shado beni or cilantro leaves

2 tablespoons ground cumin

DOUGH

2 cups all-purpose flour, plus additional for sprinkling

2 tablespoons baking powder

½ teaspoon coarse salt

1 tablespoon powdered milk

3 tablespoons canola oil

MAKE FILLING

1 Wash the split peas and place in a pot with 3 cups of water. Bring to a simmer and cook until tender but not mushy, about 20 minutes. Drain.

2 In a food processor, place the cooked split peas, turmeric, garlic, chili pepper, shado beni, and cumin. Pulse to a coarse consistency like wet sand. Set aside.

MAKE DOUGH

3 To make the dough, whisk together the flour, baking powder, salt, and powdered milk in a bowl. Gradually add some warm water, using your fingers to mix the flour and water together until you achieve a soft sticky dough that just comes together into a ball—do not knead, just gently combine the flour and water. Cover and set aside to rest for 15 minutes.

4 Flour a work surface and turn out the roti dough. Cut the dough into 4 large pieces. Flour your hands enough to be able to handle the dough and only knead long enough to form the pieces into loose balls. Let rest for 15 minutes.

MAKE DALPURI

5 Gently flatten each ball with your hand and sprinkle with some flour. Place 1 to 2 tablespoons of the split-pea mixture in the middle of each disk and pinch the dough closed around the filling, forming balls again. Let the dalpuri rest for 10 minutes.

6 Roll out each ball ¼ inch thick. Heat a tawa or cast-iron griddle. Test for readiness by splashing a few drops of water on, if it sizzles it is hot enough. Place the dalpuris on the tawa or griddle. Brush lightly with some of the oil, quickly turn over, and brush the other side with oil. Keep turning the breads quickly and often until the edges just brown and the bread puffs. Remove from the pan and serve warm.

FRY BAKE

This popular fried bread is often eaten for breakfast with Buljol (salt cod fried with onions and tomatoes, page 29) and is also an important component of the traditional Trini sandwich "Shark and Bake" (page 67). It can be a good accompaniment to any dish that is traditionally served with biscuits. Most Trinidadians make a simple dough with flour, baking powder, and salt, but I find I like the flavor the butter imparts when cut into the dough.

2 cups all-purpose flour

2 teaspoons baking powder

¾ teaspoon coarse salt

2 tablespoons cold butter or vegetable shortening

½ cup canola oil

1 Sift together the flour, baking powder, and salt into a large bowl. Cut in the butter with a fork or pastry blender until pea-sized balls form. Gradually add ¾ cup of water to form a soft dough.

2 Turn out the dough onto a floured board and knead until smooth, about 3 minutes, adding more flour as necessary if the dough is too sticky. Pinch off 2-inch pieces of dough and form balls (will make 10 balls). Flatten the balls into disks ½ inch thick with the palm of your hand.

3 Heat the oil in a large, heavy frying pan. Test the oil by sprinkling a bit of flour into the oil; if it sizzles right away, it is ready. Add the dough disks to the hot oil. Turn when puffy and golden on underside. Cook until other side is golden brown. Remove from the pan and drain on paper towels. Serve hot.

SWEET BUNS

These slightly sweet buns are yummy for breakfast with a bit of butter and jam. Of course, my father, like many Trinidadians, preferred them with that English staple—cheddar cheese.

1 cup all-purpose flour

⅛ teaspoon coarse salt

2 teaspoons baking powder

6 tablespoons butter

⅓ cup sugar

1 egg, lightly beaten

3 tablespoons milk, or as needed

1 Preheat the oven to 350°F and grease and flour a large baking sheet.

2 Sift the flour, salt, and baking powder into a mixing bowl. Add the butter and rub in with your fingers or use the paddle attachment on an electric mixer, until fine crumbs are formed. Stir in the sugar. Add the egg and mix to form a stiff dough. Add the milk as needed if the dough is too dry.

3 Turn out the dough onto a floured surface and knead gently until smooth. Divide the dough into ten balls and roll each gently between your palms to form oblong balls.

4 Place on the prepared baking sheet and gently score each bun with an X, using a sharp knife. Bake for 20 minutes, or until the buns are golden.

VARIATION: COCONUT SWEET BUNS
Add 1 cup of freshly grated or frozen grated unsweetened coconut to the dry ingredients and increase the number of eggs to two. Knead and form as above.

VARIATION: COCONUT ROLLS →
Substitute 1½ cups freshly grated or frozen grated unsweetened coconut and 1 cup of light brown sugar for the currants and white sugar.

CURRANT ROLLS

These rolls are good for breakfast or an afternoon tea snack. Mixed essence, often found in West Indian baked goods, is essential to the flavor. It is available in Caribbean markets and online. See opposite page for a delicious coconut variation.

DOUGH

2 cups all-purpose flour

Pinch of coarse salt

2 teaspoons sugar

1½ cups (3 sticks) butter, chilled and cut into pieces

¼ cup ice water plus more as needed

1 tablespoon fresh lime juice

FILLING

1½ cups currants

⅓ to ½ cup sugar

1 teaspoon ground cinnamon

1 teaspoon vanilla extract

½ teaspoon mixed essence

1 egg, beaten with 1 tablespoon water

GLAZE

2 tablespoons sugar plus extra for dusting

MAKE DOUGH:

1 Sift together the flour, salt, and sugar. Using a pastry cutter or a food processor fitted with a plastic blade, cut 1 cup of the butter into the dry ingredients until the mixture resembles coarse meal with pea-size pieces. Combine the ice water and lime juice, and gradually add to flour mixture just until it comes together in a ball. Allow the dough to rest in refrigerator for 15 minutes.

2 Dust a clean work surface and a rolling pin with flour. Roll out the dough into a 12 x 7-inch oval. Dot half of one of the short sides with about 2 tablespoons butter and fold other half over it and roll out slightly. Dot half of the dough with some butter again, and fold over and roll out slightly. Repeat this two more times, until the butter is used up, but do not roll out the last fold. Wrap in plastic wrap and chill for 2 hours.

MAKE FILLING:

3 Combine the currants, sugar, cinnamon, vanilla, and mixed essence.

ASSEMBLE AND BAKE

4 Preheat oven to 350°F. Slice dough in half and roll each half into an 18 x 7-inch rectangle. Spread half the currant mixture over each rectangle leaving a 1-inch margin all around. Brush edges of pastry with water and then roll the rectangles up from a short end away from you to make two logs. Place both logs on an ungreased baking sheet and brush with the egg wash. Bake for 45 minutes or until golden brown. Remove from the oven and cool completely.

5 While the pastries are baking, make the glaze: Combine the sugar and ½ cup of water in a small saucepan and simmer until the sugar dissolves. Remove from heat and let cool. Brush the cooled currant rolls with the glaze, then lightly dust with additional sugar. Slice and serve.

Breads 185

Bread Beloved

Whenever my father baked, my brother Ramesh's favorite was coconut bread or anything with raisins, a penchant I never understood since they looked to me like smashed bugs and I didn't like their burnt flavor. But the real truth was that Ramesh's particular favorite was anything small.

On baking days, Ramesh begged Dad to make a tiny version of at least one of the breads. Not given to whimsy, my father rarely accommodated him, but on one occasion when my brother was around four, he gave in and made him a small round coconut bread. My brother stood at the oven door watching every second of that little bread's development. In his hand, he held his favorite towel with which he intended to wrap his prize and spirit it away. While it cooled on the counter, my brother stood by its side, his head barely reaching where the bread lay. He stared at it lovingly. The minute my father said the loaf was cool enough to handle it was snatched away and we never saw it again.

We assumed, of course, that my brother had gobbled up his darling prize—an understandable, if somewhat ironic, act considering his clear adoration of the loaf. It wasn't until weeks later that we learned its true fate.

For weeks what was at first a musty odor, then a horrible smell, began to emanate from my brother's room. This plagued my mother, who was a fastidiously clean person. She cleaned the room and cleaned it again, to no avail. Finally, armed with a wash bucket of bleach water, she ripped out every piece of furniture and rolled up the rug. The source of the problem became clear. My brother had taken the little bread, swathed in his favorite towel, and tucked it in the corner behind his bed—right up against the heating vent.

Horrified, my mother asked him why he had done this. Ramesh replied that it was HIS little bread and he was going to save it forever. Unmoved, my mother wrestled the moldy mass away and threw it out—despite my brother's cries.

Years later, when we were adults, I asked him if the bread had a name. "No, I don't think I called him anything," he said. "I just know I loved him."

COCONUT BREAD

This bread is commonly eaten for breakfast or as a snack with tea. It can be compared to banana or carrot bread in its consistency and sweetness because it is a "quick bread," but in Trinidad it is an everyday bread and not a special treat.

3 cups all-purpose flour

1 tablespoon baking powder

1 cup sugar

1 teaspoon coarse salt

2 cups finely grated fresh or frozen unsweetened coconut

⅓ cup raisins (optional)

1 cup (2 sticks) butter, melted and cooled

1 large egg, lightly beaten

½ cup evaporated milk

½ cup coconut water

1 teaspoon mixed essence or vanilla extract

½ teaspoon coconut extract

Sugar for dusting

1 Preheat the oven to 350°F, and grease and flour two 9 x 5-inch loaf pans.

2 Sift together the flour, baking powder, sugar, and salt, and stir in the coconut and raisins, if using.

3 In a separate bowl, combine the butter, egg, evaporated milk, coconut water, mixed essence, and coconut extract. Add the liquid ingredients to the flour mixture, mixing gently but thoroughly so all the ingredients are well combined.

4 Pour the batter into the prepared pans, filling two-thirds full. Sprinkle the top of each loaf with sugar and bake for about 55 minutes, or until a toothpick inserted into the center comes out clean. Serve with tea.

Variation: COCONUT CHOCOLATE CHIP BREAD
Sometimes I like to make this bread more "dessert-like" by adding about ½ cup of chopped dark chocolate (E. Guittard's Chucuri is a good choice because it is made from Trinidadian Trinitario beans).

WHITE BREAD

This simple bread was my favorite of all the creations of my father's baking weekends. He formed the loaf by rolling the dough into a rectangle, dotting it with butter then rolling it up like a jelly roll. The result was that the pillowy folds could be easily torn apart—something I often did while the bread was still warm and fragrant, despite my father's admonitions that it needed to cool. (Note that you need to start making this bread the day before baking.)

1 tablespoon plus 1 teaspoon active dry yeast

2 teaspoons sugar

2 cups warm water (100–110°F)

8 cups all-purpose flour

1 teaspoon coarse salt

½ cup (1 stick) unsalted butter, cut into small pieces

Tip

Bread rising times vary by warmth and humidity of the work area. If you are baking bread on a warm humid day you will find that it rises faster, so keep an eye on any yeast-based dough while it rises. Dough that rises too much or too quickly will have a sour flavor— even after baking.

1 In a large bowl, combine the yeast, sugar, and warm water. Sift together the flour and salt, then add one-quarter of this mixture to the yeast mixture. Mix well and cover with a clean towel. Set in a warm place to form a sponge overnight.

2 The next day, cut the butter into the remaining flour mixture until the mixture resembles fine crumbs, then add it to the sponge, and knead by hand or using an electric mixer with a dough hook until a smooth, elastic dough is formed.

3 Form the dough into a ball and place it in a greased bowl, turning to coat all sides. Cover with a clean towel and place in a warm location to rise until doubled in size, about 1 hour.

4 Grease and flour two 9 x 5-inch loaf pans. Punch down the dough and knead it gently. Divide the dough in half and shape it into two oblong balls. Place the balls in the prepared pans and cover with a clean towel. Allow to rise to twice their size again, about 1 hour.

5 Preheat the oven to 350°F. Bake loaves for 1 hour, or until the bread forms a golden crust and sounds hollow when tapped. Cool thoroughly before serving.

MANGO NUT BREAD

This quick bread has a special sweet tang from the mangoes. If you cannot get fresh mangoes, frozen are available at many gourmet markets. Trader Joe's is a good brand. Alternatively, you can buy frozen mango puree made by companies like Goya.

1 large ripe mango, peeled and sliced, or 1½ cups frozen mango cubes

1 teaspoon freshly squeezed lime juice

2 cups all-purpose flour

¾ cup sugar

1 tablespoon baking powder

¼ teaspoon ground cinnamon

Pinch of nutmeg

½ teaspoon coarse salt

½ teaspoon baking soda

1 egg

2 tablespoons canola oil

1 cup (3 ounces) chopped walnuts (optional)

1 Preheat the oven to 350°F and grease a 9 x 5-inch loaf pan.

2 Combine the mango, lime juice, and 1 teaspoon of water in a blender. Puree until smooth and set aside. (Alternatively, use 1½ cups store-bought mango puree.)

3 Sift together the flour, sugar, baking powder, cinnamon, nutmeg, salt, and baking soda.

4 In a large bowl, beat together the mango puree, egg, and oil. Add the flour mixture, stirring until just combined. Add the walnuts, if using.

5 Pour the batter into prepared pan. Bake for 40 minutes, or until a cake tester inserted into the center of the bread comes out clean. Remove from the oven and cool in the pan for 15 minutes, then turn out onto a wire rack to continue cooling. Slice and serve.

CHINESE CAKES

Bean cakes made from kidney or black beans, and even sometimes black-eyed peas, are a local variation on Chinese moon cakes made from adzuki beans. Popular in Trinidad, and even more so in Guyana, I've never seen a home cook prepare these, as a number of good local bakeries usually have them on hand. Here is the recipe I've developed for these cakes which you will find varies slightly in taste and appearance from the authentic Chinese versions.

FILLING

½ cup dried black beans, soaked overnight in 3 cups of cold water, or 1 cup canned black beans

1 small star anise pod

½ cup sugar

½ teaspoon mixed essence

PASTRY

2 cups all-purpose flour

Pinch of coarse salt

½ cup (1 stick) unsalted butter, chilled and cut into small cubes

Ice water as needed

Beaten egg yolk

Red food coloring as needed

Small clean paintbrush

MAKE FILLING:

1 If using dried beans, drain soaking water. Place in a pot with 3 cups of clean water and simmer for ½ hour. Add the anise pod and simmer for another ½ hour, until very tender. (If using canned beans, drain in a colander, rinse with cold water. Place in a pot with 3 cups of clean water and the anise pod and simmer for 15 minutes.)

2 Drain the beans, remove the anise pod and discard. Place beans in a food processor and puree until smooth. Push the pureed bean mixture through a fine mesh sieve to remove any remnants of skin. Discard skins.

3 Combine the bean puree and sugar in a saucepan and place over low heat. Simmer, stirring often, until sugar is dissolved and mixture resembles a thick paste, about 15 to 20 minutes. Remove from heat, stir in the mixed essence, and set aside.

MAKE THE PASTRY:

4 Combine the flour and salt in a mixing bowl or the bowl of a food processor. Using a pastry cutter, your fingers, or the pulse setting on

the food processor, cut in the butter until pea-sized balls form. Add ice water in a thin stream, mixing until a shaggy, dry dough just forms (add just enough water so no flour remains but the dough is far from sticky). Wrap and chill in the refrigerator for 1 hour.

ASSEMBLE & BAKE:

5 Remove the dough from refrigerator and cut into 8 pieces. Form each piece into a small ball and roll out to a ¼-inch-thick disk.

6 Place 1 tablespoon of the bean mixture in the center of a disk and brush the edges with egg wash. Place another dough disk on top and using a fork or your finger, press

the seams closed. Repeat with remaining dough disks. Place cakes on a baking sheet lined with parchment paper and chill in the refrigerator for 15 minutes.

7 Preheat the oven to 350°F. Remove the baking sheet with the cakes from the refrigerator and brush the cakes with egg wash. Place in the oven and bake for 25 to 30 minutes or until they turn golden brown. Remove and cool.

8 Once cool, dip the paintbrush in the red food coloring and paint a ½-inch-wide circle or design of your choice onto the center of each cake. Serve.

M'BUSBES (KA'IK)

Mrs. Yemen Nahous serves her family this slightly sweet holiday treat during their breaks from work at her Creole restaurant on Charlotte Street, Port of Spain, Trinidad. Mrs. Nahous, who immigrated to Trinidad from Syria nearly thirty years ago, refers to these cakes as "m'busbes" as do her extended Trinidad family, but they are more commonly known in Lebanon and elsewhere as "ka'ik." M'busbes are traditionally pressed into an *aleb*, a wooden mold that creates an intricate design in the surface before baking, but you can create a design by pricking the dough with a fork before slipping them into the oven. While *m'busbes* are usually served plain, Mrs. Nahous often fills hers with ground dates.

1 teaspoon active dry yeast

¼ cup warm water (110ºF)

1¼ cups granulated sugar plus
   ¼ teaspoon

4 cups all-purpose flour

½ teaspoon coarse salt

1 teaspoon ground mahlab*

½ cup (1 stick) butter, cut into small
   cubes

½ cup cold milk, or more as needed

½ pound pitted dates (optional)

GLAZE

¼ cup sugar

1 tablespoon honey

Sesame seeds (optional)

Mahlab or ground cherry pit is available at Middle Eastern and gourmet specialty stores or online.

1 Proof the yeast by sprinkling it over the warm water in a small bowl. Sprinkle the ¼ teaspoon sugar on top of the yeast and set aside until it is bubbly, about 3 to 4 minutes.

2 Whisk the 1¼ cups sugar, flour, salt, and mahlab together in a large bowl and add the butter. Using a pastry cutter or fork, cut the butter into the flour until the mixture resembles small pea-size balls.

3 Add the yeast mixture to the flour mixture. Then add the milk a little at a time while using a fork to bring the dough together into a stiff ball. Add more or less milk as needed to achieve this consistency. Cover the dough ball with plastic wrap and set aside for 40 minutes.

4 While the dough is resting make the date filling if using: Place the pitted dates in a food processor and pulse into a thick paste. Set aside.

5 Preheat the oven to 400ºF. Flour a clean work surface and cut the dough ball into 20 equal size pieces. Roll these into balls and set aside.

6 If stuffing the m'busbes with dates, make a wide depression in a dough ball with your thumb and place about 1 tablespoon of the date paste inside. Pinch the dough ball tightly shut. Repeat with all the dough balls.

7 Using a rolling pin gently roll each ball into a circle about ¼ inch thick. If you have stuffed the m'busbes be sure to roll carefully so that the filling does not burst from the seams. You might find it easier to just gently pat the stuffed dough balls into circles about 4 inches wide.

8 Prick the m'busbes all over with a fork and place on a sheet of parchment paper on a cookie sheet. Bake until golden brown, about 10 to 15 minutes.

9 Make a glaze: Stir together the sugar, honey, and 2 tablespoons water in a small saucepan and heat until a syrup forms, about 2 minutes. Brush the warm buns with the glaze and sprinkle with sesame seeds.

SHAY SHAY TIEN'S POW

Although a relatively small part of the Trinidadian population, Chinese Trinidadians have made an indelible mark on the country's cuisine. Steamed meat buns, called "*pow*" (an adaptation of the Chinese term *bao*) are a particular favorite and it is widely agreed that the ones made at Shay Shay Tien, Trinidad's oldest Chinese restaurant, are still the best. Owner Johnson "Chin" Achong was kind enough to share their recipe.

FILLING

2 teaspoons coarse salt

1 star anise pod

¾ pound boneless pork butt or shoulder

2 tablespoons canola oil

½ medium onion, chopped

1 clove garlic, finely chopped

1½ teaspoons dark brown sugar

¼ teaspoon ground anise

1 tablespoon hoisin sauce

1 tablespoon black bean sauce

1 teaspoon red food coloring

Tip

I like the flavor of hoisin and black bean sauces, but traditionally, char siu sauce is used and you may do so here as well by simply substituting the char siu sauce for the hoisin and black bean sauces combined.

MAKE THE FILLING:

1 Bring 3 cups of water, the salt, and anise pod to a boil in a large pot. Add the pork and simmer for 25 minutes. Remove the pork, cool, and cut into ¼-inch cubes. Discard the anise pod.

2 Heat the canola oil in a large, heavy-bottomed pot. Add the onion and garlic and fry until dark brown and then remove from the oil with a slotted spoon and discard. Reduce the heat to medium. Add the dark brown sugar to the seasoned oil and let it caramelize for 1 to 2 minutes. Add the pork and stir well. Brown the pork on all sides.

3 Add ground anise, hoisin sauce, and black bean sauce. Cook, stirring constantly, until nearly dry. Add the red food coloring and mix well, so all the pieces of pork are evenly colored. Cook until totally dry. Remove from the heat and cool completely. (The meat may be made up to one day ahead and stored in refrigerator.)

CONTINUED NEXT PAGE

Tip: Pow Appetizer
To make miniature pow for an appetizer or starter for
your Chinese New Year menu (or any time of year)
cut 6 pieces from each dough rope in step 4 and
only use rounded teaspoon of filling for each pow.

DOUGH

2½ teaspoons active dry yeast

½ cup sugar plus 3 tablespoons plus
  ½ teaspoon

½ cup warm water (100°F)

3 cups all-purpose flour

1¼ teaspoons baking powder

1 egg white

1 tablespoon shortening melted with
  1 tablespoon hot water

20 (5-inch) squares of waxed paper

MAKE THE DOUGH:

4 Place the yeast and ½ teaspoon of sugar in a deep bowl, and add the warm water. Set aside until foamy. Combine the flour, baking powder, and remaining sugar together in a bowl. Add the yeast mixture, egg white, and melted shortening. Mix at high speed for 4 minutes, then at the lowest speed for 6 minutes. The dough should be smooth and highly elastic. Test the dough by pressing it with your finger—it should spring back without leaving a mark.

5 Flour a clean dry work surface. Cut the dough into 4 equal pieces. With your hands, roll the pieces of dough into long ropes about 3 inches in diameter. Cut each rope into 5 pieces. Knead each piece for 30 seconds, then form into a ball. Set the dough balls on a floured surface.

MAKE THE POW:

6 Flatten one ball of dough into a 3-inch disk. Place a heaping tablespoon of the pork mixture in the middle of the disk. Gently pull the edges of the disk around the filling and pinch together to form a sac. Then gently twist the edges together and push down into the dough ball. The pow should be a smooth, round ball. Place the filled pow, seam side down, on a square of waxed paper in a bamboo or metal steamer insert. Repeat until all the pow are filled. (Do not crowd the pow in the steamer tray; allow 2 inches of space around each pow. If you do not have a bamboo steamer with more than one tray, set some of the pow on waxed paper on a flat surface.) Allow the pow to rise until their diameter has doubled. If your kitchen is warm, this will occur by the time all the pow are stuffed. If not, cover the steamer trays with damp towels and set aside in a warm place.

7 Set the steamer trays in a wide pot with enough water to rise a quarter of the way up the bottom tray, being careful that the water doesn't seep into the tray and touch the pow. Bring the water to a simmer and steam the pow for 15 minutes. Serve warm. (Note: Pow can be reheated in a microwave for 45 seconds on high or in a 350°F oven for 20 minutes.)

Afternoon tea at
Pax Guest House

SWEETS & DESSERTS

With the wealth of sugarcane fields sweeping the island where many a colonial plantation owner found his fortune, sugar features strongly in Trinidad cooking. Sweets, candies, and desserts are so abundant that they could comprise an entire cookbook on their own, and it's rare to find a Trinidadian who doesn't have a sweet tooth.

As far as locals are concerned, when it comes to desserts, the sweeter the better. These treats are especially prolific during holidays and religious events, such as Easter and Diwali. Christmas enjoys its share of goodies too—most notably Black Cake (pages 211).

Diwali is famous for Indian sweet treats that are prepared and sold in vast quantities throughout the island. Unlike the rest of Indo-Caribbean cuisine, Indian sweets have, interestingly, remained incredibly authentic to their original form and variety. Because Diwali is a Hindu celebration, you'll find that most of these desserts do not contain eggs: in the most devout vegetarian sects, eggs are regarded as a potential life that has been extinguished, and are therefore not considered edible. Despite the fact that many Diwali celebrants in Trinidad practice a combination of reformed Hinduism and Christianity, and still others aren't Hindu at all, this custom has remained intact.

Local fruits are also the basis for many desserts, even if they are simply stewed with sugar and mixed essence as a topping for cakes or ice cream. Coconut is one of the most oft-used dessert fruits, finding its way into everything from ice cream to tarts to pudding—which brings me no end of delight since coconut is, hands-down, my favorite flavor.

COCONUT DROPS

Whenever my father set about baking and these drops were on the menu, we had a special treat. I remember nibbling them with milk for breakfast.

1 cup all-purpose flour

1 teaspoon baking powder

2 teaspoons ground cinnamon

4 tablespoons (½ stick) unsalted butter

½ cup granulated sugar

1 egg

2 teaspoons vanilla extract

2 cups fresh or frozen grated
  unsweetened coconut

½ teaspoon grated fresh lemon zest

SUGAR GLAZE

½ cup granulated sugar

Light brown sugar for sprinkling

1 Preheat the oven to 400°F and grease a baking sheet.

2 Sift together the flour, baking powder, and cinnamon.

3 Using an electric mixer, cream the butter and granulated sugar until fluffy, about 4 minutes. Add the egg and vanilla and mix well. Add the flour mixture and beat until well incorporated. Mix in the coconut and lemon zest, stirring until well combined.

4 Drop heaping tablespoonfuls of the dough onto the prepared baking sheet and bake for 20 minutes, or until golden brown. Remove from the pan and cool on wire racks.

5 Make the sugar glaze by combining the granulated sugar with ¾ cup of water in a small saucepan and simmering until the mixture attains the consistency of maple syrup, about 8 minutes (watch carefully that it doesn't burn). Lightly brush each coconut drop with the sugar syrup and sprinkle with brown sugar. Serve with tea.

COCONUT SHORTBREAD

This cookie combines the best of all worlds—the buttery, flaky texture of shortbread with the flavor of coconut. It's ideal with tea or coffee.

3 cups all-purpose flour

1 teaspoon coarse salt

1 cup fresh or frozen grated unsweetened coconut

1 cup (2 sticks) unsalted butter, softened

½ cup plus 2 tablespoons sugar

1 egg

1 Sift together the flour and salt. Mix in the coconut.

2 In another bowl, beat the butter and ½ cup of the sugar with an electric mixer until fluffy, about 4 minutes. Add the egg and mix well.

3 Add the flour mixture and mix well to form a smooth dough. Wrap the dough in plastic wrap and chill for 1 hour.

4 Preheat the oven to 325°F. Roll out the dough into a 9 x 13-inch rectangle about ½ inch thick. Slice the dough lengthwise into four equal slices, and then crosswise into six equal slices. This will give you twenty-four pieces of shortbread. Arrange on an ungreased baking sheet, leaving 1 inch between each cookie. Bake until golden brown, about 25 minutes.

5 Remove from the pan and cool on wire racks for 10 minutes. Sprinkle the shortbread with the remaining 2 tablespoons of sugar.

COCONUT PAYMEE

A delicious sweet version of paymee, like pastelles they are wrapped in banana leaves or corn husks and then steamed.

2 cups masa harina

2 teaspoons coarse salt

¾ cup sugar

4 tablespoons (½ stick) butter

2 tablespoon golden raisins (optional)

1½ cups fresh or frozen grated unsweetened coconut

½ cup grated pumpkin or butternut squash

30 (8-inch) squares of banana leaf or corn husk

Kitchen twine

1 Combine the masa harina, salt, and sugar in a medium bowl and set aside.

2 Melt the butter in a shallow frying pan and add the raisins, stirring constantly until plumped. Add the coconut and pumpkin or squash and sauté for 2 to 3 minutes, stirring occasionally.

3 Add the coconut mixture to the dry ingredients. Gradually stir in about ¾ cup of water until you have a thick, moldable dough that is not too stiff.

4 Bring a pot of salted water to a boil and blanch the banana leaves or corn husks for 30 seconds or until they are soft and malleable. Drain and rinse with cold water.

5 Place 2 heaping tablespoons of the dough on a banana leaf. Fold in the edges of the leaf so that the leaf completely covers the dough and tie with twine. Repeat with remaining dough and leaves.

6 Place a steamer basket or colander in a 6-quart saucepan and add water to the base making sure the water level is below the bottom of the steamer basket. Place the wrapped paymee in the basket, arranging in a single layer. Bring the water to a simmer and steam for 45 minutes. Serve warm.

Variation: MEAT PAYMEE
The addition of seasoned ground meat instead of coconut can make this dessert into a delicious savory dish.

COCONUT TARTS

These turnovers are an interesting departure from traditional fruit-filled versions. They make an ideal snack or dessert. Dress them up for guests with a dollop of whipped cream and dash of cinnamon.

DOUGH

2 cups all-purpose flour

⅛ teaspoon baking powder

⅛ teaspoon coarse salt

½ cup (1 stick) unsalted butter, chilled and cubed

½ cup vegetable shortening

⅔ cup cold water

FILLING

2¼ cups fresh or frozen grated unsweetened coconut

¾ cup sugar

½ teaspoon mixed essence

GLAZE

1 egg yolk

2 teaspoons milk

MAKE DOUGH:

1 Combine the flour, baking powder, and salt in the bowl of a food processor. Add the butter and vegetable shortening and pulse until crumbs the size of peas form. Slowly add the cold water until the dough just comes together. Wrap in plastic wrap and chill for at least 1 hour.

MAKE FILLING:

2 In the meantime, combine the coconut, sugar, mixed essence, and 1 cup of water in a saucepan and simmer until the sugar melts and liquid thickens to the consistency of maple syrup, about 30 minutes. Cool.

MAKE TARTS:

3 Preheat the oven to 350°F. Dust the chilled dough with flour and divide into 15 balls. Flatten the balls and then roll out to ⅛ inch thick, dusting with flour as necessary to prevent sticking.

4 Place 1 tablespoon of filling on the center of a dough disk. Lightly brush the edges of the disk with water and fold the dough over the filling to create a half-moon. Crimp the edges closed using a fork. Repeat with the rest of the dough.

5 Place tarts on a parchment-lined baking sheet. Beat the egg yolk and milk together for the glaze and brush over the tarts. Prick each tart once or twice to let steam escape. Bake for 20 to 25 minutes, or until the tarts are golden brown. Cool and serve.

COCONUT CREAM PIE

SERVES: 6 TO 8

You can use any pastry crust recipe you like for this pie, though I prefer one made with butter rather than shortening or lard, and store-bought pie shells work well, too—without all the fuss. The meringue topping makes for a lovely presentation, but it is optional.

CRUST

2 cups all-purpose flour

¼ teaspoon baking powder

Pinch of salt

½ cup (1 stick) cold butter, cut into pieces

¼ cup ice water, or more as needed

FILLING

3 egg yolks

1½ cups milk

¼ cup sugar

Pinch of grated nutmeg

Pinch of coarse salt

1 teaspoon vanilla extract

¼ teaspoon mixed essence

½ cup fresh or frozen grated unsweetened coconut

MERINGUE (optional)

3 egg whites

Pinch of cream of tartar

½ cup sugar

½ teaspoon vanilla extract

MAKE CRUST:

1 Sift together the flour, baking powder, and salt. Cut in the butter using a fork or pastry cutter or food processor fitted with a plastic blade until the mixture resembles coarse meal. Slowly drizzle the ice water into the mixture, adding just enough to bring the dough together into a loose ball. Divide the dough into 2 balls and wrap each in plastic wrap. Flatten them into disks and refrigerate for at least 2 hours. The dough can also be frozen for later use, for up to 2 months (only one disk is used in this recipe).

2 Preheat the oven to 425°F. Remove one of the dough disks from the refrigerator and roll it out ⅛ inch thick to fit an 8-inch pie plate. Line an 8-inch pie plate with the crust or a packaged pre-made crust (or if using a frozen shell, remove unthawed from its package). Chill the crust in the refrigerator while preparing the filling.

MAKE THE FILLING:

3 Lightly beat the egg yolks with the milk, sugar, nutmeg, salt, vanilla, and mixed essence. Stir in the coconut and pour into the pie shell.

4 Bake the pie for 10 minutes, then reduce the oven temperature to 350°F and bake another 15 minutes, or until the filling is firm when the pie is gently jiggled.

MAKE MERINGUE (OPTIONAL)**:**

5 Whip the egg whites and cream of tartar with a whisk
or electric beater until soft peaks form. Gradually add
the sugar and vanilla and beat until the whites hold
firm peaks.

6 Remove the pie from the oven and mound the
meringue over the filling, pulling up soft peaks with
the spoon and making sure meringue touches the
crust all around. Return the pie to the oven and bake
until the edges of the meringue are lightly browned,
12 to 15 minutes. Remove from the oven, cool
completely, and serve.

How to Crack a Coconut

Watching my father crack open a coconut was one of the most terrifying experiences of my childhood. Like most West Indians, my father split the coconut's hard shell with a long cutlass, wide and curved at the tip and nearly two feet long. It resembled something out of Aladdin and it was scary.

If the coconut was green—a delicacy only to be had on trips to Trinidad—he would hold it in his palm and level its head with the cutlass in a smooth slicing motion; or he might take angular chops around the crown. The purpose of either method was to create an opening large enough to pour out the sweet young coconut water, which is said to have high nutritional value, especially for pregnant women with morning sickness. After the water is drained, the coconut jelly is scooped out and eaten with a spoon fashioned from the chopped shell. This jelly is what hardens into the white coconut flesh as the fruit ages.

If the coconut was already aged, removing it from the green outer husk required deep slashes with the cutlass and then enormous strength to peel away the skin. In the States we could only buy dry, husked coconuts— if we were lucky—sometimes in the supermarket but more often on a trip to the Caribbean neighborhoods in Brooklyn and Queens. Today, both green coconuts and dry coconuts are readily available in many gourmet supermarkets.

To crack a dry coconut, my father again pulled out that cutlass. He held the coconut in one hand and whacked down on it with the cutlass held in the other. Every time he did this, I was sure he would cut himself, or worse, cut off his hand. He never did. Wielding a cutlass is a talent that Trinidadians seem to manage with aplomb. I myself am far too afraid to have anything to do with cutlasses, machetes, or butcher knives screaming toward objects held in my opposite hand—so I've developed my own method for draining and cracking coconuts.

Dry coconuts have three "eyes," one of which is always soft and easily pierced with a paring knife. Sometimes a second eye can be pierced as well, but this is less often the case. Once the eye is pierced, I invert the coconut onto a heavy glass or pitcher that can prop up the fruit while catching the draining liquid. I reserve this water for flavorings in breads and sauces.

To crack the coconut, I use the back of a heavy cleaver or chef's knife and holding the coconut in my opposite hand, I gently tap around the middle crosswise. This should crack the shell, allowing you to pry it apart and then pry out the meat. Nowadays, many supermarkets sell pre-scored coconuts which break open easier when you start tapping them across the middle.

Another method is to leave the coconut in a 400°F degree oven until the heat cracks the hard shell. Granted, this does change the flavor of the coconut a bit, but it is fine for baked goods since the grated coconut will be cooked anyway.

When whole coconuts can't be had, I opt for packaged, unsweetened shredded coconut—fresh-frozen is better than dry and is easily found in Middle Eastern, Indian, and Caribbean markets. If you use dry coconut, particularly in baked goods, know that you will have to increase the amount of liquid in the preparation as dry coconut products absorb a good deal of moisture.

ALTERNATE QUICK-SOAK METHOD FOR DRIED FRUIT:
Combine 1 cup raisins, 1 cup currants, 1 cup pitted prunes, 3 tablespoons mixed citrus peel, and 1 cup candied cherries in a large saucepan with 1½ cups cherry brandy and 1½ cups rum. Add 1 cinnamon stick and 2 star anise pods. Split a vanilla bean and scrape out the seeds. Add the vanilla seeds and bean to the saucepan. Place saucepan over medium heat and bring the mixture to a simmer. Simmer for 10 minutes, then cover and remove from heat. Allow to cool completely before using.

BLACK CAKE

MAKES 2

Many a culinarian has waxed prolific about the Black Cake's rich aromatic flavors and unusual texture that is something between a plum pudding and a pound cake. Although it could technically be called a fruitcake because of the candied and dried fruits that comprise its bulk, no fruitcake ever tasted this good!

Special credit must be given here to Mrs. Irma Hannays of Woodbrook, who is noted throughout Trinidad and many other Caribbean islands for her sweet hands when it comes to making special occasion cakes. Mrs. Hannays, who turns out prodigious numbers of Black Cakes every year for friends, family, and clients, developed the fast-soaking variation offered below, a great boon to Black Cake lovers who want to have their cake and eat it too—"*now for now*" as we say in Trinidad.

FRUIT

1 pound raisins

1 pound currants

1 pound prunes

¼ pound candied mixed citrus peel

½ pound candied cherries

4 cups cherry brandy or cherry wine

4 cups dark rum, such as Old Oak

1 cinnamon stick

2 star anise pods

½ vanilla bean

CAKE

2 cups all-purpose flour

2 teaspoons baking powder

1 teaspoon ground cinnamon

¼ teaspoon grated nutmeg

PREPARE FRUIT

(Note: This is the long-soak method; see alternate quick-soak method opposite page)

1 Place all the fruit ingredients except the vanilla bean in a gallon jar that can be tightly sealed—preferably with a suction lid. Split the vanilla bean and scrape out the seeds. Add the vanilla seeds and bean to the jar. Mix very well and seal. Store, unrefrigerated, in a cool, dark place for at least 3 weeks or up to 1 year.

MAKE CAKE

2 Preheat the oven to 350°F and grease two 9-inch round cake pans. Sift together the flour, baking powder, cinnamon, nutmeg, and allspice.

3 Place the butter and brown sugar in a bowl and beat with an electric mixer until fluffy, about 4 minutes. Add the eggs, one at a time, beating well after each addition. Add the mixed essence and vanilla.

CONTINUED NEXT PAGE

Sweets & Desserts 211

Black Cake Memories

For many years I thought Black Cake was a variation on English plum pudding brought to the island by English colonists. On a research trip to Ireland in 2008, I came to learn about Christmas Cake, a confection of liquor-soaked dried fruits made specifically for the winter holidays. Sure enough, further research revealed that Trinidad was among those English colonial islands that had a fairly large population of Irish indentured laborers. Black Cake only differs from the Irish versions by the liquor used and the use of burnt sugar syrup to make the cake dark.

In Trinidad, Black Cake is traditionally a Christmas cake or a wedding cake. When it is used for weddings, a boiled white icing is added. However, of late, I've noticed that it is also offered at other special occasions like graduations or christenings.

Every family has a bottle of fruit soaking for their Christmas Black Cake—usually, for some odd reason, under the kitchen sink, a fact that leads my friend Patrick Dooley to call it "under the sink cake." In fact, as soon as I'm done doing my round of Christmas baking, the jar gets refilled to soak for next year's batch. Most people have their own way of doing Black Cake, from the ingredients in the soaking liquid to whether the fruit is soaked whole or first pureed, to using white versus light or dark brown sugar. Some, as my friend Darrel Sukhdeo, like their Black Cake to be as moist as pudding while others like a more "cakey" consistency. The recipe in this book is one that I have developed based on trial, error, and personal taste and uses the creaming method for a fluffier but moist cake.

For me, Black Cake conjures up all kinds of personal lore. I remember my cousin Pinky from Tobago sending my father a Black Cake every December as a Christmas treat. She often added Guinness stout to her fruit-soaking liquid. Pinky's Black Cake arrived wrapped in tinfoil and nestled in a cookie tin, having borne the three-week boat trip totally and utterly unscathed. The long soaking in wine and rum, along with post-baking basting, kept the cake well preserved for weeks on end. It would sit, wrapped, on the kitchen table, and Ramesh and I would steal little nips of it, although we had been told to leave it alone because of its heavy alcohol content. I suspect the fact that we picked around the bits of fruit to the creamy cake itself, effectively mangling the poor loaf, didn't help our case either. My only regret is that I didn't master Black Cake until after my father died, so he never tasted my version.

Before my husband and I were married, during our first Christmas together, he watched me struggle to make ten Black Cakes for friends and relatives using an old hand mixer. I had never attempted to make such a volume before and the old machine was barely up to the task. It was a long, laborious process. Imagine my surprise on Christmas morning, when I opened a box to reveal a standing 6-quart mixer. "I just couldn't bear watching you struggle with all those cakes," was J.P.'s comment.

That mixer remains one of my most treasured gifts and it proved its mettle when I made two hundred mini Black Cakes as favors for my brother's wedding. Of course, every Christmas it sees its finest hours as I turn out batch after batch of Black Cake for eager friends and relatives.

BLACK CAKE (CONTINUED)

⅛ teaspoon ground allspice

1 cup (2 sticks) butter, softened

1 cup dark brown sugar

6 eggs

½ teaspoon mixed essence

½ teaspoon vanilla extract

1 tablespoon burnt sugar syrup *(see Tip)*

BASTING LIQUID

¼ cup dark rum

¼ cup cherry brandy

2 tablespoons sherry

Tip: Burnt Sugar Syrup

Commercially prepared burnt sugar syrup is available in West Indian markets. If you cannot find it, you can make your own by placing 2 tablespoons of dark brown sugar and 1 tablespoon of water in a dry frying pan over medium-low heat. Heat slowly, swirling the sugar in the pan until it starts to caramelize. Continue swirling until the sugar syrup becomes very dark brown—almost black. Add to batter as needed.

---

4 Using a slotted spoon, remove 5 cups of the soaked fruit from the jar (or all of the cooked fruits from the saucepan if using quick-soak method), reserving liquid. Place in the bowl of a food processor and pulse to a coarse paste. Add fruit paste to the batter and beat well.

5 Add the flour mixture ½ cup at a time, beating well after each addition. Add the burnt sugar syrup and mix well.

6 Divide the batter evenly between the prepared pans and bake for 40 minutes. Then lower the heat to 250°F and bake for another 45 to 60 minutes, or until a cake tester inserted into the middle of the cake comes out clean.

7 Remove from the oven and cool for 20 minutes in the pan.

BASTE CAKE:

8 Combine the rum, brandy, and sherry for basting (or if you used the quick-soak method use the reserved liquid for basting) and evenly brush the cooled cakes with this mixture. Allow the cakes to cool completely.

9 Remove cakes from the pans. Wrap tightly in plastic wrap and then tinfoil. You may also place the cakes in a tightly lidded plastic container. Store in a cool, dry place for at least 3 days before eating. Black cake can be stored for up to 3 months in the refrigerator. If doing so, re-baste with the basting mixture once every 2 weeks.

SWEET BREAD

This cake most closely resembles the traditional American or European Christmas fruitcakes with raisins and mixed candied fruits. However, the addition of coconut makes this loaf more flavorful. In Trinidad, sweet bread is an everyday pastry that is eaten with tea, as a snack, or at breakfast. This bread keeps for 2 weeks in the refrigerator and about a month in the freezer.

3 cups all-purpose flour

1 tablespoon baking powder

1 cup light brown sugar

½ teaspoon ground cinnamon

¼ teaspoon grated nutmeg

¼ teaspoon ground allspice

2½ cups fresh or frozen grated unsweetened coconut

1 cup raisins

½ cup candied cherries, coarsely chopped

½ cup mixed candied citrus peel

½ cup (1 stick) unsalted butter, melted

¾ cup milk

1 egg

1 teaspoon vanilla extract

½ teaspoon mixed essence

3 tablespoons currants or golden raisins, for garnish (optional)

Granulated sugar, for garnish (optional)

SUGAR SYRUP (optional)

½ cup sugar

1 Preheat the oven to 350°F and grease two 9 x 5-inch loaf pans.

2 Sift together the flour, baking powder, brown sugar, cinnamon, nutmeg, and allspice. Stir in the coconut, raisins, cherries, and candied peel.

3 In a separate bowl, combine the melted butter, milk, egg, vanilla, and mixed essence. Add to the dry ingredients and beat well. You will have a heavy batter. Divide the batter equally between the prepared loaf pans and sprinkle with currants or golden raisins, if using. Bake for 50 minutes, or until a cake tester comes out clean.

4 Remove the sweet breads from the oven and let cool in the pans for 15 minutes, then turn out onto a wire rack and cool completely.

5 While the breads are cooling, make the sugar syrup by mixing the sugar and ¾ cup of water in a small saucepan. Simmer until the sugar melts and the mixture slightly thickens to a thin syrup, about 3 minutes. Remove the pan from the heat. Brush the loaves with the sugar syrup and sprinkle with granulated sugar. Set aside to dry. Slice and serve with tea.

BUTTER CAKE

My father particularly enjoyed this cake, which is also called "sponge cake" in Trinidad, with tea and so it was another of the cakes he made on his baking weekends. To produce the best results, it's important to take the time to beat the butter and sugar until it is nearly doubled in volume.

2 cups all-purpose flour

⅛ teaspoon coarse salt

1 teaspoon baking powder

½ cup (1 stick) unsalted butter, softened

½ cup sugar

1 egg

1 teaspoon vanilla extract

1 cup milk

1 Preheat the oven to 350°F, and grease and flour an 8-inch round cake pan.

2 Sift together the flour, salt, and baking powder. Set aside.

3 Using an electric mixer, cream together the butter and sugar until light and fluffy and nearly doubled in volume. It should be pale yellow in color. Add the egg and vanilla. (The mixture may appear curdled but it will come together once the flour is added.)

4 Add the dry ingredients to butter mixture in three additions, alternating with the milk. The batter should be thick but fluid; add a little more milk if necessary to achieve this consistency.

5 Pour the batter into the prepared pan and bake for 1 hour, or until a cake tester comes out clean.

Sweets & Desserts   215

CARROT CAKE

Of course carrot cake is a popular American dessert but it is well loved in Trinidad, too. I've adapted the recipe to include flavorings and spices that I consider more Caribbean in order to make it uniquely Trinidadian. I find that this cake freezes well, so I often frost one loaf and put another aside for an "emergency" dessert or breakfast offering.

CAKE

2 cups sugar

1½ cups canola oil

4 eggs

1 teaspoon mixed essence

½ teaspoon vanilla extract

2 cups all-purpose flour

2 teaspoons baking powder

2 teaspoons baking soda

1 teaspoon coarse salt

1 teaspoon ground cinnamon

¾ teaspoon ground nutmeg

¼ teaspoon ground cloves

¼ teaspoon ground allspice

1 pound carrots, peeled and finely shredded

½ cup (2 ounces) chopped walnuts

½ cup raisins (optional)

FROSTING

3 cups confectioners' sugar

12 ounces cream cheese, softened

4 tablespoons (½ stick) unsalted butter, softened

2 teaspoons dark spiced rum

1 Preheat the oven to 325°F. Lightly grease two 9 x 5-inch loaf pans and line the bottom and sides with waxed or parchment paper. Grease the paper as well.

MAKE CAKE:

2 In the bowl of a standing mixer or using a hand mixer, beat together the sugar and oil. Add the eggs one at a time, beating well after each addition. Beat in the mixed essence and vanilla.

3 Sift together the flour, baking powder, baking soda, salt, cinnamon, nutmeg, cloves, and allspice. Beat the dry ingredients into the egg mixture. Stir in the carrots, walnuts, and raisins, if using.

4 Divide the batter evenly between the prepared pans and bake for 40 minutes or until a cake tester inserted in the center comes out clean. (The cakes should pull slightly away from sides of the pans.) Remove the pans from oven and cool for 15 minutes, then turn out the cakes onto a wire rack and cool completely. The cakes keep for one day tightly wrapped, unrefrigerated, or up to 1 month frozen (unfrosted). Frost cakes before serving.

MAKE FROSTING

5 Combine all the ingredients and using an electric mixer beat at medium-high speed until fluffy. Frost the cake(s) and serve. The frosting keeps for 1 week in refrigerator.

PAX'S LEMON CRUNCH TEA CAKES

This cake is part of the afternoon tea available at Pax Guest House (*see photo page 198*), a serene hotel set on the grounds of a Benedictine monastery in the hills above the city of Tunapuna. While regular tea service includes a nice variety of sandwiches, cakes, and teas, the silver tea service is not to be missed. If you ever get to Trinidad call ahead to make a reservation and I suggest requesting the back verandah.

CAKE

½ cup (1 stick) unsalted butter, softened

¾ cup sugar

2 eggs

Finely grated zest of 1 lemon

1½ cups self-rising flour, sifted

¼ cup whole milk

TOPPING

3 tablespoons freshly squeezed lemon juice

½ cup sugar

1 Preheat the oven to 350°F and place cupcake liners in a standard-size 12-cup or two 6-cup muffin tins. Lightly spray the cupcake liners with nonstick cooking spray.

MAKE CAKE:

2 Cream the butter and sugar with an electric mixer until light and fluffy, about 3 minutes. Add the eggs one at a time, beating for 30 seconds after each addition. Stir in the lemon zest. Gently fold in the flour in four additions, alternating with the milk.

3 Divide the batter evenly among the muffin cups, filling each cup three-quarters full. Bake for 50 minutes, or until the tops are golden and a cake tester comes out clean.

MAKE TOPPING:

4 While the cakes are baking, combine the lemon juice and sugar in a bowl for the topping. When the baked cakes are removed from the oven, immediately spoon the topping over the hot cakes and then allow them to cool completely. Serve with Darjeeling tea.

CASSAVA PONE

This is a dessert that I particularly like, largely because the coarse consistency of grated cassava is reminiscent of cornbread. It is not overly sweet, making it ideal for those who don't care for a lot of sugar.

2 cups grated cassava

1 cup grated fresh, frozen, or dried unsweetened coconut

1 cup sugar

1 teaspoon ground cinnamon

4 tablespoons (½ stick) unsalted butter, melted

½ cup evaporated milk

1 teaspoon vanilla extract

1 teaspoon mixed essence

1 Preheat the oven to 350°F. Grease an 8-inch square baking dish.

2 Combine all ingredients in a large bowl, mixing well. Pour into the prepared baking dish and bake for 1 hour, or until the top is golden brown and a cake tester inserted into the center of the cake comes out clean.

3 Let cake cool and cut into squares to serve.

SWEET RICE

The use of coconut milk and mixed essence for rice pudding, or "sweet rice," is what makes this a distinctively West Indian dish. The Angostura bitters make it totally Trini.

1 cup long-grain rice

1½ cups coconut milk

½ cup sugar

Pinch ground cinnamon

Pinch ground nutmeg

¼ teaspoon vanilla extract

¼ teaspoon mixed essence

½ teaspoon Angostura bitters

2 tablespoons raisins (optional)

1 tablespoon sweetened coconut flakes, for garnish (optional)

1 Rinse the rice in a fine-mesh sieve or colander until the water runs clear. Bring 1½ cups of water to a boil and add the rice. Simmer for 15 minutes, skimming any foam from the top of the rice, as necessary.

2 Drain the rice and return to the saucepan. Add the coconut milk, sugar, cinnamon, and nutmeg and simmer for 10 minutes. Add the vanilla, mixed essence, bitters, and raisins, if using, and simmer for 10 minutes more—the rice should be soft, and the pudding should be thick but not sticky, with some liquid.

3 Garnish with the coconut flakes and serve warm or cold.

219

KHEER

This highly traditional Indian rice pudding is very liquid because it has barely any rice! The fact that it is only slightly sweetened makes it both refreshing and smoothly soothing.

¼ cup long-grain rice

4½ cups whole milk

2 cardamom pods, slightly crushed

3 tablespoons sugar

Pinch of saffron threads, soaked in 1 tablespoon hot milk

2 tablespoons slivered almonds

1 tablespoon chopped, skinned, unsalted pistachios

1 tablespoon golden raisins

1 Put rice in a deep bowl and add enough cold water to cover by 1 to 2 inches. Swirl the rice around with your hand until the water becomes cloudy and then gently pour off the water being careful not to pour out the rice. Repeat the process 2 or 3 more times or until the rinsing water stays clear. Drain rice.

2 Place the rice in a saucepan with the milk, cardamom pods, and sugar. Bring to a boil, then lower heat and simmer, stirring, until the sugar dissolves. Continue to simmer until the rice is tender and the grains begin to split, about 30 minutes.

3 Add the saffron, almonds, pistachios, and raisins, and simmer for about 5 minutes more. Remove the pan from the heat and remove cardamom pods. Serve warm.

LAPSI

Sweet porridges like lapsi are a form of ceremonial dessert in Hindu rituals, although they may be consumed at other times as well. The addition of golden raisins or nuts makes this a celebratory dish.

1 tablespoon ghee or canola oil

1 cup bulgur wheat

2 tablespoons golden raisins

3 cups evaporated milk

¾ cup sugar

1 teaspoon ground cardamom

2 tablespoons (1 ounce) sliced almonds

1 Heat the ghee in a deep saucepan and add the bulgur wheat. Cook, stirring often, until golden brown. Add the raisins and cook until plumped, less than 1 minute.

2 Remove the pan from the heat and add the evaporated milk, sugar, and cardamom. Mix well, and return the pot to the stove. Simmer over medium-low heat, stirring constantly, until the sugar is dissolved. Continue to simmer until the lapsi has thickened like porridge, 15 to 20 minutes.

3 Serve warm, garnished with almonds.

Sweet Hands

PRASAD

When I was a child visiting Trinidad, the only way my father could persuade me to go to the many Hindu prayer meetings to which he was invited was with the promise of *prasad*, a sweet dessert that is given to guests at the end of a Hindu religious ceremony. The basic "pudding" is garnished with coconut, raisins, and nuts, which are collectively called *panjaree*. It's generally accepted that *panjaree* is only for actual religious functions although plain prasad—called *mohan bohg*—can be served any time.

2 cups ghee

½ cup raisins

2 cups farina

2 cups whole milk

3 (12-ounce) cans evaporated milk

4 cups sugar

1 teaspoon peeled and grated fresh ginger

1 teaspoon ground cardamom

GARNISHES

Raisins

Grated fresh coconut

Coarsely chopped almonds

A few cooked chickpeas

1 Heat all but 2 teaspoons of the ghee in a large, deep frying pan. Add the raisins and fry over medium-low heat until they plump. Add the farina ¼ cup at a time, stirring constantly, until it becomes light brown. Remove from heat.

2 In a separate pan, combine the whole milk, evaporated milk, sugar, ginger, and cardamom. Bring just to a boil, stirring constantly. Remove from the heat.

3 Add the milk mixture ¼ cup at a time to the farina mixture over medium-low heat, until the prasad forms semi-moist clumps. Remove from the heat.

4 Serve in small bowls and garnish with grated fresh coconut, almonds, raisins, and chickpeas.

SAWINE

Roughly a tenth of Trinidad's population is Muslim, comprising those of East Indian, African, and other mixed backgrounds. In the last decade, Muslim migration to the island from the Middle East and other areas of the Muslim world has grown. This noodle pudding is a traditional dessert for Iftar—the fast-breaking meal during the Muslim holiday of Ramadan. The cherries are a particularly Trinidadian addition.

1 (8-ounce) package vermicelli

½ teaspoon ground cinnamon

Pinch of coarse salt

6 cups evaporated milk

¼ cup sugar

½ cup (6 ounces) blanched almonds

½ cup golden raisins

½ cup candied cherries, chopped

½ teaspoon vanilla extract

1 Break the vermicelli into pieces and place in a dry skillet. Toast until golden brown and then remove from the pan.

2 Bring 2 cups of water, the cinnamon, and salt to a boil in a large saucepan. Add the toasted vermicelli and cook over low heat until most of the water has evaporated and the vermicelli is soft.

3 Add the evaporated milk, sugar, almonds, raisins, cherries, and vanilla. Simmer until all the ingredients are heated through. Serve.

VARIATION: Cooked Sawine may also be poured into a greased 9 x 13-inch baking dish and baked at 350°F until firm. Cut into squares and serve.

STEWED GUAVA

Stewed, or actually poached, fresh fruits are a simple but delicious Trinidadian dessert. You can use seasonal fruits from your own area to make the most of this recipe, choosing soft-fleshed, non-citrus fruit. Cooking fruit in sugar syrup acts as a preservative, so you can store poached fruit in a tightly sealed container in the refrigerator for up to three days.

¾ cup sugar

1 pound ripe guavas, peeled, seeded and cut into 1-inch chunks

1 cup heavy cream

⅛ teaspoon mixed essence

1 Combine the sugar and 1 cup of water in a saucepan and simmer for 4 to 5 minutes. Add the guava and continue to simmer until the fruit is fork tender.

2 In a small bowl, combine the cream and mixed essence.

3 Divide the fruit with syrup among four bowls and drizzle with the cream, as desired.

GUAVA CHEESE

My dear friend Gerard Ramsawak makes the best guava cheese I've ever had. Although guava cheese is often cut into squares, I follow Gerard's example and cut it into long rectangles, like gold bars, that can be sliced easily. I often include guava cheese on a cheese tray for a tropical touch that works well with any of the cheese that might normally be paired with quince paste.

1 pound fresh guavas, stemmed and peeled, or 16 ounces frozen guava pulp, defrosted

2 cups sugar

⅛ teaspoon ground cinnamon

⅓ cup confectioners' sugar (optional)

1 Grease an 8-inch square baking dish and dust with sugar. Set aside.

2 If using fresh guava, mash the flesh to a pulp. Rub the pulp through a fine-mesh sieve, discarding all the seeds.

3 Pour the strained pulp into a saucepan with the sugar and bring to a boil. Reduce the heat and add the cinnamon. Simmer, stirring occasionally, until the mixture begins to pull away from the sides of the pan.

4 Pour the guava mixture into the prepared pan and allow it to cool completely, at room temperature or in the refrigerator. Once cool, turn out of the pan onto a flat surface and slice in half horizontally, then cut both halves lengthwise and again crosswise. You should have eight pieces.

5 Dredge each bar with confectioners' sugar, if desired. Store in a tightly sealed container in the refrigerator for up to 2 weeks. Serve with bread, crackers, and cheese.

SUGAR CAKES

This simple confection is heavenly, especially if you are a coconut lover like I am. In my experience, freshly grated coconut is really the only way to go with this recipe, though fresh frozen will also work. Don't use sweetened shredded coconut or dried coconut however—the consistency just won't be the same. Sometimes this sweet is called "chip chip," after the popular local clams, but no one is sure why since one does not resemble the other.

1 cup sugar

4 cups fresh or frozen grated unsweetened coconut

½ teaspoon cream of tartar

1 teaspoon mixed essence

1 Grease a baking sheet and set aside.

2 Bring the sugar and 1 cup of water to a boil and cook until small bubbles appear and the mixture forms a light syrup.

3 Add the coconut and cream of tartar. Cook, stirring constantly, until the coconut mixture comes away easily from the sides of the pan. Remove the pan from the heat and stir vigorously for 3 to 4 minutes. Stir in the mixed essence.

4 Drop tablespoonfuls of the coconut mixture onto the prepared baking sheet. Allow to dry and set completely, about 6 hours.

5 Store in an airtight container at room temperature for up to 1 week.

COCONUT FUDGE

Coconut fudge is a big seller among roadside vendors but at times I find it too sweet, which is no surprise since the recipe calls for two cups of sugar, which, of course, can be reduced according to taste—by as much as half.

2 cups coconut milk

1 (15-ounce) can evaporated milk

2 cups sugar

¼ teaspoon coarse salt

2 tablespoons butter, softened

½ cup fresh or frozen grated
   unsweetened coconut

1 teaspoon vanilla extract

1 Grease a 9 x 13-inch baking dish and set aside.

2 In a large saucepan, bring the coconut milk, evaporated milk, sugar, and salt to a boil, stirring constantly. Continue simmering and stirring until the mixture becomes very thick and pudding-like. Remove the pan from the heat and allow to cool to lukewarm.

3 Pour the mixture into a bowl and add the butter, beating well with an electric mixer on medium speed, for about 5 minutes. Add the grated coconut and vanilla.

4 Pour the batter into the prepared baking dish and allow to cool completely.

5 Once fudge is cool, cut into squares and serve. Coconut fudge may be stored in an airtight container for up to 1 week.

TAMARIND BALLS

This sweet is normally made with fresh tamarind pods. Although you can find these in gourmet shops and Indian and Middle Eastern markets, it's a lot of trouble to extract the pulp and remove the seeds, especially when seeded pulp is readily available in blocks. Some people like to add a bit of hot pepper for another dimension to the sweet-and-sour taste.

8 ounces tamarind paste

2 cups sugar

¼ teaspoon finely chopped hot pepper (optional)

1 Mix the tamarind paste with 1 cup of the sugar, adding more sugar as needed to get a stiff, moldable consistency. Add the hot pepper, if using, and mix well. Cover this mixture with plastic wrap and set aside overnight at room temperature.

2 Form the tamarind mixture into 1-inch balls and place on a baking sheet lined with waxed paper or parchment. Allow them to dry for a few hours, uncovered at room temperature.

3 Roll the tamarind balls in the remaining sugar and store at room temperature in a flat container with waxed paper between the layers. Tamarind balls keep for up to 2 weeks.

CARROT BARFI

This confection is sometimes called carrot halwa. You can substitute freshly grated coconut for the carrots and garnish each piece with a candied cherry, raisin, or slice of almond.

1¼ cups sugar

2 tablespoons ghee

5 large carrots, peeled and finely grated

¼ cup condensed milk

1 cup heavy cream

20 cashews, chopped, or almond slivers (optional)

1 Grease an 8-inch square baking dish and set aside.

2 Combine the sugar and ½ cup of water in a small saucepan and simmer until the mixture reaches the consistency of syrup, about 5 minutes. Set aside.

3 Heat the ghee in a deep saucepan and add the carrots. Stir well, cover, and cook over medium-low heat until the carrots are soft and there is no liquid left in the pan.

4 Stir in the condensed milk, cream, and sugar syrup. Mix well and add the nuts. Continue to cook, stirring constantly, until the mixture comes away from the sides of the pan to form a ball.

5 Pour the carrot mixture into the prepared baking dish and spread evenly with the back of a large spoon. Allow to cool.

6 Once the barfi is cool, cut into squares or other shapes. May be stored in an airtight container for up to one week.

PAWPAW BALLS

These sweet-tart balls of cooked green papaya remind me of all-natural gumdrops.

4 green papayas, peeled, seeded, and grated

2¾ cups sugar plus additional for rolling

1 teaspoon grated lemon zest

2 tablespoons freshly squeezed lime juice

1 Place the grated papaya in a clean dish towel and twist the towel to squeeze out about half of the juice from the papaya, roughly ¼ cup of liquid. Discard the juice.

2 In a large saucepan, combine the papaya pulp, sugar, lemon zest, and lime juice. Bring the mixture to a simmer and cook, stirring, until it has a jellylike consistency, about 15 to 20 minutes.

3 Remove the pan from the heat and cool slightly. With wet hands, form the mixture into 2½-inch balls and roll in sugar. Store in a plastic container in the refrigerator.

PEERA

The consistency of this dessert is something like a stiff candy bar. The addition of cloves makes it pleasantly aromatic and spicy.

2 cups all-purpose flour

1 cup ghee

1 cup sugar

½ (12-ounce) can sweetened condensed milk

⅓ teaspoon ground cloves

⅓ teaspoon ground ginger

⅓ teaspoon ground cardamom

1 Grease a 9 x 12 baking sheet and set aside.

2 Mix the flour with enough water to form a stiff dough, about ¾ cup. Roll out the dough ⅛ inch thick and cut into 1-inch-wide strips.

3 Heat ⅔ cup of the ghee in a frying pan and add the dough strips. Fry until golden brown. Remove and drain on a plate lined with paper towels. Once cool, place the strips in a food processor and grind to the consistency of flour.

4 Combine the sugar and 1 cup of water in a deep saucepan and simmer until the sugar reaches thread stage, when a candy thermometer inserted into the mixture registers 215°F. (Test by dropping some syrup in cold water; if it becomes threadlike, it is ready.)

5 Add the condensed milk, cloves, ginger, cardamom, and remaining ⅓ cup of ghee. Add the ground flour mixture and beat well. When thoroughly combined, spread onto the prepared baking sheet, cool, and cut into 12 equal squares. Store in an airtight container for up to one week.

TOOLUM

Similar to a hard taffy or sesame candy, toolum is a type of brittle featuring coconut and citrus zest.

2 cups dark brown sugar

¼ cup molasses

2½ cups fresh or frozen grated unsweetened coconut

1 teaspoon grated orange zest

1½ teaspoons grated fresh ginger

1 Grease a baking sheet and set aside.

2 Place the brown sugar in a deep saucepan and heat over medium heat, swirling the pan, until the sugar melts. Stir in the molasses, coconut, orange zest, and ginger, and stir until the mixture leaves the sides of the pan and forms a ball. Remove the pan from the heat.

3 Drop tablespoonfuls of the mixture onto the prepared baking sheet. Set aside to cool thoroughly and harden. Store in an airtight container at room temperature. Toolum keeps for up to two weeks.

JUBJUB

MAKES 24

Jubjub is one of the confections that I ate as a child while visiting Trinidad and promptly forgot about. On a recent trip back, someone offered me some. Once the jubjub was in my mouth, all the memories that come with taste and smell flooded back and I remembered one of the neighbor children shyly offering me some near the backstairs to my father's house when I was about ten.

This candy is traditionally made with lime juice, although today, commercially prepared versions make use of many different tropical flavors. I suggest you experiment with clear tropical fruit juices of your liking. Internationally, jubjub is more commonly known as "Turkish delight."

4 tablespoons (4 envelopes) unflavored gelatin

4 cups sugar, plus extra for coating the cubes

1 teaspoon freshly squeezed lime juice

2 to 3 drops food coloring of your choice

1 Dissolve the gelatin in 1 cup of water and set aside.

2 Combine ½ cup of water and the sugar in a pan and simmer until the syrup reaches thread stage, when a candy thermometer registers 215°F. Test by dropping a little syrup in cold water; if it becomes threadlike, it is ready.

3 Remove the pan from the heat and stir in the gelatin mixture until the gelatin totally dissolves. Add the lime juice and food coloring and mix well.

4 Wet a 9 x12 baking dish (I use a spray bottle filled with water) and pour in the gelatin mixture. Refrigerate until firm.

5 Once the jubjub is firm, cut into cubes and toss in sugar to coat. Store at room temperature in a glass jar or plastic container for up to 2 weeks.

Sweets & Desserts 235

JALEBIS

Street vendors sell this fritter resembling flat curly fries year-round. It's best eaten when freshly made and still crispy.

1 teaspoon active dry yeast

2 cups plus ¼ teaspoon sugar

2 cups warm water (100–110°F)

2 cups all-purpose flour

Orange food coloring

1 cup canola oil, for frying

1 Place the yeast in a small bowl and sprinkle with the ¼ teaspoon sugar. Add ¼ cup of the warm water and set the yeast mixture aside until it bubbles.

2 Combine the yeast mixture with the flour. Gradually add the remaining warm water until the mixture achieves the consistency of yogurt. Stir in the orange food coloring drop by drop until the mixture is bright orange. Cover the bowl with plastic wrap and set aside overnight in a warm place.

3 Place 2 cups of water and the 2 cups of sugar in a small saucepan and bring to a simmer. Cook until it reaches the consistency of maple syrup, about 5 minutes. Set aside.

4 Pour the jalebi mixture into a squeeze bottle or a pitcher with a narrow spout. Heat the oil in a deep pan. Test the temperature by adding a drop of jalebi batter to the oil. If it immediately bubbles and bobs to the top, the oil is hot enough. Squeeze or pour the jalebi dough into the hot oil in overlapping, spiraling circles about 4 inches in diameter. Fry until golden brown on both sides. Remove and drain on a plate lined with paper towels. Continue until all the jalebi dough is used.

5 Transfer the jalebis to a bowl and pour the sugar syrup evenly over them so all the sides are coated. Serve immediately while warm.

LADOO

The tender yet grainy texture provided by the split peas makes this one of my favorite desserts. It is one of the few Indian Trinidadian desserts that hasn't held true to its original recipe, in that it calls for regrinding the ladoos after they are fried. Another difference is that traditional ladoos use gram (chickpea) flour or semolina flour.

1 cup dried yellow split peas, soaked overnight in 3 cups water

½ teaspoon baking powder

¼ cup evaporated milk

½ cup ghee

1 cup sugar

½ (12-ounce) can sweetened condensed milk

¼ teaspoon ground ginger

¼ teaspoon ground cloves

1 Drain the split peas and grind in a food processor or meat grinder to a coarse consistency.

2 Combine the ground split peas with the baking powder, evaporated milk, and ½ cup of water. Set aside for 2 hours.

3 Shape the split pea mixture into 2½-inch balls.

4 Heat the ghee in a deep frying pan. Test the ghee by dropping a pinch of flour into the pan; if it sizzles, it is ready. Fry the balls for 1 to 2 minutes, or until golden brown. Remove from the pan and cool on a plate lined with paper towels.

5 Once cool, place the balls in a food processor and regrind to a coarse consistency. Set aside.

6 Bring 1 cup of water and the sugar to a boil in a deep saucepan, simmering until the sugar reaches the thread stage, when a candy thermometer inserted into the mixture registers 215°F. Test by dropping some syrup in cold water; if it becomes threadlike, it is ready.

7 Remove the syrup from the heat and add the condensed milk, ginger, and cloves and mix vigorously until the mixture becomes stiff. Fold in the ground split-pea mixture and mix well.

8 Form tablespoons of the split-pea mixture into balls. Allow to set for 2 to 3 hours. Store in a sealed plastic container or dish covered with plastic wrap. Serve with tea.

MALEEDA

I received this recipe from Safiyha Ali, an attorney who blogs about food at *Lifespan of a Chenette*, and whose mom is particularly masterful at making this Muslim special-occasion dessert. Maleeda is a dessert common to Muslim communities in Central Asia, with origins in Afghanistan. Historically maleeda was made by Afghan women who said prayers while breaking up the griddle bread that is the basis of the dessert in their hands so it would become a *nazr*, a vow or serious commitment to God in Islam. In Trinidad, as in its regions of origin, maleeda is used to celebrate births, weddings, engagements, and other special occasions including Eid Al Fitr. In Trinidad, coconut, black pepper, and maraschino cherries add a twist to the original recipe.

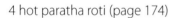

4 hot paratha roti (page 174)

1 cup flaked desiccated coconut

¾ pound brown sugar

8 ounces butter or ghee

½ teaspoon vanilla extract

½ teaspoon ground cinnamon

½ teaspoon ground cardamom

¼ teaspoon ground cloves

1 pinch black pepper

¼ cup raisins, chopped

¼ cup candied maraschino cherries, chopped

⅔ cup evaporated milk

1 Shred the parathas finely in a food processor.

2 Put shredded parathas in a mixing bowl and add all the remaining ingredients except the evaporated milk and stir to mix well.

3 Add the evaporated milk slowly stirring until the batter comes together to be able to form firm but moist balls.

4 Form the dough into balls about the size of golf balls and serve.

MISS MATTIE'S KULMA

This is a popular dessert for Diwali but is sold by street vendors year-round. Kulma most closely resemble the crunchy noodles you get in Chinese restaurants, except they are coated with sugar.

4 tablespoons (½ stick) unsalted butter

2 cups all-purpose flour

1 cup canola oil

1 cup sugar

½ teaspoon ground cinnamon

1 teaspoon mixed essence

1 Combine the butter and flour and knead into a firm dough. Roll out the dough ¼ inch thick.

2 Heat a tawa or heavy-bottomed skillet. Place the dough on the tawa and cook for about 1 minute. Flip the dough and cook for 1 minute on the other side. Remove and cut into strips about ½ inch wide. Cut each strip into 3-inch lengths.

3 Heat the oil in a 1-quart saucepan. Test the temperature of the oil by dropping a pinch of flour into the oil; if it sizzles it is ready. Add the strips of dough and fry until brown. Drain on a plate lined with paper towels.

4 Place the sugar, cinnamon, and mixed essence in a pot with ½ cup of water. Bring to a boil, stirring often, until the sugar melts. Simmer until the mixture becomes a thick syrup. Add the fried dough and toss well. Pour into a heatproof container to cool. Serve at room temperature.

The Sweetest Memories

"Just eat it," my father says, watching me as I gingerly nibble the little orange ball. He shakes his head. It is 1979, and I am 11 years old. We have come from a Hindu prayer meeting in his hometown of Chaguanas, Trinidad, site of the now-famous Hindu celebration of Diwali Nagar. I am sweating in my stiff sundress with the crinoline skirt that everyone has admired; my brother is equally turned out in a suit, a testament to my father's success in America. I shuffle behind my father in the blistering-hot street as I pick suspiciously at the sweet treat.

The ball is firm and sticky, with just enough sugar, and some taste I can't identify—something minty and familiar. Later I'll learn the spice is cardamom. But for now, a new world has opened up to me, a world of *mithai*, the Hindu name for sweets. Made from local sugar cane, they are served up in prodigious quantities every Diwali in late October or early November.

Returning to Trinidad now as a chef, I find myself in my ancestral homeland once again, on the eve of what was once my Trinidadian father's favorite holiday. Before I leave, I must satisfy my craving for *mithai*, for sugar is what largely informs our palates here on this island. But could those childhood memories of sugary treats and holiday-inspired generosity be as sweet for me today?

It is an inextricable aspect of the Indian part of heritage—my father's and mine. My great grandfather, like so many other Indians, arrived here in the nineteenth century to labor in the cane fields. The white gold they mined was largely bound for England and America, but come Diwali, the precious stuff was plentiful in Indian homes.

Though I can find the pastries anywhere, I am bound for Débé, a once sleepy backwater where residents have earned a reputation as master *mithai* makers. To feed a once-thriving sugar economy, over the years Débé locals set up small stands selling traditional pastries, cookies, and sweets as well as "doubles," sandwiches of spicy chickpeas and fried dough. It is a city built upon the fortunes of sugar.

My sentimental sweet tooth sends me on nearly a full day's travel into southwestern Trinidad, where Débé lies not far from Icacos Point, about seven miles from Venezuela. Though the day is rainy, cars throng the highway. Like me, these people know the goodies in Débé will be piled high because Diwali is coming.

This is our best chance to taste the threefold holiday: at once a devotion to Lakshmi, goddess of prosperity; the New Year; and the triumph of good over evil. While he was growing up, my father waited eagerly for Diwali, when fellow Hindus gave trays of *mithai* away, and there was no shame in taking them. It was a Hindu rite rather than an act of charity, a respite from the desperate poverty in which he was raised. Even as an adult, the thought of it left him longing for his tropical home as the leaves outside our window raged in a blast of orange and red against the sooty New York City sky.

Turning off the highway toward the center of Débé, I see Diwali preparations have started. Towers of *diyas*, traditional clay lamps, are stacked in the yards, waiting to be filled with coconut oil and placed on elaborate displays. The displays were simpler in my father's time, but he loved them nonetheless. "The *diyas* were so pretty, burning on the steps of the houses, in the balconies or along the roadside," he used to say, smiling, holding his hand up, forming a little cup with his fingers. "They were like little stars in the pitch black night."

I get out of my car and find a vendor whose small table is piled high with an assortment of *mithai* in gallon jars with tightly fitted lids. There are *gulab jamun* (mahogany-colored balls of fried cottage cheese doused in sugar syrup) and *ladoo* (deep-yellow orbs of toasted chickpea flour, sweetened and essenced with cardamom). *Barfi* squares—made from coconut flakes, pistachio or almond, sugar spices, and milk—are stacked like so many pretty tiles in alternating colors of pink, orange, and light green. All are virtually unchanged from the original recipes brought from India by our ancestors more than 150 years ago. They're balanced with the Trini creations I find here, too, like *kulma* and *chip chip* (dough sticks and coconut sugar cakes).

I buy *jalebi* first, a fritter of yeasty dough swirled through hot oil, fried crisp then dipped in sugar syrup. My father made these for us and we'd gobble them while they were too hot, burning our fingers and tongues. This time, though, I nibble a *jalebi* ever so delicately. It is still crisp under the wash of mouth-puckering sugar syrup, and I close my eyes to savor the heady taste that carries me back through years of Diwali celebrations.

When I open them again, I see a little boy of ten or eleven. He is barefoot and his T-shirt dirty. He's toting bags of sour plums as he weaves through the crowd. "Plums, salt plums!" he calls out, largely ignored, trying to compete with established pastry-mongers for their sweet-toothed clientele. I beckon him over and the child smiles. I buy some plums and tell him to keep the change, which he carefully puts in his pocket. He walks on, the bag hoisted on his shoulder, his knees knobby on thin legs, his thick, black hair standing up away from his head—so similar to my father's childhood photo. I imagine the boy taking the money he just earned to buy himself a *jalebi* or *gulab jamun*, the sticky syrup making his fingers tacky and coating his tongue as he relishes the taste of a treat well-earned.

FAT KURMA

Kurma is an incredibly popular Indo-Trinidadian sweet snack that is sold at roadside stands. However, the version that is publicly sold is hard and crunchy, widely different from the Muslim kurma that is more like a tiny donut with a crusty outside and soft center, which is the recipe I give here. This recipe is courtesy of the Trinidadian food blogger Safiyah Ali who originally wrote about it on her site *Lifespan of a Chennette*.

2 cups all-purpose flour

½ teaspoon ground cinnamon

¼ teaspoon ground cardamom

⅛ teaspoon ground cloves

3 teaspoons finely grated fresh ginger (or as desired)

½ cup (1 stick) unsalted butter

6 tablespoons evaporated milk

6 tablespoons condensed milk

4 cups of oil for frying

1½ cups granulated sugar

1 In a large bowl, whisk the flour, cinnamon, cardamom, cloves, and half of the ginger together. Add the butter and using a pastry cutter or fork, cut the butter into the flour until it looks like fine breadcrumbs.

2 Mix the evaporated milk and 6 tablespoons water together. Add to the flour mixture along with half of the condensed milk and knead the dough until it is smooth, about 5 minutes, adding extra flour as needed to prevent the dough from being sticky.

Separate the dough into 4 balls and knead each again for 2 to 3 minutes. Set aside to rest for 15 minutes.

3 Roll out one of the dough balls into a rope about ½-inch thick and about 12 to 14 inches long. Cut the rope on a diagonal into 1½-inch pieces. Repeat for each ball.

4 Heat the oil in a heavy-bottomed pot over medium heat for 4 to 5 minutes—test the temperature by dropping a pinch of flour into the oil, if it sizzles immediately the oil is ready.

5 Fry the pieces of dough in batches until golden brown and place on a wire rack or paper-towel-lined tray to drain while cooking the remaining pieces.

6 Make the sugar syrup: Put sugar and ½ cup of water in a large pot along with the remaining 1½ teaspoons ginger and boil until the sugar mixture spins a thread when dropping from a spoon. At this stage add the remaining 3 tablespoons condensed milk and boil again until the mixture spins a thread.

7 Place this sugar syrup in a large wide bowl and add the kurma. Stir continuously until they are evenly coated. Transfer to a tray to spread out a bit so that the kurma doesn't clump together.

GULAB JAMUN

Gulab jamun is probably one of the most familiar Indian desserts to Americans. It is a standard on the dessert menus of Indian restaurants and resembles donut holes floating in a light syrup.

4 cups all-purpose flour

1 teaspoon baking powder

1 teaspoon ground cardamom

1 cup (2 sticks) unsalted butter, cut into pieces

2 cups evaporated milk

1 (14-ounce) can condensed milk

2 cups oil, for frying

2 cups sugar

1 Sift together the flour, baking powder, and cardamom. Cut in the butter using a fork, or in a food processor fitted with a plastic blade, until the mixture resembles coarse meal.

2 Add the evaporated milk and condensed milk. Knead lightly to form a soft dough. Pinch off 2½-inch pieces of dough and roll into balls.

3 Heat the oil in a deep skillet. Test the temperature by dropping a pinch of flour into the oil. If it sizzles, the oil is ready. Add the dough balls in batches and fry until dark golden brown on all sides. Remove and drain on paper towels or a wire rack set over a baking sheet.

4 In a deep saucepan, bring 4½ cups of water and the sugar to a boil. Lower the heat and simmer until the mixture thickens to the consistency of a thin maple syrup. Add the gulab jamuns a few at a time and toss to coat. Serve at room temperature immediately after dipping in syrup.

MALPURA

Trinidadian East Indian desserts usually stay faithful to original recipes while savory foods have incorporated local ingredients and cooking styles from other cultures. However, a small number of desserts have also been adapted and Malpura, a fritter made with a milk-enriched dough, is one of them—it makes use of powdered milk where the traditional recipe does not.

4¾ cups powdered milk

½ cup all-purpose flour

3½ cups sugar

¾ cup ghee

GARNISHES

⅓ cup (2 ounces) chopped pistachios

2 tablespoons golden raisins

¼ cup (1 ounce) chopped almonds

1 Reconstitute 4 cups of the powdered milk according to the package directions. Pour the milk into a deep saucepan and bring to a boil. Lower the heat and simmer until thick, about 30 minutes.

2 Mix the remaining ¾ cup powdered milk with the flour and add it to the simmering milk. Remove from heat.

3 In a separate saucepan, bring the sugar and 3 cups of water to a simmer and cook until it is the consistency of thin maple syrup. Set aside over low heat to keep warm.

4 Heat the ghee in a deep frying pan. Drop tablespoonfuls of the milk dough into the pan. Flatten each spoonful with the back of the spoon and fry on both sides until golden brown. Remove and drain on a plate lined with paper towels. Continue until all the dough is used.

5 Place each malpura in the warm sugar syrup and turn gently to coat. Remove and arrange on a plate. Garnish with pistachios, raisins, and almonds. Serve warm.

RAS GULLA

Similar to Gulab Jamun (page 243), Ras Gulla are balls of dough in syrup. However, because this dough is milk-based, these are somewhat lighter and creamier.

2 cups powdered whole milk

2 tablespoons all-purpose flour

1½ teaspoons baking powder

½ cup heavy cream

1 cup canola oil, for deep-frying

2 cups sugar

1 teaspoon ground cardamom

1 Sift together the powdered milk, flour, and baking powder. Gradually add the heavy cream, mixing until the mixture can be molded into balls. Roll into 2½-inch balls and set aside.

2 Heat the oil in a deep pan until hot. Add the balls in batches, and fry until golden brown on all sides. Remove from the oil and drain on a plate lined with paper towels.

3 Combine the sugar, cardamom, and 2 cups of water in a saucepan and bring to a simmer. Simmer until the mixture reaches the consistency of maple syrup.

4 Add the ras gulla balls to the syrup and gently turn to coat. Serve warm with 1 to 2 tablespoons of syrup per ras gulla.

SOURSOP SORBET

Fruit sorbets are a perennial favorite in our house, and I like to use whatever fruit is fresh and in season to create a variety of sorbets for my daughter Sophia. I find that commercially available tropical fruit purees are a wonderful way to make sorbet with hard-to-find "home" fruits.

Another thing I like to do is to pour the sorbet mixture into popsicle trays about halfway through the churning cycle. This way the popsicle gains some of the airy, smooth quality of sorbet while being conveniently presented on a stick, which is ideal for the little ones.

½ cup sugar

1 tablespoon freshly squeezed lime juice

2 cups soursop puree (Goya is one brand)

1 Mix sugar and ½ cup of water together in a small saucepan and bring to a slow simmer. Simmer until reduced by half and then set aside to cool.

2 Mix together the lime juice, soursop puree, and the cooled sugar syrup. Pour into an ice cream maker and churn according to manufacturer's directions, usually about 40 minutes.

3 Remove sorbet from ice cream maker, pack into a quart container, and freeze overnight until hard. If making popsicles, remove halfway through the churning process and pour into popsicle trays. Freeze overnight.

Variations: FRUIT SORBETS
Soursop (or guanabana) is lovely and refreshing with an almost creamy consistency, but I encourage you to try this all-purpose recipe with any fruit you desire, simply substitute the soursop puree for a fruit puree of your choice. Guava, mango, and lulo are all very nice choices.

RUM RAISIN ICE CREAM

MAKES 1 QUART

I remember being in Trinidad in 2005 for the first ever Taste of TnT festival now held yearly in Port of Spain. One of the popular ice cream vendors had set up shop at the festival and a long line of people hovered around the stand though no one was being served. They were waiting for the homemade rum raisin ice cream to firm up, which it never quite did. When I tasted it I realized why: the rum was so prodigious fumes were practically rising from the icy confection. So take note, it's particularly important to press out the rum from the raisins if you want this ice cream to freeze!

½ cup mixed golden and dark raisins

¾ cup Royal Oak or other dark rum

1 cup heavy cream

1 cup whole milk

½ cup light brown sugar

Pinch of ground allspice

3 large egg yolks

1 teaspoon mixed essence

1 Combine the raisins and rum in a bowl and steep overnight.

2 Mix the heavy cream, milk, light brown sugar, and allspice together in a large saucepan and bring to just under a boil, stirring often to ensure the sugar is dissolved. Remove from heat.

3 Beat the egg yolks in a large bowl, and using a soup ladle, gently ladle a very thin stream of the hot milk mixture into the egg yolks while whisking vigorously. Once a full ladle of the hot milk is added, the egg yolks have been tempered enough to be added to the pot without scrambling.

Pour the egg-milk mixture into the pot of hot milk while whisking vigorously.

4 Return the pot to the burner over a low-medium heat and stir in the mixed essence. Whisk continuously but gently while the mixture is heating. Cook until it reaches a thick consistency like a very loose pudding. Remove from heat and pour into a heat-safe bowl. Refrigerate until completely cold.

5 Pour the cold custard into an ice cream maker and freeze according to manufacturers directions, until partially frozen, about 25 minutes into the process, depending on your ice cream maker.

6 Drain the raisins, reserving the rum to pour over the completed ice cream as a garnish, if desired, and pressing on the raisins to remove as much liquid as possible. Add the raisins to the ice cream and then complete the freezing process.

7 Remove ice cream from the ice cream maker and pack firmly into a quart container. Freeze overnight until solid.

COCONUT ICE CREAM

The Trinidadian version of coconut ice cream generally makes use of two ubiquitous West Indian ingredients: evaporated milk and condensed milk. I prefer to use a more traditional ice cream recipe, adding gelatin to aid thickening.

//

1 In a small bowl, sprinkle the gelatin over the whole milk and set aside to dissolve.

2 Mix the cream, coconut milk, and sugar in a saucepan. Bring to a boil, stirring to dissolve the sugar. Reduce the heat to a simmer and continue to stir until the sugar is totally dissolved.

3 Remove the pan from the heat and add the shredded coconut,, mixed essence, and coconut extract. Add the gelatin mixture and mix until totally dissolved.

4 Allow the mixture to cool completely, then pour into an ice cream maker. Freeze, following the manufacturer's directions.

5 Pack the ice cream into two 1-quart containers and freeze overnight until solid. Serve garnished with sweetened coconut, if desired.

1 tablespoon (1 envelope) unflavored gelatin

2 tablespoons whole milk

2 cups heavy cream

2 cups coconut milk

¾ cup sugar

½ cup fresh or frozen grated unsweetened coconut

½ teaspoon mixed essence or vanilla extract

1 teaspoon coconut extract

Sweetened shredded coconut, for garnish

KULFI

Kulfi is a kind of churnless ice cream, but it's not trouble-free. You have to keep removing it from the freezer as it hardens, to stir out the ice crystals. Budget plenty of time if you are making this dish.

2 cups milk

2½ cups heavy cream

3 cardamom pods, slightly crushed

Pinch of saffron threads

1 (14-ounce) can sweetened condensed milk

1 (12-ounce) can evaporated milk

1 tablespoon chopped almonds

2 tablespoons chopped unsalted pistachios

1 Bring the milk and cream to a boil in a heavy saucepan. Add the cardamom pods and saffron. Lower the heat to a simmer and continue to cook until the mixture is reduced by half.

2 Remove the cardamom pods and stir in the condensed milk and evaporated milk. Add the almonds and three-quarters of the pistachios. Pour into a deep freezer-proof bowl and let cool.

3 Once cool, place in the freezer. Remove every hour and stir to dissolve ice crystals until the kulfi is firm, about 4 hours.

4 Serve in ice cream dishes, sprinkled with remaining pistachio nuts.

SPICE BLENDS, PICKLES, SAUCES & JAMS

Next to sweets, the foods dearest to any Trinidadian's heart are hot pickles, pepper sauces, and seasoning mixes that are a part of every meal, either as a condiment or as flavoring for the pot. Today, most of these mixtures can be readily purchased pre-made from the local market or supermarket or online, but many families still make their own, or have at least one relative or friend who will prepare the mixtures for them. Making seasoning sauces and the like is not a once-a-year affair. Rather, these mixtures are made year-round as the need arises.

Personal taste has a great deal to do with the exact combination of spices and ingredients in any of these recipes. It's not uncommon to go from one neighbor's house to another and find that their curried chicken or fried fish tastes subtly but noticeably different. This is part of the beauty of Trinidadian cuisine—general cooking methods and basic ingredients may be agreed upon, but the actual composition of a recipe or dish is largely left to the creativity of the individual cook.

TRINIDAD CURRY POWDER

It's said that Trinidadians will curry anything from meat to vegetables to fruit. As in masala, green seasoning, and other spice mixtures, the ratio of spices in a curry powder is very personal. Experiment to find the proportions you like. You'll notice that hot pepper is notably absent from this mixture—unlike curry powder from Madras. Trinidadians like to add fresh hot pepper to dishes, according to taste. I find that curry leaves lend a wonderful aroma and texture, but if they are not available, simply omit.

6 cardamom pods

1 cup coriander seeds

¼ cup cumin seeds

1 tablespoon mustard seeds

1 tablespoon fenugreek seeds

10 to 15 curry leaves (optional)

¼ cup whole black peppercorns

6 whole cloves

⅓ cup plus 1 tablespoon ground turmeric

1 Break open the cardamom pods, remove the seeds, and discard the pods.

2 Place the cardamom seeds, coriander seeds, cumin seeds, mustard seeds, fenugreek seeds, and curry leaves in a heavy frying pan and toast, swirling for about 5 minutes, until the spices begin to release their aromas.

3 Place the toasted spices in a food processor or spice grinder and add the peppercorns and cloves. Grind the mixture to a fine powder. Stir in the turmeric.

4 Store in an airtight container. If stored properly, curry powder will keep for at least two months.

Tip: Curry Leaves
Fresh curry leaves are an herb with a nutty citrusy aroma and are actually not related to the spice mix used in most curry dishes. Curry leaves are available at Indian and Asian markets and these days even online.

Spice Blends, Pickles, Sauces & Jams   253

GREEN SEASONING

Green Seasoning is one of those herb mixtures that is unique to the Caribbean and differs slightly from island to island. It is used in a huge number of Trinidadian dishes. In Trinidad, it's distinguished by the use of a local herb called *shado beni* (Mexican culantro). Fresh *shado beni* can sometimes be found in West Indian markets, but if not, fresh cilantro is a good substitute.

3 tablespoons chopped fresh chives

1 tablespoon chopped fresh shado beni or cilantro leaves

2 tablespoons chopped fresh thyme

1 tablespoon chopped fresh oregano

1 tablespoon chopped fresh parsley

4 cloves garlic, finely chopped

1 Process all the ingredients in a food processor until the mixture forms a thick paste. (Alternatively, process in a blender with 2 tablespoons of vinegar.)

2 Use immediately, or store in a tightly sealed glass jar in the refrigerator for up to 1 week.

PARAMIN GREEN SEASONING

The area of Paramin, perched breathtakingly high atop the mountains of Trinidad's Northern Range, is the herb basket of the country. The steeply sloped hillsides and cool mountain air make the region ideal for growing herbs like shado beni, chives, thyme, and parsley. The Creole-descent farmers who cultivate these plants are the go-to guys for every Trinidadian cook, since their herbs are an absolute necessity for the local pantry. The addition of shallots, onions, and vinegar, and the omission of oregano, makes this blend a bit different from standard green seasoning (page 254) although you can substitute one for the other where a recipe calls for green seasoning.

4 large shallots, peeled and coarsely chopped

1 cup finely chopped fresh chives

¼ cup finely chopped fresh thyme

¼ cup stemmed and chopped flat leaf parsley

2 tablespoons finely chopped shado beni or cilantro leaves

1 medium onion, peeled and coarsely chopped

4 cloves garlic

½ teaspoon freshly ground black pepper

½ teaspoon coarse salt

2 tablespoons white vinegar

1 Place all the ingredients in the bowl of a food processor or blender and puree, adding additional vinegar as needed to achieve a smooth, somewhat liquid paste.

2 Store in a sealed container in the refrigerator for up to 1 week.

GARAM MASALA

Garam masala is, of course, most associated with true East Indian cooking and while it is used in Trinidad it is not as ubiquitous. The term "*garam*" simply means "toasted." The dry roasting of spices in this mixture adds a certain depth of flavor to the masala.

6 tablespoons coriander seeds

1 heaping teaspoon aniseed

1 heaping teaspoon ground cloves or
  ½ teaspoon whole cloves

1 heaping teaspoon cumin seeds

1 heaping teaspoon fenugreek seeds

1 teaspoon whole black peppercorns

1 teaspoon mustard seeds

2 dry hot red chilies, stemmed, or
  2 teaspoons red pepper flakes

1 heaping teaspoon ground turmeric

1 Heat a large frying pan over medium heat. When the pan is hot, place all ingredients except the turmeric in the pan. Cook, swirling the pan constantly so the spices do not scorch, for 45 seconds to 1 minute, or until the spices begin to release their aromas.

2 Place the toasted spices in a food processor or grinder and grind to a fine powder. Add the turmeric. Remove and store in an airtight container at room temperature for up to 1 month.

Tip
You can use garam masala as a substitution in any dish that might originally call for curry powder.

HOT PEPPER SAUCE

Watching my father eat was one of my most fascinating childhood pastimes—largely because of the astounding amount of incredibly hot pepper he consumed with every meal. He would either eat whole hot peppers between bites of food, each crunch releasing its tart, hot aroma, or he'd liberally dash habañero sauce on his rice, mixing it in well so that every forkful was good and spicy. One of his favorites was the yellow sauce he made from habañero peppers. I like to use it to flavor squash soups, but remember—just a little dab'll do ya!

½ pound yellow Scotch bonnet pepper or other hot chili peppers, stemmed, seeded, and finely chopped

4 fresh pimiento peppers, stemmed, seeded, and finely chopped; or 4 tablespoons finely chopped jarred pimientos

1 small carrot, peeled and finely chopped

¼ cup light brown sugar

¼ cup white wine vinegar

¼ cup mustard oil

1 tablespoon Trinidad curry powder (page 253)

1 tablespoon ground cumin

½ teaspoon coarse salt

1 teaspoon freshly ground black pepper

4 cloves garlic, finely chopped

1 Combine all the ingredients in a blender or food processor, ensuring that the lid is on tight. Pulse to a thick yellow sauce the consistency of bottled mustard.

2 Pour the sauce into a 16-ounce glass bottle and seal tightly. The sealed bottle may be stored, unrefrigerated, for up to 3 months. Once unsealed, it may be refrigerated for up to 1 month.

Tip
I always wear rubber gloves when seeding and hot chili peppers, and discard the gloves after use. However, when making this sauce, I learned the hard way that the mere smell of some pepper sauces is enough to cause serious distress: removing the food processor cover and poking my nose over the edge to check the consistency of the sauce I got a good, eye-watering, cough-inducing whiff of the stuff. The moral of the story? Hot peppers are caustic in more ways than one, so keep the sauce pointed away from your face at all times. Wash down with white vinegar all surfaces that have come into contact with hot peppers—including the outside of the sauce's storage bottle.

HOT PEPPER CHOKHA

Miss Mattie Ramroop told me a funny story involving this spicy pepper condiment. While Miss Mattie was out, our dear mutual friend Dr. Aisha Khan, who was visiting from New York, came into her house and saw a chokha-smeared roti lying on the table. Knowing that Miss Mattie would generously offer whatever food she had prepared, Aisha tore off a large bite of the roti—and scalded her mouth. Now she jokes that in the pepper-loving Trinidadian kitchen it is unwise to simply sample Trinidadian dishes without asking first!

10 Scotch bonnet peppers or other hot red chili peppers

½ head garlic, cloves separated and peeled

¼ teaspoon coarse salt

½ small onion, finely chopped

1 teaspoon canola oil

1 Prepare a grill or preheat the broiler. Place the hot peppers and garlic on the grill or under the broiler. (Alternatively, place them directly in the flame of a gas burner.) Cook until the garlic is lightly browned and the peppers become brown and blistered. Allow to cool, and then stem and finely chop the peppers and mash the garlic.

2 Combine the peppers and garlic with the salt, onion, and oil. Mix well and refrigerate if not using immediately. The chokha will keep for up to 1 week. Use as a condiment with any curry or stew served with rice or roti.

PIRI-PIRI SAUCE

This sauce has its origins in the condiment of the same name from Africa and was no doubt originally brought to Trinidad by enslaved peoples. Piri-piri sauce is generally used on its own as a condiment, but can be added to barbecue sauces or marinades. I find the oil used in the Trinidadian version gives the sauce more ability to stick to the food—which is good if you choose to use it in a marinade. Authentic piri-piri, however, does not make use of oil but uses vinegar.

3 cups canola oil

2 Congo or bird peppers, stemmed, seeded, and finely chopped

1 teaspoon grated lemon zest

1 teaspoon coarse or kosher salt

2 bay leaves

1 Combine all the ingredients in a jar and seal tightly. Refrigerate for 2 weeks, shaking the jar every 2 days or so.

2 Serve as a condiment with any food. Store refrigerated for up to 2 months.

Tip: Hot Peppers
 Remember to use gloves when handling hot peppers. Or if you prefer not to use gloves, don't touch your eyes or face and wash hands immediately after handling, using plenty of hot water and soap! Wash down any surfaces that the peppers may have touched with white vinegar as well.

MASALA PASTE

It's impossible to say for sure whether East Indian spice mixtures like this masala are absolutely authentic, in large part because India is such a vast country that a particular spice blend might have come from a single indentured laborer who hailed from a small village off the beaten track. Additionally, although the ingredients are standard Indian spice-box issue, the ratio of individual spices can vary from area to area and cook to cook. You may want to experiment with this mix until you find a combination you really like.

6 tablespoons coriander seeds

1 heaping teaspoon aniseed

1 heaping teaspoon whole cloves

1 heaping teaspoon ground turmeric

1 heaping teaspoon cumin seeds

1 heaping teaspoon fenugreek seeds

1 teaspoon whole black peppercorns

1 teaspoon mustard seeds

2 fresh hot red chilies, stemmed

3 cloves garlic

1 medium onion, chopped

1 Place the coriander seeds, aniseed, cloves, turmeric, cumin seeds, fenugreek seeds, peppercorns, and mustard seeds in a food processor or grinder and grind to a powder.

2 Add the chilies, garlic, and onion and process into a paste, adding water as necessary to achieve a paste-like consistency. Store, refrigerated, in an airtight container until needed, for up to 1 week.

Tip
You can substitute masala paste in dishes that call for curry powder for a different, more aromatic, taste.

COCONUT CHUTNEY

This chutney is South Indian in origin, and outside of Trinidad, can be found in restaurants as an accompaniment to *dosas* (crepes made from rice or lentil flour and stuffed with spiced vegetables).

2 cups fresh or frozen grated unsweetened coconut

3 cloves garlic, finely chopped

1 teaspoon coarse salt

2 hot red chilies, stemmed, seeded, and finely chopped

2 tablespoons finely chopped shado beni or cilantro leaves

1 Place all ingredients in the bowl of a food processor and puree to a coarse paste.

2 Serve as a condiment with vegetarian dishes such as Aloo Talkari (page 129). Store in a sealed glass container in the refrigerator for up to 1 week.

LIME PEPPER

Lime pepper can really be served with anything, but it is best with fish dishes. This recipe is very close to the original recipes from India that are still produced today.

¾ cup freshly squeezed lime juice, skins reserved

10 Scotch bonnet peppers or other hot red chili peppers, chopped

1 tablespoon coarse salt

3-inch chunk bitter melon, cut into small pieces

1 small carrot, peeled and cut into small pieces

1 Combine the lime juice, hot peppers, salt, melon, and carrot. Cut the lime skins into small pieces and add to the mixture, stirring well.

2 Place the mixture in an 8-ounce glass jar and seal lid tightly. Place the jar on a sunny window ledge or outside in direct sunlight for at least 2 hours and up to 3 days. Store in a dry place. Lime pepper keeps for up to 2 months.

MOTHER-IN-LAW

This is a relatively new recipe in Trinidad and can be likened to a spicy condiment paste of carrot and bitter melon along with prodigious hot chili peppers. No one is quite sure who or where it was developed, but it started out as a wedding condiment that represented the "hot" tongue and temper of a mother-in-law. It is served with roti and rice dishes and is now also a regular at most Hindu prayer meetings.

3 Scotch bonnet peppers or other hot red chili peppers

2 tablespoons chopped shado beni or cilantro leaves

2 bitter melons, peeled and finely chopped

2 carrots, peeled and finely chopped

4 tablespoons freshly squeezed lime juice

½ teaspoon coarse salt

1 onion, finely chopped

1 Grind the peppers and shado beni in a food processor or blender to a coarse paste. If the mixture is too dry to process, add 2 tablespoons of the lime juice. Add the remaining ingredients and pulse to a coarse consistency like wet sand.

2 Store in a sealable container in the refrigerator for up to 1 month. Serve as a condiment with rotis and rice dishes.

SHADO BENI SAUCE

MAKES 2 CUPS

This sauce is often found on tables at food stands right next to the ketchup. Trinidadians put it on almost anything, but particularly on the Shark and Bake sold at Maracas Bay Beach (page 67).

½ cup shado beni or cilantro leaves, finely chopped

4 cloves garlic

2 teaspoons canola oil

1 Scotch bonnet pepper or other hot red chili pepper, stemmed and seeded

1½ cups white vinegar

1 Place the shado beni or cilantro, garlic, canola oil, and hot pepper in the bowl of a food processor or blender and pulse to a smooth paste. Add the vinegar and pulse once or twice more.

2 Store, refrigerated, in a tightly sealed glass jar.

CHOW-CHOW

C how-chow was brought to Trinidad by the English who learned how to make it from the Dutch. In sections of the United States, as in Trinidad, "*chow*" refers to a pickled fruit or vegetable mixture that is very spicy. You can decide which vegetables you'd like to use but this is a fairly standard recipe. Trinidadians eat chow-chow as a snack but I like to use it as a condiment with grilled foods.

2 tablespoons coarse salt

½ cup bite-size cauliflower florets

½ green papaya, peeled and chopped into 1-inch pieces

1 medium carrot, peeled and chopped into 1-inch pieces

1 small onion, coarsely chopped

2 stalks celery, chopped into 1-inch pieces

½ English cucumber, coarsely chopped

1 small green Italian sweet pepper, stemmed, seeded, and coarsely chopped

¼ cup all-purpose flour

½ cup prepared yellow mustard

¼ cup sugar

1 teaspoon ground turmeric

3 cups white vinegar

2 Scotch bonnet peppers or other hot red chili peppers, stemmed, seeded, and finely chopped

1 Bring 6 cups of water to a boil in a large pot. Add 1 tablespoon of the salt, the cauliflower, papaya, carrot, onion, celery, cucumber, and sweet pepper. Blanch for 10 minutes, drain, and set aside.

2 In a deep saucepan, combine the remaining 1 tablespoon of salt, the flour, mustard, sugar, and turmeric. Mix well and then whisk in 1 cup of water. Bring to a simmer, whisking constantly, until the mixture thickens.

3 Continue whisking and pour in the vinegar in a steady stream. Bring the mixture to a boil. Add the chili peppers and blanched vegetables. Stir well and remove from heat.

4 Pour into sterilized mason jars and seal. Serve as a condiment with any grilled food.

Tip

Heating vinegar releases its pungent, potentially lung irritating odors. Don't put your face directly over the pot when adding the vinegar to chow-chow or any other preparation.

TAMARIND SAUCE

Although also called a "chutney," this is really a smooth sauce. As with other tamarind recipes in this book, I use tamarind concentrate rather than going through the hassle of reconstituting fresh pods or dried paste.

2 tablespoons tamarind concentrate

1 cup hot water

1 teaspoon coarse salt

2 teaspoons dark brown sugar

1 teaspoon ground cumin

¼ teaspoon fennel seeds, ground

2 cloves garlic, finely chopped

1 small Scotch bonnet pepper or other hot red chili pepper, stemmed, seeded, and finely chopped

2 tablespoons finely chopped shado beni or cilantro leaves

1 Combine the tamarind concentrate and hot water in a bowl and allow to cool. Stir in the remaining ingredients.

2 Serve as a condiment with Shark and Bake (page 67), Meat Patties (page 56), or any other savory turnover or fritter. Store in a glass jar with a tight lid.

KUCHELA

This condiment of spiced green mango can be eaten with roti (pages 174-177), doubles (page 51), or any stew dish. It is my brother's favorite, and whenever anyone visits from Trinidad they are obliged to bring back a few jars of homemade kuchela for him, although it is readily available in West Indian markets. Matouk's is a good brand.

5 small green mangoes, peeled

1 head garlic, peeled

2 or 3 Scotch bonnet peppers or other hot red chili peppers

¼ cup canola oil

⅓ cup achar masala

½ teaspoon coarse salt

½ cup mustard oil

1 Grate the mangoes through the large holes of a grater. Squeeze the juice from mango pulp using your hands, or by placing the pulp in a strainer and pressing on it with the back of a spoon until all the juice is released. Discard the juice. Place mango pulp in a bowl.

2 Place the garlic and chili peppers in a food processor and grind to the consistency of wet sand.

3 Heat the canola oil in a large, deep skillet. Add the ground garlic and chili peppers and fry for 1 minute. Add the achar masala and salt and mix well. Add to the mango pulp and mix well. Stir in the mustard oil.

4 Place in a glass jar and seal tightly. Allow to sit unrefrigerated for at least 5 days and up to 3 months.

TRADITIONAL MANGO CHUTNEY

This chutney recipe provides an excellent use for any leftover green tomatoes from your summer garden. It is ideal as a condiment with any Indian curry or rice dishes.

2 medium green mangoes, peeled and sliced

1 large onion, coarsely chopped

2 medium green tomatoes, cored and coarsely chopped

½ cup raisins

1 cup dark brown sugar

1 teaspoon coarse salt

4 whole cloves

4 small Scotch bonnet peppers or other hot red chili peppers, stemmed, seeded, and finely chopped

¼ teaspoon whole peppercorns

2 cups white vinegar

1 Place the mango slices, onion, and green tomatoes in the bowl of a food processor or blender and process until finely chopped. (If the mixture is too dry to process easily in a blender, add 2 tablespoons of the vinegar.) Add the raisins and pulse a few more times to chop the raisins.

2 In a medium saucepan, combine the mango mixture with the dark brown sugar, salt, cloves, hot peppers, and peppercorns. Mix well and simmer for 30 minutes.

3 Add the vinegar and simmer over low heat for 2 hours more.

4 Pour the chutney into a sterilized (1-quart) jar, 2 (1-pint) jars, or sealable plastic containers, and refrigerate. Keeps up to 1 month.

MANGO ACHAR

This spicy condiment is generally eaten with roti and other Indian dishes, however, like most spicy condiments, folks add it to whatever they feel like. More curry powder can be added to taste—it is then called "Curried Mango."

5 green mangoes, unpeeled

2 teaspoons canola oil

1 head of garlic, separated, peeled, and crushed

1 teaspoon Trinidad curry powder (page 253) mixed with 1 teaspoon water

2 or 3 Scotch bonnet peppers or other hot red chili peppers

10 shado beni or cilantro leaves

1 cup brown sugar

3 tablespoons achar masala

1 teaspoon coarse salt

1 Using a heavy, sharp cleaver, cut each mango lengthwise into eight equal pieces, straight through the pits.

2 Heat the oil in a large, deep skillet. Add the garlic and fry for 30 seconds. Add the curry powder, chili peppers, and shado beni, mix well, and cook for about 1 minute.

3 Stir in the green mango slices, brown sugar, achar masala, and salt. Add 2 cups of water and cover. Simmer, stirring occasionally, for about 20 minutes. Remove from the heat and cool. Once cool remove any mango pits.

4 Place mixture in a sealable 1-quart jar or 2 (16-ounce) jars and refrigerate. Mango achar keeps up to 2 weeks.

MANGO SALSA

This condiment is different from a chutney in that it isn't cooked and the mango isn't sweetened.

1 large green mango, peeled

½ teaspoon coarse salt, or to taste

½ Scotch bonnet pepper or other hot red chili pepper, stemmed, seeded, and finely chopped

Freshly ground black pepper to taste

3 cloves garlic, finely chopped

1 tablespoon coarsely chopped shado beni or cilantro leaves

1 tablespoon fresh lime juice

1 Grate the mango using the large holes of a box grater. Place mango in a bowl and stir in the remaining ingredients. Cover and chill for 1 hour.

2 Serve as a condiment with rice dishes and stews. Store in a sealable glass container in the refrigerator for up to 1 month.

MANGO JAM

Jams and jellies are a popular breakfast offering in Trinidad, no doubt because of the long English influence on the island. Instead of traditional American jams like strawberry and raspberry, however, in Trinidad jams are made from the wide variety of locally available tropical fruits.

2 medium half-ripe mangoes, peeled, seeded, and chopped

¾ cup sugar

4 tablespoons fresh lime juice

1 In a saucepan, combine the mangos, sugar, lime juice, and ½ cup of water. Bring to a simmer and cook until the mango is soft and pulpy and the syrup reaches thread stage, when a candy thermometer inserted into the mixture registers 215°F—test by dropping some syrup in cold water; if it becomes threadlike, it is ready.

2 Pour into hot, sterilized mason jars and seal tightly.

GUAVA JAM

Guavas are plentiful in Trinidad and guava jam is one of the most practical and popular uses for them. While grape jelly or strawberry preserves may be the breakfast standard in the United States, guava jam graces almost every Trinidadian breakfast table. It is made fairly regularly when guava is in season, from spring to fall—in other words, as soon as a family runs out, more guavas go into the pot!

1 pound fresh guava, peeled and seeded, or 2 cups frozen guava pulp, thawed

¾ cup sugar

1 tablespoon freshly squeezed lime juice

1 If using fresh guava, place in a saucepan with water to cover and bring to a boil. Reduce to a simmer and cook until soft. Press the cooked guava through a fine-mesh sieve into a saucepan.

2 Add the remaining ingredients to the guava pulp and simmer until thickened to the consistency of jam.

3 Bottle in sterilized mason jars if you are storing for later use. For immediate use, pour into a tightly lidded container and refrigerate.

GUAVA JELLY

The traditional recipe for guava jelly is a time-consuming process that requires hanging a bag of guava pulp to drain overnight. For the sake of tradition, I offer that recipe here but also include the alternative of using commercially expressed guava juice.

1 pound fresh guava, peeled and seeded, or 2 cups frozen guava pulp, thawed, or 2 cups bottled pure guava nectar (such as Goya brand)

¾ cup sugar

1 tablespoon freshly squeezed lime juice

1 If using fresh or frozen guava, place them in a saucepan with water to cover and bring to a boil. Reduce to a simmer and cook until soft. Press the cooked guava through a fine-mesh sieve. Pour the guava pulp into a muslin cloth gathered to form a bag. Tie securely at the top. Hang the bag from the kitchen sink faucet or some other hook and place a large bowl below it. Allow the pulp to drip into the bowl overnight. Discard the pulp remaining in the bag, while reserving the liquid in the bowl.

2 Place the extracted guava liquid or bottled nectar in a saucepan with the remaining ingredients. Cook over medium heat, stirring constantly, until the sugar is dissolved.

3 Raise the heat to medium-high, and cook, stirring occasionally so the pot does not boil over, until the mixture reaches the thread stage, when a candy thermometer inserted into the mixture registers 215°F. Test by dropping some syrup in cold water; if it becomes threadlike, it is ready. Remove from heat.

4 Pour the hot liquid into hot, sterilized mason jars and seal tightly.

BEVERAGES

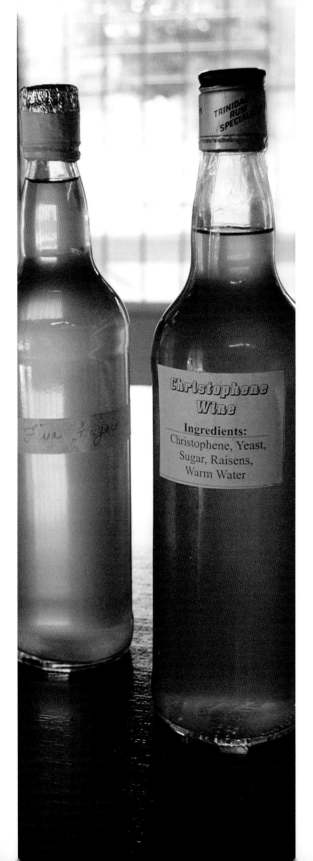

Christophene
Wine

Ingredients:
Christophene, Yeast,
Sugar, Raisens,
Warm Water

Trinidad claims many national drinks, the most famous of which are rums and Carib and Stag, the locally made beers. The rum shop, an old-style bar similar to a social club, was once the preferred venue for drinking and men could be found at any hour of the day sipping rum and chasing it with Carib, talking and joking loudly or playing All Fours, a game similar to bridge on which big money bets were often made.

Because of Trinidad's wealth of local ingredients, there are many other nationally notable drinks. There is Mauby, a tree-bark brew reminiscent of root beer; and Sorrel, a steeped, sweetened drink made from a type of hibiscus. Any number of teas and tisanes brewed from local flowers, herbs, and fruits also exist and are collectively called "bush tea." They are usually credited with medicinal properties as well.

Cocoa tea—what we would call hot chocolate—is another regionally specific drink. Although it does exist in other parts of the Caribbean, chocolate only grows in an area within twenty degrees of the equator, so not every Caribbean island produces it. However, Trinidadian cocoa tea is made from locally produced beans and spices.

The libation I remember most distinctly as a regular feature in my father's house is tea. Served for breakfast, along with a snack, or just before bed, tea is a quintessential part of Trinidadian cuisine. Although it was 165 years of British Colonial rule that brought tea to Trinidad, it was no doubt also a welcome reminder of home for more than 140,000 East Indians who came to the island as indentured laborers between 1857 and 1917. Eventually, tea drinking became as standard to Trinidadians as to the English, with many brands to choose from, many straight from India.

Today, however, Lipton's is the most widely consumed tea in the country. After brewing, it is usually sweetened with gobs of condensed milk. Trinidadians like their tea, as they do most of their nonalcoholic drinks, incredibly sweet. In fact, as a child visiting my father's family, I often found the morning tea served with breakfast to be so cloyingly sweet that barely any tea flavor was discernible.

But I've always heard that teatime in Trinidad was once an elegant and sophisticated affair with silver tea services, lovely little cakes and tarts made from fresh local fruits, and petite sandwiches that paired traditional British egg or chicken salad with a dash of Trinidad curry. In my fancies, formally attired attendants always served this stylish repast on a cool verandah.

Alas, while today teatime is honored at many locales throughout Trinidad, it is usually a quick affair gulped down with a sweet bun or some cookies. However, on a trip back "home," I managed to find the teatime of my dreams. Nestled in the compound of the Mount St. Benedict Monastery perched in the Northern Range, Pax Guest House, a small inn housed in a historic building, still allows travelers a taste of tropical teas of yore.

Established in 1916 by the Benedictine brothers as a way stop for weary travelers, Pax's scenic verandahs overlook the lush valleys below. Today, managers Gerard Ramsawak and Oda Van Der Heijden continue the tradition of high hospitality with both a regular afternoon tea and silver service tea from 3:00 to 6:00 p.m. daily. Replete with a full range of Indian, Chinese, and tropical brews as well as a plethora of tea cakes and sandwiches, including *pow* from Mr. Gerard's cousin Chin at Shay Shay Tien (page 195) and Miss Oda's secret family recipe for Frozen Dutch Chocolate Cake, tea at Pax Guest House is a sublime experience. Visitors are encouraged to linger at their table, sipping tea and enjoying the refreshing mountain air, while the rest of Trinidad hustles by below. (See photo page 198.)

COCOA TEA

Trinidadian chocolate is considered to be among the finest in the world, and large chocolate manufacturers from Europe buy the crop to flavor more widely produced but inferior chocolates from Africa and South America. Cocoa tea is made from "cocoa sticks," which are 100 percent Trinidad cocoa beans ground into a paste with local spices. The sticks are then dried and grated into boiling water to create a "tea" that is then flavored with condensed milk. Because pure Trinidad chocolate is not readily available outside of the country, I have adapted this recipe to use cocoa powder from producers that use a high percentage of Trinidad chocolate in their product.

COCOA MIX

2 cups dark unsweetened Valrhona chocolate powder; or 2 (4-ounce) Valrhona Gran Couva, finely chopped

1 teaspoon ground cinnamon

¼ teaspoon ground nutmeg

⅛ teaspoon ground bay leaf

¼ teaspoon ground ginger

COCOA TEA (per serving)

2 tablespoons cocoa mix

1 cup boiling water

Sweetened condensed milk to taste, or regular milk and heavy cream to taste

1 drop vanilla extract

MAKE COCOA MIX:

1 Combine all the ingredients. Store in a glass jar with a tight lid.

MAKE INDIVIDUAL SERVINGS:

2 Mix 2 tablespoons of the cocoa mix into the boiling water. Stir well and return to a boil. Remove the pot from the heat. Add condensed milk to taste and the vanilla extract. (Use the regular milk and heavy cream to taste if the mix is made with chopped chocolate bars.)

King Cocoa in Trinidad & Tobago

The story of cocoa in Trinidad is one of ambition, ingenuity, greed, glory, suffering, and sustenance. Cocoa first came to Trinidad in the 1500s with Spanish colonialists who planted a *criollo* of a native Central and South American variety. By the 1700s, cocoa was an abundant crop garnering high prices. Later in that century, the Spanish government gave Catholics from France and Spain willing to settle in Trinidad free land grants in the form of prime cocoa land in the Northern, Central, and Southern ranges, as well as tax amnesty on imported enslaved people to work that land. The crop flourished further and many fortunes were made.

However, it was adversity that ultimately created a cocoa bean native to Trinidad that would become one of the most prized cocoa beans in the world. In 1727, a pestilence called Witche's Broom destroyed much of the *criollo* crops. *Forastero*, a much heartier native cocoa from Venezuela, was brought to Trinidad and hybridized with the *criollo* to form *Trinitario*, which had the aroma and fruit of *criollo* and the heartiness of *forastero*.

The cocoa industry continued to make magnates and reign as the primary moneymaking crop, along with sugarcane exported from Trinidad, but historical events were to change its standing. The abolition of slavery in 1820 and the end of indenture from India and China in 1917 dried up free and cheap labor sources respectively. Still, advances in cocoa science, such as the Dutch process method of removing cocoa butter from cocoa liquor, fueled the demand for beans and the period of 1866 to 1920 is largely known as the Golden Age of Cocoa in Trinidad.

But by the 1930s periods of disease, poor production methods, and labor issues had crippled cocoa, and the rising petroleum industry in Trinidad, which is rich in both oil, pitch, and liquid natural gas, replaced brown gold with black.

Today, Trinidad remains one of only ten countries that produce what is recognized in the world cocoa forum as 100% Fine Flavor Cocoa. In other words, these beans are used to add superior flavor to mass-market cocoa, usually of the *forastero* variety. It is a favorite among high-end chocolatiers such as Valrhona (which maintains a partnership with one of the few remaining large estates in the prized Monsterrat/Gran Couva region), Guittard, Pralus, and others.

Trinidad cocoa can be likened to beluga caviar in terms of its value among connoisseurs: it's rare, expensive, and rapidly disappearing from the world market. The reasons are many, from government regulations that are restrictive to the small planter to the inability of estate owners to procure dependable labor, as cocoa is a crop that still requires hand picking. Cocoa picking is hard work and like most agriculture jobs in Trinidad & Tobago, not high on the list of chosen professions.

A small group of intrepid souls fight daily to keep the Trinidad cocoa industry alive. From the Cocoa Research Unit at the University of the West Indies at St. Augustine, which houses the largest genome bank of cocoa in the world, and dedicated Ministry of Agriculture scientists like Kamaldeo Maharaj, to major planters like Prism Agri and San Juan Estate, to the smallest farmer cooperatives formed by devoted planters like Jude Lee Sam, whose production is small though precious, to the individual boutique producers making artisan chocolate bars and cocoa powder, a hearts-and-minds campaign is being waged today in Trinidad to change the view of cocoa from a "slave crop" to a unique commodity that is responsible both directly and indirectly for the rich cultural influx and heritage that make up the nation of Trinidad & Tobago.

TRINI MOCCACHINO

My husband, photographer Jean-Paul Vellotti, noticed the chocolatey notes of locally grown coffee in Trinidad and had the idea of making a local "moccachino." Here is my interpretation of his idea. Starbucks—eat your heart out!

1 tablespoon Cocoa Tea mix (page 277)

1 cup hot strong brewed Colombian or other South American coffee

½ cup whole milk, scalded

Sugar to taste

Dash of ground cinnamon, to taste

1 Place all ingredients except the cinnamon in a blender and froth until well incorporated, being careful that lid is secure to hold in the hot liquid.

2 Serve hot with a dash of cinnamon on top.

Preserving Old Traditions

The oil that makes Trinidad a rich country is both a boon and a bane. The money that comes from this resource offers a quality of life that is generally better than that of other Caribbean islands, and in fact, those at the top of the class structure are very rich indeed. Another benefit is that the use of computers is making it easier to preserve and warehouse documents dating well back into the eighteenth century. New structures, like the National Library on Hart and Abercromby streets in Port of Spain, are a marriage of architecture and technology seldom seen even in the United States.

However, the downside to all this ready money is that, not surprisingly, mechanization and modernization have replaced many old traditions, but for the efforts of a few intrepid, and not a little stubborn, souls like Mr. Felix, a village leader of Brasso Seco, in the hills above Arima.

Brasso Seco (which means "dry branch" in Spanish) was once an enclave rich with cocoa plantations. Driving up the narrow mountain road, you'll find more than a few cocoa drying sheds in various states of decay. Largely inhabited by Creole descendants, the village is tiny, spotlessly clean, and has a lovely open-air schoolhouse for its thirty or so children.

Among the main products once produced for local use in Brasso Seco was cocoa sticks, used for cocoa tea. Other local delicacies include "buccaneer" smoked meats, and fruit wines.

Working with the Trinidad Industrial Development Corporation, Mr. Felix and a few other villagers provide demonstrations on local cooking methods and cocoa processing. Among these is a view of a cocoa shed, a building with a pitched roof that rolls back on casters to expose the cocoa beans to sunlight. Later, the beans are polished in a process called "dancing the cocoa," in which one walks through the cocoa barefoot, rubbing the beans under the soles of one's feet to bring them to a high polish. The beans are then roasted and ground for cocoa sticks.

We enjoyed freshly made cocoa tea at Miss V's home after she demonstrated the cocoa-stick-making process. Our visit took place just after school hours, as Miss V and her family are the village schoolteachers and administrators. We sipped cocoa tea, and enjoyed talk of the Old Trinidad, including a lesson in the local Spanish still spoken by many of the elders.

While there I was lucky enough to re-experience something I had forgotten some time ago, when Miss V's grandnephew stepped into the house for a short visit and she greeted him by saying, "God bless you, Marlon." Long ago,

Lighting of a candle for the celebration of Diwali, a five-day festival of lights

it was common for a younger person entering an older relative's house to be greeted this way. Although practiced little today, it's one of the sweetest memories I have of visiting older folks in Trinidad when I was a child.

In Tobago, efforts are being made to preserve West African traditions, and demonstrations of African-style weddings sometimes take place. Sometimes, if you are lucky, you can still get a glimpse of an old mud-brick oven in someone's yard, the once-preferred method of baking bread for poorer people without ovens or even kitchens.

Trinidadians of East Indian descent are well known for the preservation of their heritage, which, interestingly, has remained static over the 150-odd years that they have been denizens of the island. In speaking with friends who hail directly from India, I'm often struck at how much more modern they are in their religious practices and view of family dynamics.

Despite such pockets of cultural preservation, Trinidad as a whole is heading dangerously close to cultural subjugation to computers and televisions. As time wears on, Trinidad's population will no doubt continue to struggle with the double-edged sword that is modernization—my only hope is that technology is used to its best advantage in the preservation of a culture whose rich and unusual mosaic is not found elsewhere in the world.

PEANUT PUNCH

Peanuts and peanut butter aren't widely used in Trinidad, and when they are, they are most likely a West African influence versus an American one as many think. Peanuts are native to Africa where they are called groundnuts and are widely used.

Almost all recipes I've seen for Peanut Punch call for smooth peanut butter, but I imagine that at some point freshly ground peanuts were the original ingredient. To strike a balance I call for natural peanut butter in this recipe.

½ cup natural peanut butter

2 cups evaporated milk

Dash of angostura bitters

Pinch of cinnamon

Pinch of nutmeg

¼ cup light brown sugar or more to taste (optional)

1 Combine all ingredients in a blender and puree to a smooth shake.

2 Serve over crushed ice.

Variations: CASHEW PUNCH / ALMOND PUNCH

I've tried Peanut Punch using cashew butter and almond butter as a substitution for those with a peanut allergy and found the result to be just as delicious. Nut butters of various kinds are readily available in health food stores and organic supermarkets.

MAUBY

This popular cold drink is made from the boiled bark of the carob tree and tastes very much like root beer. Bottled Mauby is available in Caribbean stores and online, as is the dried bark.

1 tablespoon crumbled dried mauby bark

1 teaspoon dried orange peel

2 whole cloves

½ cinnamon stick

Pinch of mace

2 cups light brown sugar

1 Place the mauby bark, orange peel, cloves, cinnamon stick, and mace in a saucepan with 1 cup of water. Simmer for 5 minutes. Remove from the heat and allow to cool completely.

2 Combine the mauby brew with 23 cups of water and the brown sugar. Mix very well.

3 Strain the mauby into sterilized glass containers, seal tightly, and store in a cool, dry place for 3 days. Mauby can be stored, refrigerated, for up to 2 weeks.

TAMARIND JUICE

Tamarind is a tropical fruit that originated in Africa, made its way along the spice route to India and the Middle East, and eventually wound up in the southern half of the Western Hemisphere. In Trinidad, it is the basis for many sweets and for this drink.

2 tablespoons tamarind pulp

¼ cup sugar, or to taste

1 Place the tamarind pulp in a pot with 4 cups of water and bring to a boil. Lower the heat and simmer for 25 minutes.

2 Remove the pot from the heat and pour the liquid through a strainer, pressing with the back of a spoon to extract all the liquid.

3 Mix in the sugar, adjusting the quantity to taste. Mix well and cool completely. Serve over ice.

SORREL

A traditional must-have Christmas beverage, Sorrel has a warmly aromatic and spicy flavor thanks to the addition of cinnamon and cloves. On its own, sorrel, a member of the hibiscus family, is quite tart, but the drink, which is a lovely ruby red color, is pleasantly sweet-tart thanks to sugar. In Jamaica, ginger is added to the mix, but not in Trinidad—I find I prefer it with rather than without, so you decide. I also like my Sorrel on the tarter side, but you may choose to add more sugar. Some folks like to add rum or vodka to Sorrel to make a hibiscus cocktail.

1 cinnamon stick

6 cloves

1 cup dried sorrel flowers*

1 cup sugar

1-inch piece fresh ginger, sliced (optional)

_____

*Dried sorrel flowers can be found in Caribbean markets and online.

1 Place 10 cups of water and all ingredients in a saucepan and bring to a boil. Simmer for 5 minutes. Remove the mixture from the heat, cover, and allow to steep at least 2 hours, but preferably, overnight.

2 Pour the mixture through a fine mesh sieve into a pitcher or glass bottle and store in the refrigerator. Serve chilled. Sorrel keeps for up to 1 week.

Tip

You can simmer the ingredients longer to achieve a more potent, darker-colored drink that may be cut with water as desired for the individual drinker's taste.

CHRISTOPHENE WINE

Winemaking in the "true" sense doesn't exist in Trinidad since the climate is inhospitable to grapes. However, a variety of cordials and liqueurs are made from local fruits and vegetables. Christophene (chayote) and other fruit wines are made at home and not sold in liquor stores.

6 cups sugar

4 christophenes (chayote), peeled and grated

3 cloves, slightly crushed

Pinch of mace

1 Dissolve the sugar in 3 quarts of water. Add the grated christophene, cloves, and mace.

2 Pour into a glass jar and seal tightly. Store at room temperature in a dry place for 10 days.

3 Strain the liquid into sterilized glass containers and store in the refrigerator for up to 1 week.

MANGO WINE

Another locally made liqueur, the tangy sweet flavor of mango wine makes it a perfect cooler for a summer cocktail party.

6 cups sugar

2 large green mangoes, peeled and grated

3 whole cloves, slightly crushed

1 Dissolve the sugar in 3 quarts of water. Add the grated mango and cloves. Pour into a glass jar and seal tightly. Store at room temperature in a dry place for 10 days.

2 Strain the liquid and pour into sterilized bottles. Store refrigerated for up to 1 week.

SUGARCANE WINE

Sugarcane wine, made from free running sugarcane juice can be compared to a light agricole rum—although it is faster to make and the alcohol content is lower.

6 cups sugar

3 pounds sugarcane, peeled and chopped

1 teaspoon active dry yeast

1 Place all ingredients in a sterilized gallon jar with 3 quarts (12 cups) of water. Seal tightly and store in a cool, dark place for 10 days.

2 Strain the liquid and place in a clean bottle. Store for another 2 weeks in a cool, dark place. Sugarcane wine keeps refrigerated for up to two weeks. Serve cold.

DAD'S GINGER BEER

My first memory of ginger beer is of three-quart apothecary jars set out on the front stoop to steep on the scorching cement on hot summer days. Ginger beer was brewed only on blisteringly hot summer days, when the New York City heat was so brutal it could rival Trinidad's. It was a cloudy, pale yellow liquid swirling with a mass of shredded ginger and protruding vanilla beans that looked to me like big black worms. Dad described this concoction to me by saying that it was "something like ginger ale." My five-year-old mind immediately delighted at the thought that I could drink ginger ale—just like Schweppes—whenever I wanted, because my dad had the secret recipe.

I eagerly took my first sip and was thrown for a loop by the throat-scorching heat of the ginger. And a bigger shock: no bubbles. Like many older Trinidadians, my father grew up in the Depression era, a time during which expensive, bubble-giving yeast was reserved for baking bread. I didn't understand that nuance then, though. My disappointment at the lack of carbonation was so great that, for years after that first taste, I rarely drank his brew at all.

---

8 ounces fresh ginger, peeled and grated on the large holes of a box grater

2 tablespoons fresh lime juice

¼ teaspoon ground mace

1½ cups light brown sugar

½ vanilla bean, split lengthwise

12 cups boiling water

6 sprigs mint

Tip

For those interested in bubbly and slightly alcoholic ginger beer, time will do the trick. Store the ginger beer for 3 weeks in a tightly sealed mason jar at room temperature. It will ferment to produce a true "beer."

1 Put the ginger, lime juice, mace, and ¾ cup of the brown sugar into a wide-mouthed gallon glass or ceramic jar. Scrape the seeds from the vanilla bean into the jar and add the pod.

2 Add 12 cups of boiling water to the jar and stir until the sugar dissolves. Set the ginger mixture aside to steep and cool to room temperature. Cover the jar tightly and refrigerate for 1 week.

3 Line a large sieve with a double layer of cheesecloth. Strain the ginger mixture through the sieve into another wide-mouthed gallon glass or ceramic jar, firmly pressing on the solids with the back of a spoon to extract as much flavor as possible. Discard the solids.

4 Add the remaining ¾ cup of brown sugar to the ginger beer and stir until dissolved. Serve in glasses over crushed ice, garnished with mint sprigs. Ginger beer may be stored in a sealable glass jar, refrigerated, for up to 2 weeks.

PONCHE CREMA

Ponche Crema is a type of eggnog popular throughout the Caribbean. It is delicious served over ice as a creamy summer cocktail. This is my family's recipe, which uses coconut milk and resembles Coquito. I suspect my father learned to make Ponche Crema in this way in the Spanish islands during his time as a traveling gold jewelry salesman throughout the Caribbean. For the more traditional Trinidadian version, omit the cream of coconut.

4 eggs

1 (14-ounce) can sweetened condensed milk

¼ cup cream of coconut

¼ cup coconut milk (optional)

1 cup evaporated milk

¾ cup good-quality dark rum, such as Myer's

1 teaspoon Angostura bitters

¼ teaspoon mixed essence

¼ teaspoon ground nutmeg

⅛ teaspoon ground cloves

Whipped cream, for garnish

Ground cinnamon, for garnish

1 Blend the eggs in a blender at high speed for 20 seconds. Add the condensed milk, cream of coconut, coconut milk, evaporated milk, and about half the rum. Blend again for 10 seconds. Add the remaining rum, bitters, mixed essence, nutmeg, and cloves. Pulse in the blender once more.

2 Refrigerate and serve cold, over ice cubes, with a dollop of whipped cream and dusting of cinnamon.

Rum

As with other sugar-rich islands, rum is a major part of Trinidadian life and culture. Enslaved people and indentured laborers received a ration of rum along with their general provisions—a practice that sadly led to rampant alcoholism that continues today.

Because rum comes from molasses or free-run sugarcane juice and sugar cane is a plant that is highly affected by the mineral composition of soil, the flavors of local rums can vary dramatically from island to island in the West Indies. Rums that make use of the agricole method, which is the fermentation of fresh uncooked cane juice, are considered the most purely flavored. Perhaps because it was the first liquor I really tasted or that I am simply accustomed to it, I find Trinidad rum has a smooth and fruity flavor that can also be discerned in the local chocolate and coffee and no doubt can be attributed to the soil.

Rum is still copiously drunk in Trinidad—often chased with Carib or Stag beer, a practice that originated in rum shops of yore. Over-proof rums, called "*puncheon*," a derivation of the Irish word "*potcheen*," referring to pot still alcohols containing no less than 75 percent alcohol, are part of a cultural tradition of their own and those who drink *puncheon* neat are considered "tough" or manly.

Of late, Trinidad is producing high-end boutique rums like 1919 and 1824, both from Angostura Ltd. The latter is hand-bottled from a selection of fine rums aged in oak barrels formerly used to cure Jack Daniels Tennessee Whiskey.

Sugarcane

TRINIDAD RUM PUNCH

Rum punch is a standard party libation, and in 2004, Angostura, the bottlers of the famous bitters and a major rum manufacturer, began bottling various versions for mass distribution. Convenient though this may be, a rum punch recipe is a family tradition and I doubt many folks will abandon theirs. Here is mine.

1 small mango, peeled and chopped, or 1 cup frozen ripe mango, thawed

1 cup sliced fresh or frozen strawberries

1 cup fresh or canned pineapple chunks

1 (4-ounce) can mandarin orange slices with juice

¼ cup maraschino cherries

½ teaspoon coconut extract

¼ teaspoon mixed essence

2 teaspoons Angostura bitters

½ pint dark rum (such as Old Oak or Myer's), chilled

½ pint coconut rum, chilled

2 cups tropical fruit juice (such as Welch's Tropical Passion Juice from concentrate)

1 liter ginger ale, chilled

2 cups sparkling white wine (such as Freixenet), chilled

1 navel orange, unpeeled and sliced into ¼-inch rounds

1 star fruit, sliced horizontally (¼ inch thick)

1 In a large punch bowl, combine the mango, strawberries, pineapple chunks, mandarin orange slices with their juice, and maraschino cherries. Add the coconut extract, mixed essence, Angostura bitters, and rum. Place the bowl in the refrigerator or set over crushed ice, and allow the fruit to macerate for at least 1 hour and up to overnight.

2 When ready to serve, stir the tropical fruit juice into the fruit mixture. Gently pour in the ginger ale and sparkling wine so as not to lose too much carbonation. Float the orange slices and star fruit slices on top. Serve over crushed ice.

SOURSOP PUNCH

Soursop is also known as guanabana. While the fresh fruit isn't always readily available, companies such as Goya offer the frozen pulp and juice. I have adapted this recipe accordingly to make use of the frozen fruit.

1 (14-ounce) package frozen soursop pulp, thawed

2 cups evaporated milk

¼ cup sugar

Pinch of coarse salt

6 tablespoons sweetened condensed milk

2 tablespoons Angostura bitters

1 Place all the ingredients in a blender with 2 cups of water and puree until smooth.

2 Serve the punch over crushed ice.

Angostura Bitters

Nearly every American supermarket has a touch of the Trinidadian. It's in the drinks aisle, right alongside the mixers—Angostura bitters. This famous tool in the kit of any bartender worth his salt has been manufactured by a secret process in Trinidad since 1824. The name Angostura refers to the small Venezuelan village where Dr. Johann Gotthilf Benjamin Siegert first bottled his aromatic bitters before being driven out of that country and fleeing to Trinidad, where he set up shop.

At any given time, only five people know the secret recipe to the bitters, a recipe that is never written down and is prepared under total lock-down by workers who pour out the ingredients from unmarked bags. So precious is this recipe that the bitters ingredients arrive by ship to Port of Spain and are stored in a special warehouse that is guarded at all times. There are never any markings on any bag, box, or label to give even a hint as to the contents of those precious containers.

To further preserve the sanctity of the recipe, Angostura never makes its bitters on a set schedule. Instead, they are simply made when the warehouse stocks are deemed to be running low.

SEA MOSS DRINK

To me, what's most interesting about Sea Moss or Irish Moss drink is that it seems to be one of the few remaining connections to the Irish indentured laborers who were prevalent on Trinidad, Jamaica, Montserrat, and other English colonies in the Caribbean. On a trip to Ireland, I tasted Carrageen Pudding, made from milk and sugar and thickened with dried Irish sea moss. From the first spoonful, I noticed the resemblance to Sea Moss Drink which is a version of the same pudding using evaporated instead of fresh milk and with a shake-like consistency. Both the pudding and the drink are something of an acquired taste and are thought to be a constitution fortifier in both lands.

2 ounces dried sea moss (available in Caribbean markets and online)

1 tablespoon freshly squeezed lime juice

4 cups evaporated milk

½ cup sugar

2 teaspoons Angostura bitters

1 Place the sea moss in a bowl with the lime juice and ½ cup of water. Allow to soak overnight.

2 Drain the sea moss and put it in a saucepan with 2 cups of water and bring to a boil. Lower the heat and simmer until the sea moss looks like a wad of jelly. Remove the pan from the heat and cool.

3 Place the sea moss mixture in a blender with the evaporated milk and sugar. Puree until smooth. Add the bitters and serve over crushed ice.

GLOSSARY

Achar	Any condiment prepared with achar masala, for example, Mango Achar (page 268)
Achar Masala	A spice blend for pickled or peppered condiments that also acts as a preservative
Aji Dulce	A variety of sweet pepper found in Latin America and the Caribbean. It has a fruity flavor with only a little heat. If you can't find them, a pimiento pepper or a red bell pepper would be good substitutes.
Aloo	The Hindi word for potato
Bake	A fried biscuit, very much like a savory beignet (page 183)
Breadfruit	A starchy tree fruit that was considered a "ground provision" in the past, often served to enslaved people and indentured laborers as a filling meal
Buljol	A breakfast dish of fried salt cod, onions, and tomatoes (page 29); generally eaten with bake (page 183)
Burnt Sugar Syrup	A highly caramelized sugar syrup (page 213) added to cakes to create a darker color. It gives Black Cake (page 211) its very dark brown appearance
Buss Up Shut	A fluffy griddle bread that is shredded like a "burst-up shirt" and eaten with curries (page 175)
Caraili	A bitter melon resembling a light green cucumber with a knobby skin
Casareep	A seasoning syrup made from boiled cassava and spices; often used in stews
Cascadura	Local freshwater fish, resembling catfish in looks. A good substitute is swordfish.
Channa	The Hindi word for chickpea
Chataigne	(pronounced *Shah-tyne*) The Trinidadian name for breadnut, a starchy tree fruit that is similar to breadfruit in taste and family, but closer to chestnut in appearance. Also called jackfruit or by the Indian name of *katahar*, chataigne is available in most Asian, Indian, and Caribbean markets.
Chip Chip	A local variety of clam; also a popular coconut dessert (Sugar Cakes, page 228)
Chokha	The term "*chokha*" actually refers to any dish of vegetables roasted over a fire or scorched in hot oil, then mashed into a paste, and usually eaten with roti.

Coal pot	A huge iron pot that was used to cook over an open fire
Coconut milk	A liquid extracted from fresh coconut meat. It is available canned at most supermarkets.
Coconut water	The juice found inside a young coconut. It is available canned (Goya is one popular brand).
Creole	People descended from Spanish and French colonials who mixed with native Caribbeans. The term has come to mean anything that is mixed, from people to food. Creole food refers to Trinidadian food that is more European in nature rather than African or Indian-influenced.
Dal	The Hindi word for split peas
Dalpuri	A fluffy griddlecake with split pea powder baked inside, similar to a traditional Indian paratha (page 180)
Diwali	The Hindu festival of lights in honor of the goddess Laxshmi, generally observed in October
Doubles	A popular street food eaten for breakfast or as a street food; comprised of spiced chickpeas folded between two small disks of fried dough (page 51)
Fig	A local Trinidad & Tobago term for banana
Flying Fish	A local sweet-fleshed fish generally found in the waters between Barbados and Tobago
Ghee	Clarified butter, available at Indian markets, many natural food stores, and online (or you can make your own, see how on page 129)
Green Seasoning	A seasoning paste made from fresh herbs, including shado beni, oregano, parsley, thyme, garlic, and chives (pages 254, 255)
Ground Provision	A category of starchy vegetables and fruit that includes plantains and green bananas, breadfruit, cassava, yam, and taro
Kuchela	A condiment of shredded green mango, hot peppers, and achar masala (page 266)
Mauby	A drink made from the bark of the carob tree (page 283)
Mixed Essence	A baking flavoring of almond, pear, and vanilla extracts which is often used in West Indian baked goods. It is available in Caribbean markets and online.
Oil-Down	A cooking method in which coconut milk is simmered with meats and vegetables until it evaporates
Pastelles	A traditional tamale-like snack made at Christmastime (pages 62-65)
Pawpaw	Local term for papaya

Pimiento peppers	A mild pepper best known in the United States in their jarred form. You can substitute 1 tablespoon chopped jarred pimiento for 1 fresh pimiento pepper. In its dried, ground form the pimiento pepper is the common kitchen spice paprika.
Plantain	Large cooking banana
Pomerac	A tree fruit resembling a red pear, with a soft, white, sweet/tart flesh (see page xii)
Prasad	A dry pudding made from farina, served at Hindu festivals and prayer meetings (page 223)
Pumpkin	Calabaza or West Indian pumpkin are used in Trinidad; cheese pumpkin or butternut squash are the best substitutes
Roti	A puffy griddle bread for curries and Indian stews (pages 174-178)
Ruku	Annatto seed; used as a coloring agent and seasoning spice
Sadha Roti	An Indian griddle bread that is not fluffy (page 176)
Scotch Bonnet Pepper	A small extremely hot pepper that is yellow or red and squat in shape (if you prefer less heat use other milder chili peppers in its place). Tip: Remember to use gloves when handling hot peppers. Or if you prefer not to use gloves, don't touch your eyes or face and wash hands immediately after handling, using plenty of hot water and soap! Wash down any surfaces that the peppers may have touch with white vinegar as well.
Seasoning Pepper.	*See* Aji Dulce
Shado Beni	A local Caribbean herb, most closely related to cilantro
Shark and Bake	Famous beach food of deep-fried shark strips served between fried bread (page 67)
Soharee	A broad leaf that is used as a plate at traditional Hindu events
Sorrel	A type of hibiscus flower from which a drink of the same name (page 285) or bush tea is made
Tawa	A flat iron griddle on which Indian breads are cooked

INDEX

var. = variation

Index   303

ABOUT THE AUTHOR

RAMIN GANESHRAM was born in New York City to a Trinidadian father and Iranian mother. She is a journalist and professional chef trained at the Institute of Culinary Education, and author of several cookbooks including *Future Chefs* (IACP Cookbook Award winner) and *Cooking with Coconut* which won an Honorable Mention in the Readable Feast Awards in 2017. Her writing has been featured in the *New York Times, Newsday, Saveur, Gourmet, Bon Appetit,* and on epicurious.com, as well as *National Geographic Traveler, Forbes Traveler,* and many other publications. Ganeshram has appeared as a judge on the Food Network's "Throwdown! with Bobby Flay." She resides with her family in Connecticut.